On The Poverty Of Student Life

On The Poverty Of Student Life Considered In Its Economic, Political, Psychological, Sexual, And Particularly Intellectual Aspects, With A Modest Proposal For Its Remedy

Members of the Situationist International and Students from Strasbourg
Edited by Mehdi El Hajoui and Anna O'Meara
French translations by Nadège LeJeune and Zoé Crochon

ISBN: 978-1-94217-357-1 | EBook ISBN: 978-1-94217-365-6
Library of Congress Number: 2022933984

10 9 8 7 6 5 4 3 2 1

Common Notions
c/o Interference Archive
314 7th St.
Brooklyn, NY 11215

Common Notions
c/o Making Worlds Bookstore
210 S. 45th St.
Philadelphia, PA 19104

www.commonnotions.org
info@commonnotions.org

Discounted bulk quantities of our books are available for organizing, educational, or fundraising purposes. Please contact Common Notions at the address above for more information.

Cover design by Josh MacPhee / Antumbra Design
Layout design and typesetting by Morgan Buck / Antumbra Design
with Graciela "Chela" Vasquez / ChelitasDesign

Printed by union labor in Canada on acid-free paper

On The Poverty Of Student Life Considered In Its Economic, Political, Psychological, Sexual, And Particularly Intellectual Aspects, With A Modest Proposal For Its Remedy

Members of the Situationist International and Students from Strasbourg

Edited by Mehdi El Hajoui and Anna O'Meara

Brooklyn, NY
Philadelphia, PA
commonnotions.org

Contents

III Cataloging *On the Poverty of Student Life*

I
Situating *On the Poverty of Student Life*

Preface

"The Most Scandalous Pamphlet of This Century"

> "We might very well say, and no one would disagree with us, that the student is the most universally despised creature in France, apart from the priest and the policeman."[1]

Thus opens *De la misère en milieu étudiant, considérée sous ses aspects économique, politique, psychologique, sexuel et notamment intellectuel et de quelques moyens pour y remédier* [*On the Poverty of Student Life: Considered in Its Economic, Political, Psychological, Sexual, and Particularly Intellectual Aspects, with a Modest Proposal for Its Remedy*], also adapted as *Ten Days That Shook the University* and *On Student Poverty*, a 9,000-word tract published by a student association at the University of Strasbourg in November, 1966.

Following this opening salvo, the pamphlet uses a similarly provocative tone to explain how university students, through their passivity and subservience, perpetuate the existing social and economic order. The student is nothing but a bourgeois-in-training: "he has a provisional part to play, a rehearsal for his final role as an element in market society as conservative as the rest."[2] But *On the Poverty of Student Life* is also a powerful call to action, a rude awakening that inspired students to protest trends of disempowerment in political change and emerge as the vanguard of a new social order: "The revolt of youth against an imposed and 'given' way of life is the first sign of a total subversion. It is the prelude to a period of revolt—the revolt of those who can no longer live in our society."[3]

On the Poverty of Student Life had the effect of a jolt for the placid teens and twenty-somethings at the (then sleepy) University of Strasbourg. The incendiary brochure later made its way to the newly founded Paris Nanterre University and the hallowed halls of the Sorbonne. By some accounts, over 300,000 copies of the pamphlet circulated in the years immediately following its publication.[4]

But how did *On the Poverty of Student Life* get to a point of such popularity? In 1966, a handful of students intent on causing disruption were miraculously elected to lead the University of Strasbourg's student association, AFGES

(*Association Fédérative Générale des Étudiants de Strasbourg*). The Situationists saw an opening; Mustapha Khayati put pen to paper and wrote the bulk of what would soon be advertised as "the most scandalous pamphlet of the century."[5] 10,000 copies were printed, using up the entire budget of the student union, then distributed at the ceremony marking the beginning of the 1966 academic year. A scandal soon ensued, with the young Turks appearing on the front page of local newspapers and being featured in nationwide dailies like *Le Monde* and in periodicals like France's *L'Express*, Italy's *L'Europeo*, and more. The operation also made it possible for the Situationist International (SI)—then an underground political and artistic movement—to emerge from the confines of the avant-garde. A year and a half before massive student occupations and protests involving over 11 million workers would paralyze the country, the SI stood behind what might be considered the first major expression of student discontent in 1960s France.

This short preface aims to set some broad context around *On the Poverty of Student Life*, showcase the motivation behind this project, and provide an overview of the content the editors have chosen to include. It is followed by an introduction by Anna O'Meara, who explores the critical significance of the pamphlet and its global ramifications. Specifically, O'Meara dives into the connections between the Situationist International and the Zengakuren, a Japanese national student association. The Zengakuren showed radical organizations what a student group could do: it launched extraordinary protests of the "Red Purge" and US occupation that ended in riots, it violently battled the police (and won), and it drew enormous numbers and support from fellow students and Japanese citizens alike. But could such radical action possibly happen through UNEF, the French national student union, especially given its past collaboration with Vichy France and ongoing attempts to maintain colonial authority over African student organizing? Next is an interview with Mustapha Khayati, the primary author of the text. Though a collective endeavor—Christine Ballivet, André Bertrand, Guy Debord, Roby Grunenwald, Daniel Joubert, Mustapha Khayati, André Schneider, Bruno Vayr-Piova, and perhaps Christian Millot all contributed in one way or another[6]—*On the Poverty of Student Life* is almost entirely the work of Debord, Khayati, and Joubert. Among the three, Khayati played the biggest role by far, holding the pen and drafting nearly all the content. In a letter to Pascal Dumontier dated November 19, 1990, Joubert writes, "it seems to me perfectly appropriate to attribute the authorship of this text to Mustapha Khayati, while indicating that he benefited from the help of several Situationists and students from Strasbourg."[7]

From his arrival in Strasbourg in 1961 to his encounter with Debord and decision to join the Situationist International, Khayati describes the circumstances in which *On the Poverty of Student Life* came to be. He also explains how the writing occurred in a matter of weeks and he sheds light on the ideas that influenced him. Next, the former Situationist provides a vivid account of that fateful day of November 22, 1966, when thousands of copies of the pamphlet got into the hands of students, faculty, and the city's local dignitaries. Khayati then reflects on the trajectory of the text, from humble provincial roots (the source of a local scandal) to national recognition (a key intellectual guidepost for May '68 students) and, ultimately, global dissemination. Finally, the Tunisian writer shares his perspective on how *On the Poverty of Student Life* has influenced generations of students, and whether it continues to be relevant to this day.

Next is a text by Allan Antliff, based on discussions with Lorraine Perlman, that sheds new light on the Black & Red translation of *On the Poverty of Student Life*. Black & Red played a critical role in the transmission of radical texts and Situationist ideas in the United States, for example, with the publication of the first English-language edition of Guy Debord's *The Society of the Spectacle* in 1970.

We have also chosen to reprint the pamphlet *On the Poverty of Student Life* itself, both in its original French and in an English translation. The French text is a verbatim copy of the original brochure—the one that scandalized Strasbourg's professors, students, and bourgeois establishment when they found it on their chairs at the university's opening ceremony. Also included is a facsimile version of a draft of the first chapter, courtesy of Khayati and Yale University's Beinecke Library. For the English translation, we have chosen to reproduce Donald Nicholson-Smith and T.J. Clark's adaptation of the French pamphlet under the title *Ten Days That Shook the University*. It is preceded by a short introductory note by Nicholson-Smith, where he explains that, in lieu of a literal translation, he chose to partner with Clark to adapt the text, making it more accessible and relevant to English-speaking readers.

The heart of this book is an illustrated bibliography of known editions of *On the Poverty of Student Life*. It is intended to help reveal the extent to which the text has circulated since its initial publication in November 1966. Most editions are the work of anarchist collectives, students, or small groups of individuals and meant for distribution at local universities or in the community. This organic dissemination is very much in the spirit of the original pamphlet, with the first edition stating that "no copyright is held on the text, it can be reproduced by anyone in any form whatsoever." In fact, the commercial reprint of the text by Editions Champ Libre in 1976 gave rise to a conflict between Khayati and the publisher, Gérard Lebovici. After hearing about the planned release, Khayati wrote to Lebovici, "This text is not intended for the commercial distribution that you want to give it. . . . It is necessary to let this text circulate through many pirate editions."[8]

Excluding digital-only editions and reprints of the text as part of anthologies, we have been able to locate over one hundred editions of *On the Poverty of Student Life*, written in over eighteen languages. Together, they provide evidence that the text was read throughout Europe, the Americas, Asia, and Australia. Each entry consists of a description of the physical item, followed by a short commentary on its particular significance. We also include a scan of the front wrapper (or cover) and, occasionally, interesting visual content found within the text. While expansive, this bibliography is not comprehensive: we invite readers to alert us to other editions they might have encountered, so that they may be included in a revised edition of this book.

This volume, in a nutshell, is a tribute to one of the most politically and culturally significant pamphlets of the second half of the twentieth century. It serves as an homage to a tract that played a pivotal role in social history and, fifty-five years on, continues to inspire generations of students. For those readers already familiar with *On the Poverty of Student Life*, I hope this book illuminates interesting or otherwise neglected facets of the text. And for those who are new to it, get ready to be punched in the face by "the most scandalous pamphlet of this century."

Mehdi El Hajoui
September 2021

Notes

1   All quotations are from the English translation by Donald Nicholson-Smith and T.J. Clark, *Ten Days That Shook the University: The Situationists at Strasbourg* (London: BCM/ Situationist International, 1967).

2   Nicholson-Smith and Clark, *Ten Days That Shook the University*.

3   Nicholson-Smith and Clark, *Ten Days That Shook the University*.

4   "When taking into account international distribution, *On the Poverty of Student Life*'s total print run likely stood somewhere between 250,000 to 300,000. Of those, 70,000 copies were published directly by the SI. The other copies were produced by other revolutionary groups and by radical newspapers or publishers." [Internationale Situationniste, *Internationale Situationniste* 12 (September 1969): 103.]

5   See André Bertrand, *Le retour de la colonne Durutti* (Strasbourg: AFGES, October 1966).

6   André Bertrand and André Schneider, *Le scandale de Strasbourg mis à nu par ses célibataires, même* (Montreuil: l'Insomniaque, 2018), 177.

7   Bertrand and Schneider, *Le scandale de Strasbourg*, 326. Pascal Dumontier is the author of *Les situationnistes et mai 1968 : théorie et pratique de la révolution (1966–1972)* (Paris: Gérard Lebovici, 1990). He exchanged letters with Debord in the early 1990s.

8   Mustapha Khayati, "Letter to Champ Libre, October 12, 1976," in *Champ Libre, Correspondance*, Vol. 1 (Paris: Champ Libre, 1978), 31.

Introduction

Zengakuren: How a Japanese Student Union Influenced the SI

Anna O'Meara

"[Zengakuren] is the most important group in the world,"[1] argue members of the Situationist International (SI) in the first edition of *On the Poverty of Student Life*.[2] Why did the SI enthusiastically support a Japanese student union, while they mocked and derided the French student group, Union Nationale des Étudiants de France (UNEF)? And, if Zengakuren was so important, then why, by the 1970s, was it almost entirely ignored in discussions related to the SI and May '68? Why was even the mention of Zengakuren omitted from subsequent translations of *On the Poverty of Student Life*? In this introduction, I will consider: (1) the role of UNEF, which was infiltrated by the SI in order to print *On the Poverty of Student Life*;[3] (2) the influence of a sect of Zengakuren, the Revolutionary Communist League (RCL), on its production and diffusion. Communication between the SI in France, the RCL, and student activists in Berkeley from this period creates a complex yet interwoven story from three distant parts of the globe. As a result of such global connectivity, what the SI found as lacking in the French UNEF's passivity, they found inspiring, for a short time, in a Japanese student union, despite significant language barriers and cultural differences. However, after the initial publication of *On the Poverty of Student Life* in November 1966, differences between the ideas of the SI and Zengakuren came to light. As a result, members of the SI removed any mention of the Japanese group from the 1970 Chinese edition and further discouraged appreciation for Zengakuren among American pro-Situationist movements in Northern California, specifically, the Council for the Eruption of the Marvelous (CEM).

UNEF: The "Years of Slumber"

The Union Nationale des Étudiants de France (UNEF) was founded in 1907 and soon became the largest French student union. In its constitution, the organization resolved to act apolitically. Over the course of the twentieth century, UNEF's attempts toward apoliticism became, at times, means of supporting existing political powers and, at other times, apoliticism was simply an impossibility.

Up until the 1950s, UNEF was reputed for elitism, corporatism, conservatism, and during World War II, a complacent attitude toward fascism. This is not to say that French students always held the same complacency. In fact, many students were involved in radical organizations outside of the university. Between 1900 and 1926, the French student population doubled, making way for a somewhat more diverse group in terms of class, national identity, and race. This divide between a controlling elite and growing enrollment would continue to escalate and exacerbate tensions up until the student riots of 1968. Nevertheless, UNEF's origins as a small elite of mostly wealthy students, along with its oligarchical structure, continued to characterize the student union's culture and predominantly conservative political attitudes for the first half-century after its founding.[4]

Despite claims of apoliticism, UNEF cooperated with dominant power structures in both world wars, which became particularly contentious during World War II. Although it made a deliberate effort to hold no position, UNEF established a relationship with the authoritarian Vichy government that "even went as far as collaborating with its program of compulsory youth work camps in Germany."[5] It's possible that UNEF's complacency allowed the organization to survive under Vichy, but this complacency would necessarily define negative attitudes toward UNEF after the liberation of France in 1944, when conflict and factionalism in worldwide francophone student organizations related to UNEF unraveled up to the breaking point of May '68. Perhaps it was UNEF's harmful apoliticism that *On the Poverty of Student Life* had in mind when it stated, "What is unforgivable is not so much [the student's] actual misery, but his complaisance in the face of the misery of others."[6]

Another political narrative in the history of UNEF involves their resistance to the decolonization of the former French Empire. In the 1940s, UNEF also focused on maintaining its power over the student unions of "greater France" by disbanding student organizations in Africa, including the Conseil National des Etudiants Coloniaux (CNEC) in 1941. UNEF also saw ongoing conflict with the Association Générale des Etudiants de Dakar.[7] The fact that UNEF made so many efforts to maintain its hold over African student organizations backfired, becoming a catalyst for the organization's political shift in the 1950s: "Delegations from numerous foreign student organizations attend[ed] UNEF Congresses. . . . Some of the more notable objects of condemnation [included]: continued French colonialism."[8]

Nevertheless, throughout the Algerian War (1954–1962), UNEF would not take an official position on the war. The organization's apparent opposition to the war came as a response to UNEF's subsect in Algiers, composed primarily of non-Arabs who favored a "French Algeria." Thus, UNEF's vocalization of support for Algerian liberation was intended to silence the overt support for colonialism within the Algerian sections of their own organization.[9] It's possible that UNEF's decision to support Algerian liberation was essentially damage control; a means of saving face following accusations of collaboration with fascist organizations. Regardless of intent, it was this moment of support for decolonial struggles that agitated Charles De Gaulle in such a way that it heightened the organization's role in political affairs and put UNEF in a position where it could act as a mouthpiece that would reach the French presses for the foreseeable future.[10]

After the Algerian War, UNEF found itself in disarray. Factionalism between leftist tendencies broke from the organization's last hold on the vestiges of their right-wing past. It was in this environment of confusion that possibilities for change ripened. The Situationist International would embrace the possibility of such drastic changes that could undermine the power of universities, along with the disassembly of UNEF's supposedly "apolitical" complacency that supported colonial and bureaucratic power structures. When pro-Situationist students were able to gain power over the oligarchical authority of the Strasbourg section of UNEF, Situationists saw an opportunity for political action that would instigate radical change.

While the Situationist International didn't expect UNEF to change, one might nevertheless wonder what happened to it over time. Today, they remain a large student organization. On the surface, it may appear as though UNEF has become more progressive: leadership has indeed moved from a white male elite to a more diverse demographic. However, certain conservative tendencies within the union remain revered by people in power, such as France's current national education minister, Jean-Michel Blanquer. Blanquer remembers and aims to uphold the student organization's conservative past. In April 2021, *The New York Times* published an article on UNEF titled, "An Outspoken Student Union Positions Itself at the Vanguard of a Changing France." The article's authors' state:

> To its critics, the UNEF is the incarnation of the threat coming from U.S. universities—importing ideas that are fundamentally challenging relations

between women and men, questioning the role of race and racism in France, and upsetting society's hierarchies of power.[11]

Blanquer agrees with these sentiments, and also that he has "led the government's broader pushback against what he and conservative intellectuals describe as the threat from progressive American ideas on race, gender, and postcolonialism."[12]

The idea that "progressive ideas" are specifically "American" gives a sense of the reductive regional approach of both the mentioned critics and *The New York Times*, as though postcolonialism were a specifically American concept. Furthermore, while Blanquer argues that race, gender, and postcolonialism are major threats to the traditionally conservative French UNEF, a solidification of power takes place and shifts focus from advocating for the rights of all students (including women and people of color) to a struggle merely to become equally considered in an oppressive system. *On the Poverty of Student Life* saw a similar struggle take place in 1966:

> In the apartheid of the temporary problems of a healthy pluralism (compare and contrast the 'woman question' and the 'problem of racism'). In reality, if there is a problem of youth in modern capitalism it is part of the total crisis of that society. It is just that youth feels the crisis most acutely. (Not only feels it but tries to give it expression.)[13]

Considering the problematic bureaucracy of the French school system and recent unsuccessful efforts to dismantle it, along with the nature of many other bureaucratic institutions, one might question whether efforts against these oppressive powers made *real* strides toward a more empowered world for the many or simply just for the few. Or perhaps what we are now seeing is an extension of the deeper "total crisis" that is the focus of *On the Poverty of Student Life*?

Japan and Paris: A Passionate Rapport, Attempts at Understanding

> Japan is the only industrialized country where this fusion of student youth and working-class militants has already taken place. Zengakuren, the organization of revolutionary students, and the League of Young Marxist Workers joined to form the backbone of the Communist Revolutionary League. The movement is already setting and solving the new problems of revolutionary organization. Without illusions, it fights both Western capitalism and the bureaucracies of the so-called socialist states. Without hierarchies, it groups together several thousand students and workers on a democratic basis, and aims at the participation of every member in all the activities of the organization. . . . *At present, [Zengakuren] is the most important group in the world.*[14]

On the Poverty of Student Life indicts student passivity and alienation, particularly in the context of politics. However, the manifesto provides a model intended to be reproducible: it is based on the SI's understanding of and communication with a sect of Zengakuren [All-Japan Federation of Student Self-Government Associations] that had been organizing massive student uprisings since Hiroshima and Nagasaki. As such, it behooves us to consider the history of this group as inspiration for events following the publication of *On the Poverty of Student Life* in Paris, in May '68. Along with the League of Young Marxist Workers, Zengakuren was "the best attempt at the time" for how "youth revolt can only become revolutionary if it unites with workers' struggles."[15]

While Zengakuren has been widely researched, the connections between the Situationist International and Californian translators of *On the Poverty of Student Life* have been notably underrepresented in scholarship, especially given that the SI wrote that the group was "the most influential group in the world" in *On the Poverty of Student Life*.

From at least March to November of 1963, two Japanese delegates from Zengakuren named Tsushi Kurokawa and Toru Tagaki stayed with SI founder, Guy Debord, and Debord's partner, Michèle Bernstein, in Paris.[16] During this time, Kurokara and Tagaki were able to assist in translating Situationist texts into Japanese. Archival records from the Beinecke at Yale further show that, in 1966, the Situationist International corresponded with a Tokyo sect of Zengakuren called the Japan Revolutionary Communist League (RCL) in order to exchange international contacts with groups such as Students for a Democratic Society (SDS) in Chicago, the Vietnam Day Committee in California, and organizations in Switzerland, Belgium, France, New Zealand, Germany, and England. In 1965, Guy Debord made contact with RCL founder Kan'ichi Kuroda, and he was familiar with the Zengakuren periodical, *Zen-Shin*.[17] The RCL sent photos of their struggles at Waseda University. The Situationist International sent detailed handwritten analyses of Marx that denounced the USSR and Stalin's theory of "socialism in one country"[18] in 1966, and updates on the student riots across France in 1968. The latter were signed by Debord, Khayati, and Vaneigem. Historically, the RCL likewise denounced Stalinism and the Soviet Union. In May 1970, what seems to be the first Japanese translation of *On the Poverty of Student Life* appeared in the Japanese anarchist journal *Structure*.[19]

Founded in the late 1940s, Zengakuren—unlike the French UNEF—had significant radical tendencies. In particular, it had a long history of left-leaning Japanese student organizations involved in labor organizing. As early as 1919, the student organization Shinjinkai established a tradition of connecting university students and labor organizing movements. By the 1930s, anti-Marxist professors at many Japanese universities "found themselves mercilessly jeered." The demographics of these student organizations show that these students were not wealthy, and their funds tended to be minimal.[20] Throughout the history of Japanese student organizations, student leaders represented the middle and working class, unlike the historically elite oligarchy that ran UNEF. Zengakuren's founding in 1948 was initiated "in the midst of struggle against higher tuition."[21] From 1965 until 1970, it divided into various radical sects, many of which would stage their own revolts. From 1971 to 1975, Zengakuren was characterized by struggles for hegemony between these sects.[22]

Zengakuren's post-Leninist sects were of interest to the Situationist International for a short time, despite the fact that the group faced limitations in understanding. Because of the SI's influence on May '68 and world uprisings, it is therefore transitively imperative to consider Japanese student activism, and to put into question existing conceptions that Paris was a starting point for student uprisings across the world. Though May '68 was an inspiration for many, it was not born in a vacuum. Around the world, protests of the university model cried for alternatives to student life: students in both Japan and France were making radical calls to "End the University" [大学の終焉], and this similar line of thinking was perhaps what solidified connections between these two distant countries, along with correspondence between RCL and the Situationist International.[23] *On the Poverty of Student Life* acted as inspiration for international demonstrations, and it was this text of *On the Poverty of Student Life* that tells us Zengakuren contributed to making "Japan . . . the only industrialized country where this fusion of student youth and working-class militants has already taken place."[24]

While the Situationist International was inspired by Zengakuren, there was a significant degree of ignorance among many regarding its full composition and ideas. Situationist Attila Kótanyi was convinced that Zengakuren was related to Zen Buddhism. René Viénet "took hours to detail that Zen Buddhism and Zengakuren were totally different kanji."[25] Nevertheless, Guy Debord's correspondences reveal many letters concerning meetings with Japanese delegates that include some degree of detail, as well as attempts to apply Zengakuren's strategies.

The RCL, in particular, identified its tendency as distinctly to the left of Trotsky, which appealed to the Situationist International. In other words, the RCL considered aspects of Trotsky's theories, but redefined their approach toward a more anti-authoritarian tendency. This inspiration encouraged a spirit of internationalism, and so the RCL established correspondence with international student organizations to organize global student advocacy. Zengakuren became members of the International Union of Students (IUS), a group that Zengakuren member, Akio Ohno, saw a necessary internationalist response to "postwar" antifascism. Ohno encouraged worldwide student organizations to resolve their disagreements, but he also considered how alternative organizations to IUS were funded by the CIA like the International Student Conference (ISC) or the Indonesian Students Action Union, which was created to police other radical elements in student organizations.

In an effort to distribute *On the Poverty of Student Life*, Debord and Khayati worked with the Zengakuren delegates they'd met in Paris. Khayati sent a telegram ending with the following:

> LONG LIVE THE JAPANESE REVOLUTIONARY COMMUNIST LEAGUE.
>
> LONG LIVE ZENGAKUREN.
>
> ALL POWER TO THE INTERNATIONAL WORKERS' COUNCILS.[26]

Further, in May '68, Zengakuren's tactics were applied in the riots in the Latin Quarter:

> The Shagakudo, who like to fight in the Kanda area of Tokyo, have been strongly influenced by the French students' Latin Quarter style of street fighting and are always trying to emulate this with street barricades and liberated areas to get the ordinary citizens involved too. In France, on the other hand, there were instances when the students armed themselves with sticks (like '*gebabo*') and tried snake-dance demonstrations, although these may not have been so successful.[27]

The Situationists furthermore worked to ensure that the political strategies and activities of Zengakuren would be discussed and applied outside of Paris, and outside of just the internal networks of Situationist correspondence. The Danish translation of *On the Poverty of Student Life*, which was produced by the Situationist International, included photographs of Zengakuren's demonstrations in November 1968, and featured an image of a Japanese translation of "Politics and Art" [政治と芸術] by the Shadow Group [影組]. "Politics and Art" is a translation of a text by Guy Debord that considers Danish radicalism.[28] In nearby Denmark, Situationist J.V. Martin "had great success protesting in the street in the style of Zengakuren. Two days later, he burned down his house," according to Guy Debord.[29] A few years earlier, Debord had requested that Martin host an art opening, with cocktails where images would have titles like: "President Eisenhower Shamefully Fled the Strong Zengakuren Protests."[30]

Omission of Zengakuren in Global Editions of *On the Poverty of Student Life*

On the Poverty of Student Life found worldwide reception. Many groups around the world discovered the Situationist International for the first time through this text. For others, it inspired a completely new approach to their grievances against society and university institutions.

The text's afterlife should not simply be approached as an extension of its original intent and context. Especially because *On the Poverty of Student Life* was created to be free from copyright restrictions, and the text itself could be changed at will. Even the earliest editions by Situationists like Donald Nicholson-Smith encouraged translation written more to invoke a response from a specific new audience rather than stay true to original wording. In considering significant changes to the text, one of the most prominent trends that occurs is omission, particularly of the mention of Zengakuren. The following stories account for reasons for the omission of Zengakuren in Chinese editions, as well as reasons for omissions and additions to Chapter 2 in an American edition by Council for the Eruption of the Marvelous (CEM).

Omission in a Chinese Edition

Some translations of *On the Poverty of Student Life* omitted the original text's references to Zengakuren altogether. In the 1972 foreword to the Chinese edition, an unnamed Chinese translator argues that the actual nature of the Japanese organization wasn't really understood by the Situationist International. It goes on to specifically criticize "Western American" (presumably Berkeley) students, as well as the tendency within Chinese and Asian radical movements to look to the West for some type of guidance. The foreword mentions that Zengakuren was removed from the text, but nevertheless encourages the cultivation of a specifically Chinese understanding of student poverty that can wage critiques on students in Hong Kong, as well as provide a Chinese alternative to mere mimicking of Western leftism. These qualms were articulated because René Viénet "pointed out to the translator" that, in Hong Kong, there were "illusions about Trotskyism and the more recent Californian phase."[31] Viénet, a former Situationist, facilitated the 1972 Chinese-language edition in Hong Kong under the Champ Libre imprint. He is also a filmmaker, and a scholar of twentieth-century Chinese history who spent time in Hong Kong and Taiwan.

By 1970, the Zengakuren had transitioned from a period of many autonomous sects to a struggle for hegemony. When Viénet traveled to Japan for the first time in 1969, where he met the RCL, they had shifted from an ultra-leftist stance to a more typical Leninist tendency. Viénet vehemently felt this tendency to be incompatible with Situationist ideas, and he ensured that this concern was communicated in the introduction to the 1972 Chinese edition:

> [The translation] reproduces Mustapha Khayati's text as it was issued in Strasbourg in 1966, with the exception of some forty lines concerning a Japanese Leninist organization.[32]

This introduction was signed "Lu Zhishen" (a pseudonym taken from the fourteenth-century Chinese novel *Water Margin* [水滸]). It goes on to discuss how Japanese radical tendencies had been misunderstood by the Situationist International.

Initially, Viénet, like other Situationists, also corresponded with Zengakuren. He dispatched many telegrams during May '68 through the Council for Maintaining the Occupations (CMDO), including the following message that was sent to the Tokyo Zengakuren (RCP), as Viénet had previously met one of their delegates in Paris. The telegram references a Diderot and Meslier correspondence that circulated during the French Revolution: "Men will never be free until the last king is strangled with the entrails of the last priest."[33]

LONG LIVE THE STRUGGLE OF THE JAPANESE COMRADES WHO HAVE OPENED COMBAT SIMULTANEOUSLY ON THE FRONTS OF ANTI-STALINISM AND ANTI-IMPERIALISM STOP LONG LIVE FACTORY OCCUPATIONS STOP LONG LIVE THE GENERAL STRIKE STOP LONG LIVE THE INTERNATIONAL POWER OF THE WORKERS COUNCILS STOP HUMANITY WON'T BE HAPPY TILL THE LAST BUREAUCRAT IS HUNG WITH THE GUTS OF THE LAST CAPITALIST STOP OCCUPATION COMMITTEE OF THE PEOPLE'S FREE SORBONNE.[34]

Viénet reflects on how the Situationist understanding of the French Revolution was "superficial" at the time. He was familiar with Meslier's *Testament* and wrote a similar quotation to one from the telegram on the paintings inside the Sorbonne: "Humanity won't be happy until the last bureaucrat is hung with the guts of the last capitalist" [Figure 1]. Viénet affirms that he was "one of the authentic Eleuthéromanes," but at a time when he was unaware of certain problematic aspects of the French Revolutionaries, including their treatment of women.[35]

While there was support for the RCP in 1968, Viénet's less than positive visit to Japan in 1969 provided a reason to bury the influence of Zengakuren. Guy

Debord was eager to hear about this meeting, writing that Viénet was visiting Japan and would report back on a visit with Zengakuren member Nemoto, though other francophone Zengakuren delegates were in prison.[36] However, Viénet did not have anything positive to report, and it seems that many other Situationists were not as adamant about contesting Zengakuren in the 1980s. According to Viénet, "[Debord] appears to have asked that the Chinese edition of *On the Poverty of Student Life* be removed from Champ Libre's catalogue [...] after contesting the removal of the aberrant and unwelcome praise of the demented Trotsky-Maoist Zengakuren."[37] After Viénet lost touch with Debord, a friend informed him that it was Debord who approached Champ Libre to remove the Chinese translation of *On the Poverty of Student Life* from production, along with several other Chinese-language books due, he said, to the fact that, three Chinese characters for student [大學生] were printed upside down [ㄚ畚天]. In 1975, Guy Debord wrote Gérard Lebovici of Champ Libre, saying:

> Regarding the regrettable Chinese edition of *On the Poverty of Student Life* that I showed you the other day, Alice pointed out to me that three of the seven characters in the title have been printed upside-down! . . . The "Bibliothèque Asiatique" should not be making such mediocre mistakes in service of sinology.[38]

Apparently, Debord did not recognize the deliberate choice and allusion related to the decision to print characters this way; a decision that took several minutes to typeset. Viénet hypothesizes that this could be due to the fact that Khayati was listed as the primary author of the pamphlet more than the apparent criticism that Debord vaguely related to Chinese historiography. Debord expressed such authorship concerns during the production of Viénet's *Enragés et situationnistes* in 1968.[39] The footnotes of Debord's letters in *Correspondance, volume 5*, emphasize that it may have had to do with the exclusion of Zengakuren from the text.[40]

In line with the Champ Libre edition, the 1986 Chinese translation by the *Spectacular Times* included the 1972 introduction by Lu Zhishen, including the same explanation about the omission of the Zengakuren passage.

The Rewritten Chapter of the CEM Edition

In a Californian reprint of *On the Poverty of Student Life* by the Council for the Eruption of the Marvelous (CEM), Chapter 2 was nearly entirely rewritten, with passages on Zengakuren—along with the Dutch Provo—replaced with critiques of California in the 1960s and '70s. This shows how CEM didn't view Zengakuren (or all of Chapter 2 of *On the Poverty of*

Student Life) as key elements for a *texte de combat* that would be effective in an American context.

Isaac Cronin of CEM remembers that not all members of the group agreed with the changes. Rather, according to Cronin, another author "[edited the text] on his own . . . an almost incomprehensible version of the 1966 Situationist classic [of] *On the Poverty of Student Life*."[41] Cronin continued, "It added little to the content. It would be like rewriting *The German Ideology* and substituting a critique of Switzerland."[42] A sense of distance and lack of understanding also influenced opinions of Zengakuren within CEM, and later, the Bay Area pro-Situationist group Contradiction.

Cronin was first introduced to the texts of the Situationist International through *On the Poverty of Student Life* in 1967 when he was a student at UC Santa Cruz. At the time, he was studying Freudian psychology and witnessing "Stop the Draft" and the Vietnam Day Committee, but he was dissatisfied with the radicalism around him. He called *On the Poverty of Student Life* a "prophetic moment": "I made a vow to myself that I was going to meet the Situationists as soon as possible. These are the best ideas I'd come across."[43]

Cronin and CEM's Dan Hammer later presented the CEM translation to Viénet at a Situationist meeting during their 1970 visit to Paris. As Cronin recalls, Viénet asked why the text was changed: "I am sure we did not have a very good answer. We had broken with [the original translator] over his mystical/artistic perspective earlier."[44] Cronin discussed how the Situationists seemed to perceive the work of the Berkeley pro-Situationists as a form of, in Cronin's words, "PR." As he recalls, Debord was not present and Vaneigem was in Belgium at the time, but other Situationists, including Viénet, attended the meeting.

In CEM's rewrite of Chapter 2, trends include critiques of anarchists, "counterculture," "mysticism," and "bastardized Zen." One of the most prominent sections in the rewrite states:

> This attitude [of escapist revolt] is evident in those Europeans and
> Americans who follow Fidel and Mao like gods. Their refusal to con-
> front the realities of advanced capitalist society is no less escapist
> than the mystic's. Tortured by guilt for living in imperialist countries,
> revelling [sic] in the scum of their own inadequacy, they desire only
> complete self-destruction. They trill to the prophesies of their own an-
> nihilation: believing the racist alarums about advancing yellow hordes,
> they run to prostrate themselves at the feet of the attacking conquerors.
> Their guilt is surpassed only by their impotence.[45]

It seems that, perhaps, an inclusion of Zengakuren in this text would be seen by CEM as too attractive to Californians who fetishized Eastern thought. Bigger questions arise regarding how Americans coped with race relations at the time, particularly in relation to the Vietnam War and the US occupation of Japan.

This is not to say that members of CEM disregarded the atrocities of the Vietnam War. In fact, the reality was quite the opposite. Their rewrite of *On the Poverty of Student Life* criticized Californian protesters. The main issues in their edition were "impotence," "escapis[m]," "inadequacy," and untrustworthy motivations, including "racis[m]" and "thrill[ing] to the prophesies of their own annihilation."[46] Cronin remembers frustration with the incredible student passivity toward the atrocities in Vietnam and otherwise in the University of California schools. At UC Santa Cruz, he recalls, "We were just attacking the place." He remembers burning down his house to create a Molotov cocktail, then later, sending a letter to a professor telling him to kill himself. The letter contained a razor blade. This act was investigated by the FBI as domestic terrorism. But why did they send it? Because the professor contributed to the invention of napalm. "We were as angry at professors as we were at the military," said Cronin.[47]

Despite its disinclusion from the editions of *On the Poverty of Student Life*, Zengakuren was significantly influential for the American left in the 1960s, particularly for the Students for a Democratic Society (SDS).[48] Guy Debord noted how SDS was a great example of how to apply techniques developed by Zengakuren,[49] although Situationists launched critiques of SDS elsewhere, including in Viénet's *Enragés et situationnistes*.[50]

Student Life Today

It's true; student life has changed since the 1960s. Still, the fact that *On the Poverty of Student Life* continues to be translated and discussed around the world is evidence of its continued relevance to ongoing problems in society and education. Taking the example of UNEF today, repressive actions toward the already extremely limited powers of students echo trends of longstanding power structures. In the United States, issues like the school-to-prison-pipeline, police brutality, and racism remain rampant. Title IX concerns and the student debt crises are mere symptoms of major social inequities. Today, we are truly living in a world in crisis, whether or not we are personally in a position to recognize that crisis.

Figure 1. René Viénet, *Enragés et situationnistes dans le mouvement des occupations* (Paris: Galllimard, 1968), 93.

Notes

1   Situationist International, *Ten Days That Shook the University: The Situationists at Strasbourg* (London: BCM/Situationist International, 1967).

2   Situationist International, *Ten Days That Shook the University*, 16.

3   Situationist International, "Our Goals and Methods in the Strasbourg Scandal," *Situationist International Anthology*, trans. Ken Knabb (Berkeley: Bureau of Public Secrets, 2006), 263.

4   A. Belden Fields, *Student Politics in France* (New York: Basic Books, 1970), 115.

5   Jean-Pierre Worms, "The French Student Movement," in *Student Activism: Town and Gown in Historical Perspective*, ed. Alexander DeConde (New York: Charles Scribner's Sons, 1971), 76.

6   Situationist International, *Ten Days That Shook the University*.

7   UNESCO, *The Role of African Student Movements in the Political and Social Evolution of Africa from 1900 to 1975* (Paris: UNESCO Publishing, 1994), 185, 194.

8   Fields, *Student Politics in France*, 91.

9   Fields, *Student Politics in France*, 32.

10 Alain Monchablon, *Histoire de l'UNEF* (Paris: Presses Universitaires de France), 1983.

11 Norimitsu Onishi and Constant Méheut, "An Outspoken Student Union Positions Itself at the Vanguard of a Changing France," *The New York Times*, April 6, 2021, https://www.nytimes.com/2021/04/04/world/europe/france-student-union-unef-racism.html.

12 Onishi and Méheut, "An Outspoken Student Union."

13 Situationist International, *Ten Days That Shook the University*, 11.

14 Situationist International, *Ten Days That Shook the University*, 16.

15 Mustapha Khayati, interview with Mehdi El Hajoui, September, 2021.

16 Guy Debord, *Correspondance, volume 2 : septembre 1960 - décembre 1964* (Paris: Librarie Arthème Fayard, 2005), 110.

17 Debord, "Letter to to J.V. Martin, May 8, 1963," *Correspondance*, Vol. 2, 20.

18 Mustapha Khayati Papers, GEN MSS 1480, Box 3f, *International Situationist*, Khayati Papers, Beinecke Rare Book and Manuscript Library, Yale University.

19 "About the Misery of Student Situations" [学生の情況の悲惨さについて], 構造 [*Structure*] 2, no. 29 (1970): 182–201.

20 Henry Dewitt Smith, *Japan's First Student Radicals* (Cambridge: Harvard University Press, 1972), 79, 204.

21 Mustapha Khayati Papers, GEN MSS 1480, Box 3f, *International Situationist*, Khayati Papers, Beinecke Rare Book and Manuscript Library, Yale University.

22 Michiya Shimbori et al., "Japanese Student Activism in the 1970s," *Higher Education* 9, no. 2 (March 1980): 139–154.

23 石田 靖夫, アンテルナシオナル・シチュアシオニスト 1 状況の構築, Tokobon, 1994.

24 Situationist International, *Ten Days That Shook the University*, 16.

25 René Viénet, email message to Anna O'Meara, October 13, 2021.

26 André Bertrand and André Schneider, *Le scandale de Strasbourg* (Montreuil: L'Insomniaque, 2018), 198.

27   Stuart J. Dowsey (ed.), *Zengakuren: Japan's Revolutionary Students* (Berkeley: The Ishi Press, 1970), 236.

28   Guy Debord, "The Situationists and the New Forms of Action in Politics and Art" (1963), trans. Ken Knabb, *Bureau of Public Secrets*, http://www.bopsecrets.org/SI/new-forms.htm.

29   Guy Debord, "Letter to Mustapha Khayati, March 31, 1965," *Correspondance, volume 3 : janvier 1965 - décembre 1968* (Paris: Librarie Arthème Fayard, 2005), 19.

30   Guy Debord, "Letter to J.V. Martin, March 28, 1962," *Correspondance, vol. 2* (Paris: Librarie Arthème Fayard, 2005), 133.

31   René Viénet, email message to Anna O'Meara, October 13, 2021.

32   論大學生之貧乏 [*On the Poverty of Student Life*], ed. René Viénet (Paris: Champ Libre, 1972).

33   René Viénet, email message to Anna O'Meara, October 13, 2021.

34   Occupation Committee of the People's Free Sorbonne University, "Telegrams," *Situationist International Online*, trans. Ken Knabb, 1980, https://www.cddc.vt.edu/sionline/si/telegrams.html.

35   René Viénet, email message to Anna O'Meara, October 13, 2021.

36   Guy Debord, "Letter to Gianfranco Sanguinetti, November 13, 1969," *Correspondance, volume 4, janvier 1969 – décembre 1972*, 145–148.

37   René Viénet, email message to Mehdi El Hajoui, September 4, 2021.

38   Guy Debord, "Letter to Gerard Lebovici," *Correspondance, volume 5, janvier 1973 - décembre 1978* (Paris: Librarie Arthème Fayard, 2005), 153.

39   René Viénet, *Enragés et situationnistes dans le mouvement des occupations* (Paris: Galllimard, 1968), 219. And René Viénet, email message to Anna O'Meara, January 29, 2021.

40   Debord, "Letter to Juvénal Quillet and Bernard Schumacher, July 11, 1973," *Correspondance, vol. 5*, 192.

41   Isaac Cronin, *Nothing Happened: An American Situationist Memoir* (New York: Delancey Street Press, 2021).

42   Isaac Cronin, email message to Anna O'Meara, September 26, 2021.

43   Isaac Cronin, Zoom interview with Anna O'Meara, October 9, 2021.

44   Isaac Cronin, email message to Anna O'Meara, October 2, 2021.

45   Situationist International, *On the Poverty of Student Life* (Berkeley: Council for the Eruption of the Marvelous, 1970), 14–15.

46   Situationist International, *On the Poverty of Student Life* [CEM 1970], 14–15.

47   Isaac Cronin, Zoom interview with Anna O'Meara, October 9, 2021.

48   Dowsey, *Zengakuren*, 223.

49   Guy Debord, "Letter to Christopher Gray and Donald Nicholson-Smith, November 25, 1967," *Correspondance, volume 0, septembre 1951 - juillet 1957* (Paris: Librarie Arthème Fayard, 2005), 356.

50   René Viénet, *Enragés et situationnistes dans le mouvement des occupations* (Paris: Galllimard, 1968), 37–39.

On the Poverty of Student Life, Past and Present

Mustapha Khayati interviewed by Mehdi El Hajoui

Mustapha Khayati and Mehdi El Hajoui

Translated with the help of Nadège LeJeune and Zoé Crochon

The Origins of *On the Poverty of Student Life*

Mehdi El Hajoui: *The year is 1966. Under what circumstances did* On the Poverty of Student Life *come to be? You were studying philosophy in Strasbourg when you became a member of the Situationist International. . . .*

Mustapha Khayati: To answer this question, let's first go back to the "Situationist" group in Strasbourg. This was, first and foremost, a group of friends who shared the same theoretical and political beliefs. It was made up of Edith Frey, her brother Théo Frey, Jean Garnault, Béchir Tlili, and myself. We were first introduced to the "Young Marx" in Henri Lefebvre's elective course at Sciences Po, which opened with an examination of "Marx as Philosopher." In some ways, we were able to dodge the leftist detours of the time. Henri Lefebvre had openly pursued an (at-the-time controversial) approach that sought to distance Marx's ideas from Marxism-Leninism. In one of his lectures, Lefebvre mentioned the journal *Socialisme ou Barbarie*, as well as *Internationale Situationniste*, which only Béchir Tlili knew about at the time. During his first year in Paris, Béchir had been able to learn about and associate with some of the most radical groups, like Socialisme ou Barbarie (S ou B) and the Situationist International (SI). At the time, he still exchanged letters with Guy Debord, and he lent us a copy of the SI journal.

There was a general excitement; we wanted to know everything, right away. The presentation of the journal, its stunning aluminum foil wrappers, really stood out to us. Then, there was the content—inspired by Marxist theory and Socialisme ou Barbarie's analyses of bureaucratic capitalism, while introducing the critique of everyday life, which built on the subversive project of modern art and poetry. . . .

In 1963, Béchir Tlili introduced me to Guy Debord during a trip to Paris, but there wasn't any agenda for the meeting. Our small Strasbourg group didn't really care to have a relationship with the Situationist International, and even less so to become members of the group. The journal was enough for us. A bit later, I started writing to Debord, just as a sympathizer. In hindsight, Debord already seemed to think of us as an organized group, while we were just a bunch of friends with shared ideas.

In March 1965, Edith, Théo, Jean, and I launched our first Situationist-inspired action with the release of the pamphlet *La tortue dans la vitrine* [*The Tortoise in the Tank*], opposing the work of cyberneticist Abraham Moles. At that time, we were looking to break out from a strictly intellectual approach and move into the realm of action. This shift to practice drew us closer to the SI and also led to a break with Tlili, who had refused to join in this operation as he wanted to focus on his studies.

We got to know Moles because he was a professor of Sociology at the University of Strasbourg, and through "Correspondence with a Cybernetician," published in issue #9 of *Internationale Situationniste* (August 1964). We got the idea to distribute the pamphlet along with a copy of the "Correspondence" to disrupt a conference Moles was organizing with the artist Nicolas Schöffer. The two specialized in cybernetics, which is a technical science that intends to control beings, machines, and society. We had a small print run of 100 or 200 copies. We attended the conference and, as we were passing out the leaflet, we heckled a bit, shouting, "Down with robots! Down with cybernetics!" People were a bit taken aback, but the conference wasn't disrupted much. In the crowd were some of the students who would later partake in the "Strasbourg scandal." These students were the first to witness our actions and, most likely, the first in Strasbourg to be introduced to the SI.

A few weeks later, Debord wrote to us, "You're the only Situationists in Strasbourg."[1]

This is how Debord and Vaneigem made us—without our asking—full members of the SI. From then on, we started participating in the group's activities. We drafted the pamphlet *Address to Revolutionaries of Algeria and of All Countries*, which was distributed clandestinely in July 1965 and subsequently reprinted as a supplement to issue #10 of the journal. It is possible the *Address* contributed to a broader dissemination of Situationist ideas in political circles before it got even wider. *On the Poverty of Student Life* further amplified this propagation.

MEH: *Could you explain what drove you to write this incendiary pamphlet?*

MK: It's quite a roundabout story. Besides our group, there was another Strasbourg anarchist student organization led by Daniel Joubert, a Theology student and Protestant. He was one of the editors of *Le Semeur*, the voice of dissident Protestant students, all of whom were followers of Jacques Ellül. Joubert knew about the SI and had even met Debord, who had made it clear to him that he couldn't be associated with the movement until he recanted his faith. We saw a bunch of the people from this group at Le Minotaure, a café we visited every day, but we didn't talk to them.

Joubert and his friends would initiate the project, after having taken over the AFGES Bureau out of cynicism and mockery. Some of the group's members were officially elected to the Strasbourg-based student union on May 4, 1966, with the support of a handful of voters (and the tacit consent of a largely indifferent student population). They immediately thought of leveraging this "takeover" to orchestrate an action with the Situationists. They reached out to Debord through one of their friends, André Bertrand, who was a student in Toulouse at the time.[2]

Bertrand and Sean Wilder met Debord in June of 1966 at the Cinq Billards café in Paris.[3] Bertrand explained his friends' idea to Debord and suggested that they could tap into funds that may benefit the SI. These funds—really the student union's entire budget for the year—were indeed available to them and could have been used to pay back the SI's mounting printing debts following the publication of many pamphlets and a lengthy issue #10 of *Internationale Situationniste*. Instead, Debord suggested to Bertrand and Wilder that they produce a critical text on student poverty which could then be published in the SI's journal. Yet, during the 7th conference of the Situationist International, which took place in Paris a few weeks later, Debord didn't say a word about this project, even though there were plenty of opportunities to do so.

It wasn't until midsummer of 1966 that I got a letter from Debord saying, "What did the 'neo-Strasbourgers'[4] do?" He added: "Make it clear that anyone who can help the SI, but hesitates to do so, will never be considered a friend."[5] This is how I came into contact with the other group, which I had only known in passing at Le Minautore. It was summer and I was alone in Strasbourg. It had been two years since I'd been to Tunisia as a result of my actions against the Bourguiba regime. Garnault was in Paris with his family, while Théo and Edith were with theirs in Mulhouse.

Joubert, who knew the Situationists well, and was the only one capable of articulating a critical theory, put pen to paper. He wrote a first draft, but it was found to be lacking; Joubert himself agreed with this. I was part of a few discussions meant to improve the text, but soon began to write on my own and started a new draft. I wrote to Debord: "We're talking, without much progress, and the current text doesn't hold much water. I'm struggling to see how this might lead anywhere."

Debord then proposed that I write about student life and students' despicable status. He suggested challenging the commonly accepted notion that students were both free and subversive; instead, students' illusion of freedom and subversiveness is precisely what makes them despicable. Debord's own (deliberately interrupted) educational experience, and the repulsion it inspired in him, likely explain the lasting scorn he had for that milieu. So Debord sent me some unedited notes. He wrote, "For a beginning, this is a shocking way of taking the herd of students head-on." Then, he gave valuable advice, "Use a cold and unemotional style."[6]

MEH: *How did you write the text? It was quick, a couple of weeks at most I believe. Who else was involved in the writing and editing?*

MK: I wrote about ten pages that I first wanted to discuss with the Paris group. I traveled back and forth. Then, I discussed it with the AFGES group, including Joubert, André Schneider, Christine Ballivet, and, if I remember correctly, Bruno Vayr-Piova.[7] We would talk about the text, and then I would write some more, either in Paris or in Strasbourg. The AFGES group made a few suggestions, added some corrections, and contributed a few phrases—but didn't make any objection.

The more I wrote, the more I knew how I wanted to organize the text. I finally settled on three sections. First, the student, his misery, the reality of that misery. . . . The question wasn't about whether to pursue higher education so much as it was about playing the role of "the student": someone who, because he is (on average) more educated and operates outside the workforce, likes to believe that he's part of a unique social group, that he is free from constraints. This pamphlet sought to denounce the fantasy of the bohemian intellectual student. The first part was the most aggressive, as well as the most difficult. I didn't have anything to draw from; I had to come up with it all. I relied on what we saw, and who we always made fun of: Strasbourg students, by-and-large bumpkins who fancied themselves intellectuals. All the violence in the first part, which is undoubtedly the real cause of the scandal, derives from the fact that it was based on real student life at Strasbourg, and that it attacked all institutions—academic, religious, and cultural—of a provincial town run by and made up of profoundly conservative leaders.

Having taken stock of the student situation, I next had to consider youth protest movements in both their strengths and weaknesses. On a trip to London a few weeks earlier, I'd gathered some of the most radical American and English publications of the time. Conversations I'd had with Chris Gray and Charles Radcliffe during that stay were also fresh in my mind. I had to demystify the dominant idea that youth revolt was a quasi-biological reality, linking it back instead to its historical roots and connecting it to emerging protest movements around the world. I criticized the *blousons noirs* [greasers]—as the Situationists had already done—as well as the Provos in Amsterdam, who claimed to be influenced by both greasers and anarchists but were led by individuals we viewed as untrustworthy, such as the artist Constant [Nieuwenhuys] and Bernhard De Vries, who had just been elected city councillor of Amsterdam. Because of the Vietnam War, American youth protests, especially in Californian universities, were far more developed than in France, where the Stalinist-Trotskyist tendency prevailed among politically motivated students. The most radical students, however, were drawn to the Vietnamese and Chinese models. *On the Poverty of Student Life* criticized that confusion, as well as the hippie lifestyle and the belief in the liberating power of drugs. I concluded that youth protests, no matter how large, never led to a holistic critique of the system; they attacked the symptoms but didn't tackle the root causes.

The third part tries to outline a future for revolution: youth revolts can only become revolutionary if they come together with workers' struggles. As an example of this possible union, I discuss the Japanese revolutionary movements, Zengakuren, and the League of Young Marxist Workers, which were the furthest along at the time, at least as far as we were aware.[8] This is how the pamphlet came together. There were some edits, a few words or concepts to define or correct, as well as some additions to the first part. There were very few discussions about the second and third parts. The writing was easy for me and didn't take me as long as the first part. The whole thing took less than two months.

MEH: *What were some of the key influences on the text?*

MK: There were some books I'd read, but also the sardonic attitude of our group, which had cemented our friendship and had set us apart from other students, the majority of whom came from Alsatian villages which had remained quite backward, especially in terms of religion. . . . There was also our hostility toward most professors, who were largely conservative and religious, and then there was our pamphlet against Moles. All this contributed to the text. When it came to the analysis, two books about the end of the university by Georges Gusdorf, who had been my professor in 1964, played a role. *Why Professors?* and *The University in Question* made a justified but obviously very elitist and reactionary critique of the "democratization" of education, particularly in the teaching of the social sciences, which was just beginning to emerge. Gusdorf must have read Schopenhauer, who felt contempt for professors and engaged in a critique of institutional knowledge. When Gusdorf asks the question, "Why professors," he assumes that knowledge can be obtained in other ways. What he has in mind is an aristocratic knowledge, which finds its end in itself and not in the training of future senior government officials and company executives. Akin to the contempt for students, *On the Poverty of Student Life* expresses this contempt for teachers in a rather forceful manner.

MEH: *How was the text finalized?*

MK: I reread it with the Paris group, then with the AFGES group in Strasbourg, and then it was approved. Garnault attended a few final meetings when he came back to Strasbourg. In the AFGES group, there were a few jokers who suggested phrases like "menopause of the mind," which I think came from Joubert, and "when they don't piss in his crack" from Roby Grunenwald.[9] In Paris, too, we had a blast trying to find the right phrases, particularly for the first part, which was the most controversial. We had so much fun writing this text.

MEH: *How did you come up with the title?*

MK: I got the idea from bibliographies of eighteenth-century texts, which I found at the *Bibliothèque nationale de France* [National Library of France] and the Strasbourg library. I thought the title should be as long as it was in those days. We needed to show our hand right away; there could be no mistaking our intent. After talking about it, we finally settled on—*On the Poverty of Student Life: Considered in Its Economic, Political, Psychological, Sexual, and Especially Intellectual Aspects, and a Modest Proposal for Its Remedy.* The title turns students' ambitions into miseries, with intellectual ambition being the greatest of all miseries.

MEH: *Were you aware of the impact this text could have?*

MK: We all agreed that this text was important because, and for the first time, it was going to be distributed directly to the people whom it was about. We had a chance to be heard, but no one had any idea how it was going to go. There are always circumstances, along with chance, that make it so that at any given time, things may or may not take. We couldn't imagine how this would cause an unprecedented scandal, because, for years, leftists had been talking about student protests and few people were interested. Had this text first circulated in Paris, it would never have had the resonance it had in Strasbourg. It's only because the local press took interest in it and framed it as scandalous that it became scandalous. This forced the authorities to take repressive steps which, in my view, they originally had no intention of taking.

The Strasbourg Scandal

MEH: On the Poverty of Student Life *was printed quickly in a run of 10,000 copies. How did you find a printer and manage the logistics?*

MK: We found a small printer named Weibel, who took care of the layout. I would go to the printer to correct the proofs and track the progress of the printing process. We had settled on a print run of 10,000 copies. The result was great. The printer was very skilled and did an excellent job: the result was a beautiful 32-page pamphlet, with the first 1,000 copies bound in dark green wrappers with a beautiful typeface. (Coincidentally, the cover resembled that of the first German edition of *The Communist Manifesto*). It was a legitimate, typeset print job, while most other publications were mimeographed at the time. Of course, this was a reference to the *Internationale Situationniste*, but in this case, the pamphlet was going to be given away and not sold. The text was published under the aegis of AFGES; its officers were therefore legally responsible for it. The pamphlet was ready by the end of October. The start of the academic year, which was a major event in Strasbourg, seemed to me like the perfect opportunity to disseminate it.

MEH: *Can you describe the distribution of the text during the start of the 1966–1967 academic year?*

MK: Starting in 1919, the ceremony marking the beginning of the academic year would take place on November 22nd—the same day that the University of Strasbourg was reopened as a French institution of higher learning, following Germany's defeat in World War I. Every year, Strasbourg's local dignitaries, senior government officials, and prominent citizens would be in attendance. Most copies of the text were meant to be distributed to students in front of university cafeterias once the ceremony was over.

Doors opened at about 9:30 or 10:00 a.m. The four of us (Edith, Théo, Garnault, and I) came in an hour early, along with some AFGES representatives.

Other AFGES members (including Schneider), who were afraid of potential academic sanctions, had refused to distribute the pamphlet on the first day of the academic year and were therefore not involved with this action. We put a copy on each chair and then waited in the lobby. We started to see dignitaries filtering in. They'd take their seats, find the pamphlet, and put it on their laps. Because it was a fine-looking book, they didn't throw it away. Then, the ceremony began, and went on for two or three hours. At last, people filtered out, all holding the brochures, all in official attire: soldiers in uniforms, priests in robes, professors in gowns. . . . It was a unique, exhilarating moment to see all these bourgeois from Strasbourg holding *On the Poverty of Student Life* against their bellies, with no clue as to what was inside! It's too bad no photograph captured this moment. . . . Two years later, Bayen, the rector of the University, recalled this episode during his inaugural speech for the 1968 academic year.[10] Then, the pamphlet was widely distributed at university cafeterias, including the popular Cafétéria La Petite Gallia.

MEH: *Local papers were appalled by the action, and even* Le Monde *wrote about you! What happened in the weeks that followed the text's publication?*

MK: It all started with a press conference, called for by AFGES on the day following the text's distribution. Only three journalists showed up. I had prepared some notes and it was Schneider, on behalf of AFGES, who said, "We seized power, as one of UNEF's sects, in order to criticize the world and disclose the role played by students in modern society. Student unionism is nothing but a caricature of labor unionism, which isn't at all what this pamphlet is about. Instead, it should be read as a critique of society as a whole. AFGES, which is a reputable and well-resourced institution, served as a springboard for disseminating our ideas."[11] I then took the floor to explain what the Situationist International really stood for. The next day, newspapers voiced their outrage: first *Les Dernières Nouvelles d'Alsace*, then *Le Nouvel Alsacien*. The first journalists held back a bit, but, soon enough, other newspapers started to rile each other up. They started attacking the authors, calling them "weirdos," "madmen," and "beatniks." What really kicked up a storm were some of the most provocative lines from the first part. The rest was barely mentioned. In the end, it was the media that created enormous publicity by showing huge outrage. There was what we would now call a "buzz." National newspapers like *France-Soir* felt the need to echo this and the far-right jumped at the opportunity to lash out at UNEF and the left.

Journalists vaguely understood that the ideas put forth in the book were the

SI's, so they started looking for articles about the group. None of them, though, bothered to look at the SI's journal, *Internationale Situationniste*. They all parroted the phrase "Secret International Society," which was first used in an article in *Le Figaro Littéraire*.[12] They spoke of sexual debauchery, of the theft of union funds, and basically made moral indictments that would rile their readers. People were most shocked by the first few sentences, with their crass charges against religion and professors and their praise of book theft—in other words, blasphemy against everything that defined the institution of the university. Reactionary journalists were therefore the first to "advertise" the brochure and to make it a selling point for newspapers in France and elsewhere. . . .

One hundred copies were mailed to the Paris group. Debord shared with me the SI's press contacts, a list of subscribers and friends, so that I could send them one, five, or ten copies each. Several problems came up that had to be addressed quickly. First, as journalists started pouring in, the issue of the press. Who was going to speak to them? Debord panicked a little and said that a sharp distinction had to be made between Situationists and others. We agreed that I would represent the Situationists, and that I would be paired with Schneider, then AFGES' president. We spoke to journalists together.

MEH: *How did the interviews with the press go?*

MK: Our goal was to set the facts straight and explain what the SI stood for. As a result of the scandal, journalists had to compete for information, so I spoke openly and at length, and they paid close attention. There were different journalists every day. After a few articles were published in Italy, student protesters from Torino showed up, followed by a team from the Italian public broadcasting company Radiotelevisione italiana (RAI). Two students, Luisella Passerini and Mario Perniola, told us about the political unrest in Torino, where protesters opposed the Italian Communist Party—then one of the largest in Europe—and "Togliatism."[13] Perniola had just published a text that praised the SI, but this was the first we'd heard of Italian protest groups. We spoke for a while, then they took a bunch of copies of *On the Poverty of Student Life* and said, "We'll try to get these ideas out there, but we should also talk about it more." I stayed in touch with Luisella Passerini, who would become one of the translators of *On the Poverty of Student Life*. We were both surprised and excited that Giangiacomo Feltrinelli, who had been a Stalinist dissenter, kind of like François Maspero in France, agreed to publish the translation in May 1967.[14]

The RAI journalist who came to Strasbourg was a former Stalinist in his forties who had broken rank with the party. He was happy to find someone to back up his fight. I talked to him, and he said, "I've read the text. I found it really interesting, even moving. I found ideas that I had when I was in the Communist Party. You're absolutely right when you say that bringing down Stalinism is the first critical step for launching a new proletarian revolution." He asked me to detail the pamphlet's ideas and my idea of revolution, on camera. Then, he interviewed other students. I spoke as though I were in front of a crowd, and the interview was broadcasted in its entirety on Italian TV on Christmas Day, December 25th! It might have been convenient for Christian democrats because Stalinists—who were quite powerful in Italy at the time—were being attacked. It was on that day that seventeen-year-old Gianfranco Sanguinetti became a Situationist.[15] I found a short letter from Perniola saying that he had watched the broadcast, that it was great, that it was uncut, and that it reflected all the key ideas. I never had a chance to watch it myself.

Soon after, about forty professors and several student organizations filed a lawsuit. They hired lawyers and requested that the AFGES Bureau be placed under the supervision of a judicial administrator, which the court granted. Judge Llabador's justification for his decision provides quite an extraordinary articulation of our goals and our actions. It was one of the clearest texts about who we were and what we stood for.[16] Separately, the university's rector, Maurice Bayen—who was completely out of touch—had found himself overwhelmed by the situation but lacked an excuse to crack down on us. He ended up giving the most reactionary speech, worthy of the stupidest journalists, stating that the authors of the text and the organizers of the action were in need of psychiatric help, that they would have to be locked up in a madhouse.[17] If we lived in the USSR, that's definitely where we would have ended up.

Around December, things started to get worse for me after the French weekly *L'Express* published an article where "MK" was presented as the "brains" behind the operation.[18] The journalist from *L'Express* had come with a photographer who took a picture of us without our knowledge or consent. This picture, where I am shown next to Schneider, would be reprinted in *The Times*.[19] We thought this might make me susceptible to deportation. That's when the Paris group—especially Debord—said, "Mustapha must come back to Paris."

The UNEF General Conference was held in in Paris in mid-January 1967. The Strasbourg group was in attendance. I was also there and together we drafted a motion that called for the dissolution of UNEF.[20] Three groups voted in favor of the dissolution. This was the beginning of our relationship with the Nantes group and with Yvon Chotard, who would stir things up in Nantes for a couple of years.

A second edition of *On the Poverty of Student Life* was distributed across France, then reproduced everywhere.[21] We received letters from different groups telling us about their own actions and projects. On the other hand, Stalinists, Catholics, and others promptly took steps to end the scandal and tear UNEF away from the claws of a group of "unleashed anarchists" who were seen as "eccentric" and "irresponsible."

Leading up to May '68

MEH: On the Poverty of Student Life *ends with the famous phrase: "Proletarian revolutions will be festivals or nothing, for festivity is the very keynote of the life they announce. Play is the ultimate principle of this festival, and the only rules it can recognize are to live without dead time and to enjoy without restraints." The slogan "live without dead time, enjoy without restraints" was adopted in May '68.*

Let's talk about the way the pamphlet made its way from Strasbourg to Nanterre. René Riesel was, I think, very influenced by On the Poverty of Student Life. *The text was soon distributed in Nanterre by the Enragés group.*

MK: When it comes to the Enragés, but also other radical groups, it's fair to say that *On the Poverty of Student Life* found the readers it had hoped to reach: people ready to translate theory into action. Throughout 1967 and the beginning of '68, we expanded our outreach to individuals and groups who supported the ideas put forth in *On the Poverty of Student Life* and who played an active part in the text's dissemination. Most were disenchanted anarchists who had become hostile to the Anarchist Federation's leadership; they had sided with the Situationists in the controversy against *Le Monde libertaire* [*Libertarian World*], which had fallen under the ownership of Maurice Joyeux and Suzanne (Suzy) Chevet.[22] The May '68 revolution was the unforeseeable outcome of all of these protest movements, with *On the Poverty of Student Life* acting as a catalyst.

MEH: On the Poverty of Student Life *then reached the Sorbonne and it's often said that it was the spark that ignited May '68. What do you think?*

MK: Thanks to its style and because of the stir it caused, *On the Poverty of Student Life* broadened the reach of Situationist ideas. But the Situationist phrase "these ideas are in everyone's heads" isn't just a slogan. The Enragés, among others, appropriated the ideas in *On the Poverty of Student Life* because they identified with them. With no input from the SI, they came up with their own subversive actions, which in turn appealed to a lot of students. At the time, most militant students (except for those in a few, very small political groups) were fighting for coed housing, and their demands were limited to university life.

Starting in January of '68, the Enragés set a very high bar: the destruction of universities as the first step toward a broader social revolution, especially since Nanterre was the iconic "new" modernized university. Because of its provocative and antagonistic stances, the group stood out among anarchist and leftist groups. The poster "Waiting for Cybernetics, the Cops" was produced after Dean Grappin called the police to the University following one of their activities. While their slogans covering the walls of Nanterre (for example, "Never Work," "Take Your Desires for Reality," "Unions are Brothels") and their song "La Grapignole" drew from Situationist ideas, the group developed them on its own. We were never involved; instead, we followed things from a distance. No one knew what would become of the Nanterre movement. It was thanks to the Enragés—to their radicalism and their imagination—that the movement soon became insurrectionary.

There were only three of us in Paris: Debord, Viénet, and me. Vaneigem visited sometimes. We were working on distributing issue #11 of *Internationale Situationniste*. Following the scandal caused by *On the Poverty of Student Life*, we came into contact with a lot of people in France and some in Europe. As a result, we supported the folks in Nanterre and others in Nantes and Lyon; we talked to them about what they were doing or provided them with copies of *On the Poverty of Student Life* if they wanted to pass them around. But most of what they did, they did on their own.

MEH: On the Poverty of Student Life *advocates for not only political but also cultural revolution. For example, it reads, "[The student] is so 'eccentric' that he continues–thirty years after [Wilhelm] Reich's excellent lessons–to entertain the most traditional forms or erotic behavior, reproducing at this level the general relations of society." To what extent does* On the Poverty of Student Life *anticipate the cultural revolution at the end of the '60s and throughout the 1970s?*

MK: Before May '68, people already knew that anything that doesn't kill power makes it stronger. And indeed, power became stronger by taking away the weapons that were turned against it, and by seizing a minority of "sixty-eighters," particularly among the pitiful Maoists, and then deploying them in various parts of the spectacle. Sexual liberation and what you refer to as the "cultural revolution" naturally came out of people's broad participation in May '68. However, it took less than a decade for the lifestyle and values of a subversive minority to be popularized, legitimated, and even set up as a model—in other words, to fall prey to large-scale recuperation. The "bitter victory" of this subversion coincided with the integration into capitalism and its "new spirit" of what sociologists refer to as "artistic critique"—which is, in fact, neither "artistic" nor a "critique." Each step of this amalgamation has been accompanied by an ideology and a new market for "cultural products," which allow the system to overcome its backwardness by sucking the lifeblood from the most vibrant and novel aspects of the revolutionary movement. After half a century, permissiveness, license, the pleasure mandate, and the prohibition to forbid have become the new norm and been consecrated by the law. This norm weighs on the millions of alienated individuals who populate the so-called Western world.

Publishing Flows: Translations and Reprints

MEH: *On the Poverty of Student Life was a huge success, with 250,000 to 300,000 copies printed before 1970.[23] In 1976, the publisher Gérard Lebovici undertook a controversial reprint of the text through his publishing house, Champ Libre. In a letter dated October 12, 1976, you wrote to him, "This text is not meant for the commercial distribution you intend to give it. It is necessary to let it circulate through many pirate editions."[24] Can you tell us more about the need for* On the Poverty of Student Life *to continue circulating freely?*

MK: All I can say is that, of those hundreds of thousands of copies in circulation, I never received a dime of royalties, and that was the point. I gave Sulliver the permission to reprint the text during France's general strikes of 1995, but at the condition that it would be sold at cost.[25] I was opposed to the 1976 Champ Libre reprint and, with the support of a few friends, I tried to squash it by writing a short response to Lebovici's extremely arrogant letter (which was no doubt penned by Debord).[26]

Another sneaky attempt was made by Debord's widow, who tried to have *On the Poverty of Student Life* included in *The Complete Works of Guy Debord*, published by Gallimard in 2006. It was drawn to my attention in time for me to halt the operation, thanks to Antoine Gallimard's discernment; he was used to these sorts of foolish claims.

The last commercial edition to date is from a small Protestant publishing house, which is the only religious one I know about.[27] The author of the preface even had the audacity to stake a claim to *On the Poverty of Student Life* (through his close friendship with Daniel Joubert), while conveniently skipping over the fact that Joubert, in his renunciation of Protestantism, had dragged him through the mud![28]

MEH: *The first edition of* On the Poverty of Student Life *states, "This text may be freely reproduced even without indication of origin." French (1967), Belgian (1968), and Swiss (1974) pirate editions quickly surfaced as a result. The text was also promptly adapted into English (1967) by Donald Nicholson-Smith and T.J. Clark, then translated into Spanish, German, Portuguese, Italian, Dutch, Danish, Swedish, Serbo-Croatian, Indonesian, Chinese. . . and more recently into Russian and Korean. Did some of the reprints or translations stand out to you? For instance, what about the Chinese edition edited by René Viénet and published in Hong Kong in 1972?*

MK: *On the Poverty of Student Life* took on a life of its own after its initial publication, and I hardly followed the history of its distribution and translations, except when I personally knew the editors. Other than the first English translation/adaptation that was produced by former comrades,[29] the oldest translation was the Italian version produced by semi-sympathizers of the Situationists whom I knew personally.[30] At the end of the '60s, I met a young woman from the Madrid Acratas group who told us that her group had released a Spanish version of the text.[31] Finally, I used to know Pierre Gallissaires, a well-known translator, who produced one of the German translations of *On the Poverty of Student Life* in the 1970s.[32]

On the Poverty of Student Life Today

MEH: *To this day,* On the Poverty of Student Life *remains in print, largely through pirate editions. There are now over a hundred editions that we know of in at least eighteen languages. Why, fifty-five years later, does this text continue to be so influential?*

MK: I have two hypotheses. One is about the text's publication history and the other is about history more generally.

After the successes the book found around the world, despite neither deliberate advertising nor specific means of dissemination, *On the Poverty of Student Life* has become, in a way, a classic of subversion. Small publishers view the text as a bit of an oddity that is worth putting out there: it is connected to a university scandal, to a group that became famous among the cultural avant-garde, and finally to a revolutionary movement that now has its place in museums.

The second hypothesis, which is far more interesting to me, is the echo this text may still find today among groups and individuals looking for ways to make sense of and wage a struggle against the world they live in. The notion of "poverty" continues to be highly relevant because it embodies all of the misfortunes of men in the era of the ubiquitous commodity spectacle. *On the Poverty of Student Life* is a mirror that everyone can look into and recognize their own miserable condition, then cry out, "What are they doing to me and what the hell am I doing here?" The people who started May '68 were the ones who refused to resign themselves to the monster they saw in the mirror. Similarly, those proclaiming "We want to live, not just survive!" are the ones rising up around the world today. In their greatest poverty, the seed of life remains, whereas the overwhelming power of the world of commodities only carries the seed of death in the superstore of "rights" that are tossed away to perpetuate survival.

MEH: *What would you like to say to the students who read* On the Poverty of Student Life *today and embrace its ideas?*

MK: Absolutely nothing! The students described and mocked in 1966 no longer exist. Of all of their poverties, only economic poverty has grown. A segment of society whose future was once assured by the economic system has proliferated and dissolved into the large mass of "precarious workers." Today, students no longer deserve the contempt that *On the Poverty of Student Life* once had them shoulder.

If one were to write a new version of *On the Poverty of Student Life* today, it definitely would not take students as its target. Other actors—often less poor, more pretentious, and more indoctrinated (perhaps students who have succeeded?)—have claimed their rightful place as potential objects of contempt: the universe of the so-called "counterculture," of the "alternative," has become, after a lengthy detour, one of the dominant ideologies of our time. An ideology that holds the illusion that it is possible to live "differently" and "on the margins" of the world as it is, without the need to undertake its unavoidable destruction.

Notes

1 Guy Debord to Mustapha Khayati, June 9, 1965, *Correspondance, volume 3, janvier 1965 - décembre 1968* (Paris: Librarie Arthème Fayard, 2003), 39–40.

2 André Bertrand authored *Le retour de la colonne Durutti* (1966), a famous détourned comic strip announcing the publication of *On the Poverty of Student Life*.

3 Sean Wilder was the only American subscriber to the *Internationale Situationniste*. Prior to 1966, he had been asked to translate *The Decline and the Fall of the Spectacular-Commodity Economy*, an unsigned tract on the Watts Riots that is now attributed to Guy Debord. It first appeared in issue #10 of *Internationale Situationniste*.

4 "Neo-Strasbourgers" was a moniker used by Guy Debord to describe Strasbourg students who were involved in the *On the Poverty of Student Life* scandal but were not bonafide members of the SI.

5 Debord to Khayati, August 10, 1966, *Correspondance, vol. 3*, 158.

6 Debord to Khayati, September 9, 1966, *Correspondance, vol. 3*, 161–162.

7 André Schneider was elected president of the AFGES Bureau and Bruno Vayr-Piova served as vice president. AFGES was the local Strasbourg section of France's largest national student union, UNEF.

8 The reference to Zengakuren was omitted in a Chinese translation of the text produced by René Viénet in 1970.

9 Roby Grunenwald was a member of AFGES and a medical student.

10 "We weren't altogether surprised by protest movements that startled France. The unrest caused by a few Situationists who had taken over key leadership roles in the student union was a warning shot. You may remember that, at the ceremony marking the beginning of the 1966 academic year, Situationists had put copies of the pamphlet *On the Poverty of Student Life* on every chair." See André Bertrand and André Schneider, *Le scandale de Strasbourg mis à nu par ses célibataires, même* (Montreuil: L'Insomniaque, 2018), 206.

11 The above quotation is reminiscent of what is stated in "The Communiqué of the Last Bureau of the AFGES," November 23, 1966. For a verbatim transcript of the communiqué, see: Bertrand and Schneider, *Le scandale de Strasbourg*, 298.

12 Dominique Jamet, "La prise de pouvoir des 'situationnistes' à Strasbourg," *Le Figaro Littéraire* (December 1, 1966): 11.

13 Palmiro Togliatti was the founder and leader of the Italian Communist Party from 1927 (except for a short period) until his death in 1964. He had a close relationship with the Soviet Union, having become a Soviet citizen in 1930.

14 Internazionale Situazionista, *Della miseria nell'ambiente studentesco considerata nei suoi aspetti economico, politico, psicologico, sessuale e specialmente intellettuale e di alcuni mezzi per porvi rimedio* (Milan: Feltrinelli, 1967). Anna Bravo, Giovanni Butrico, Daniela Marin, and Luisella Passerini translated the text and edited the preface.

15 Gianfranco Sanguinetti would only become a bonafide member of the Situationist International a few years later. He cofounded the Italian section of the Situationist International in January 1969.

16 The Summary Order was issued on December 13, 1966, by the Strasbourg District Court, with Judge Llabador presiding. Some editions of *On the Poverty of Student Life* feature excerpts from the text (for instance it appears on the rear wrapper of several Black & Red editions).

17 "These students are insulting their professors. They belong in a madhouse." Rector Maurice Bayen, as quoted by Jacques Clauvel, *L'Aurore*, November 26, 1966.

18 Jean Girbas, "A Strasbourg, les Etudiants Déhcouvrent la Démocratie," *L'Express* 807 (December 5–11, 1966): 110–111.

19 The unsolicited photo of Khayati and Schneider that originally appeared in *L'Express* and *The Times* is also reproduced in Bertrand and Schneider, *Le scandale de Strasbourg*, 181.

20 "Association Fédérative Générale des Etudiants de Strasbourg. Projet de motion en vue de l'Assemblée Générale de l'UNEF des 14–15 janvier 1967." Reproduced in the Appendix of Bertrand and Schneider, *Le scandale de Strasbourg*, 300–301.

21 *De la misère en milieu* étudiant, *considérée sous ses aspects économique, politique, psychologique, sexuel et notamment intellectuel et de quelques moyens pour y remédier* (Paris: Internationale Situationniste), 1967. Second edition, without the "psyschologique" spelling mistake from the 1966 edition. 10,000 copies were printed.

22 For a detailed account of the relationship between anarchist groups and Situationists in the 1960s, see: Miguel Amorós, *Les Situationnistes et l'anarchie* (Villasavary: Éditions de la Roue, 2012).

23 "Taking into account international distribution, On the Poverty of Student Life's total print run likely stood somewhere between 250,000 to 300,000. Of those, 70,000 copies were published directly by the SI. The other copies were produced by other revolutionary groups and by radical newspapers or publishers." See Internationale Situationniste 12 (September 1969): 103.

24 Champ Libre, Correspondance, vol. 1 (Paris: Champ Libre, 1978), 31.

25 *De la misère en milieu* étudiant, *considérée sous ses aspects* économique, *politique, psychologique, sexuel et notamment intellectuel et de quelques moyens pour y remédier* (Aix-en-Provence: Sulliver, 1995).

26 Mustapha Khayati, "A propos de la réédition de la misère en milieu etudiant," in *Champ Libre, Correspondance, vol. 1*, 34–37.

27 *De la misère en milieu* étudiant, *considérée sous ses aspects* économique, *politique, psychologique, sexuel et notamment intellectuel et de quelques moyens pour y remédier* (Maisons-Laffitte: Éditions Ampelos, 2018).

28 Jean Baubérot wrote the preface for the Ampelos edition of *De la misère en milieu étudiant*.

29 *Ten Days That Shook the University: The Situationists at Strasbourg* (London: BCM/ Situationist International), 1967.

30 See note 14.

31 We were unable to locate a copy of this edition.

32 Über *das Elend im Studentenmilieu* (Hamburg: Nautilus, 1977).

De la misère en milieu étudiant, hier et aujourd'hui

Entretien avec Mustapha Khayati, par Mehdi El Hajoui

Mustapha Khayati et Mehdi El Hajoui

Aux origines de *la Misère*

Mehdi El Hajoui : *Nous sommes en 1966. Dans quelles circonstances as-tu écrit* la Misère *? Tu étudiais la philosophie à Strasbourg, et faisais déjà partie de l'*Internationale Situationniste...

Mustapha Khayati : Pour répondre à ta question, il faudrait faire un petit retour en arrière : le groupe « situationniste » de Strasbourg, constitué d'Edith Frey, son frère Théo, Jean Garnault, Béchir Tlili et moi-même, était d'abord un groupe d'amis partageant les mêmes convictions théoriques et politiques. Nous avions découvert le jeune Marx à travers un cours facultatif que donnait Henri Lefebvre à Sciences Po et qui commençait par l'étude du « Marx philosophe », qui allait, pourrait-on dire, nous permettre d'échapper à toutes les errances gauchistes de l'époque. Henri Lefebvre s'inscrivait clairement dans une démarche polémique cherchant à séparer la pensée de Marx du marxisme-léninisme. Dans un de ses cours, il a évoqué la revue *Socialisme ou Barbarie*, et l'*Internationale Situationniste*, que seul Béchir Tlili connaissait à l'époque. Béchir avait, lors de sa première année à Paris, pu connaître et fréquenter les courants les plus radicaux comme Socialisme ou Barbarie (S ou B) et l'Internationale Situationniste. Il était alors toujours en correspondance avec Guy Debord et nous a prêté un numéro de la revue.

Ça a été un enthousiasme commun et nous avons voulu tout de suite tout connaître. Ce qui nous a marqués, c'est d'abord la forme de la revue, cette couverture étonnante en papier métallisé. Puis le propos, qui avait pour arrière-plan théorique tout Marx, les analyses de S ou B sur le capitalisme bureaucratique, mais qui introduisait aussi la critique de la vie quotidienne, héritière du projet subversif de l'art et de la poésie modernes.

En 1963, Béchir Tlili m'a fait rencontrer Guy Debord lors d'un passage à Paris mais sans objectif précis. Notre petit groupe de Strasbourg n'avait pas particulièrement envie d'avoir des relations avec le groupe situationniste et encore moins d'en devenir membre, la revue nous suffisait. Un peu plus tard, j'ai commencé à correspondre avec Guy Debord mais ça ne dépassait pas la sympathie. Avec le recul, il semble que Debord nous percevait déjà comme un groupe constitué alors que nous nous vivions comme une bande d'amis avec des idées communes.

C'est en mars 1965 que nous avons débuté, avec Edith, Théo et Jean Garnault, nos activités d'inspiration situ avec le tract *La Tortue dans la Vitrine* contre Abraham Moles. Nous voulions à ce moment-là sortir de la démarche purement intellectuelle et réaliser une action. C'est ce passage à la pratique qui nous a engagés dans la voie de l'IS et nous a séparés de Tlili qui a refusé de s'associer à cette opération. Il ne voulait plus s'occuper que de ses études.

Nous connaissions Abraham Moles comme professeur de sociologie à Strasbourg et à travers la « Correspondance avec un cybernéticien » publiée dans le numéro 9 de *Internationale Situationniste*. L'idée nous était venue de distribuer ce tract avec la correspondance et d'ainsi perturber la conférence qu'il organisait avec le sculpteur cybernétique Nicolas Schöffer. Tous deux étaient adeptes de la cybernétique, techno-science capable de gouverner les êtres vivants, les machines et la société. Nous avions fait un petit tirage de cent ou deux cents exemplaires. Nous sommes allés à cette conférence et, en même temps que nous distribuions le tract, nous avons un peu chahuté en criant « À bas les robots ! A bas la cybernétique ! » Les gens étaient un peu interloqués mais leur réunion n'a pas tellement été sabotée. Il y avait probablement parmi eux une partie de ceux qui, par la suite, participeront au scandale de l'AFGES. Ils ont sans doute été les premiers à remarquer notre intervention et l'introduction de l'IS à Strasbourg.

Quelques semaines plus tard, Debord nous dit dans une lettre : « Vous êtes, vous, les seuls situationnistes à Strasbourg. »[1] C'est ainsi que Debord et Vaneigem ont fait de nous, sans qu'on le leur demande, des membres à part entière de l'IS. A partir de là, nous commençons donc à participer aux activités du groupe, notamment avec la rédaction du tract *Adresse aux révolutionnaires d'Algérie et de tous les pays*, publié en juillet 1965, puis dans le numéro 10 de la revue. *L'Adresse* est peut-être l'élément qui a permis une plus large diffusion des thèses de l'IS dans les milieux politiques et puis cela s'est un peu élargi. La *Misère* ne fera qu'amplifier ce mouvement.

MEH : *Pourrais-tu expliquer ce qui t'a motivé à écrire ce brûlot ?*

MK : C'est une histoire très indirecte. Parallèlement à notre groupe, il y avait à Strasbourg un groupe d'étudiants anarchisants animé par Daniel Joubert, alors étudiant à la Faculté de Théologie Protestante et un des rédacteurs du *Semeur*, organe des étudiants protestants contestataires, tous disciples de Jacques Ellül. Joubert connaissait l'IS et avait même rencontré Debord, qui lui avait clairement déclaré que tant qu'il n'avait pas abjuré, il ne pouvait prétendre avoir des relations avec l'IS. Nous voyions plusieurs personnes de ce groupe au café Le Minotaure que nous fréquentions tous quotidiennement, mais sans nous parler.

C'est ce groupe qui sera à l'origine du projet, après que par cynisme et dérision, il s'est emparé du bureau de l'AFGES, la Fédération des étudiants d'Alsace, légalement élu le 4 mai 1966 devant une poignée d'électeurs et dans l'indifférence générale des étudiants strasbourgeois. Ils ont tout de suite pensé à utiliser cette « prise de pouvoir » pour faire un coup avec l'IS. Par l'intermédiaire d'un de leurs amis, André Bertrand,[2] alors étudiant à Toulouse, ils ont contacté Debord.

Bertrand, accompagné de Sean Wilder,[3] a rencontré Debord en juin 1966 au café Cinq Billards à Paris et lui a exposé l'idée de ses amis, en laissant aussi entendre qu'il y avait de l'argent dont il serait possible de faire profiter l'IS. Cet argent, dont ils disposaient par l'AFGES, aurait effectivement pu contribuer au financement de la revue, c'est-à-dire à payer les dettes qui s'accumulaient auprès de l'imprimeur, surtout après la publication de plusieurs tirés à part et du numéro 10, qui avait été plus coûteux en raison de son volume. Debord a alors suggéré de publier un texte critique sur le thème de la misère étudiante et d'utiliser librement la revue pour cela. Pourtant, lors de la VIIe Conférence de l'IS, réunie quelques semaines plus tard à Paris, Debord n'a pas dit un mot de ce projet alors que les occasions ne manquaient pas pour le faire.

Ce n'est qu'au milieu de l'été 66 que je reçois une lettre de lui me disant : « Qu'ont donné les néo-strasbourgeois ? »[4] Ajoutant cette remarque « Bien faire comprendre que celui qui peut aider l'IS, et hésite à le faire, ne sera jamais traité par nous en ami. »[5] C'est ainsi que je suis entré en contact avec le groupe, que je connaissais de loin au Minotaure. C'était l'été et j'étais seul à Strasbourg, c'était la deuxième année que je ne rentrais plus en Tunisie, en raison de mes activités contre le régime de Bourguiba. Garnault était à Paris avec sa famille, et Théo et Edith avec la leur dans la région de Mulhouse.

Joubert, qui connaissait bien l'IS et qui était le seul capable d'élaborer une pensée théorique, a commencé à rédiger. Il a fait un premier jet mais personne ne l'a trouvé assez bon et lui-même l'a admis. J'ai participé à quelques discussions en vue d'améliorer la chose, puis je me suis mis à écrire seul en entamant un autre brouillon. J'avais écrit à Debord : On est en discussion, ça n'avance pas beaucoup, le texte déjà existant ne tient pas la route. Cela me semble un peu difficile d'aboutir à partir de cette base.

Il m'a alors envoyé quelques notes : la situation de l'étudiant, son statut méprisable. L'idée proposée par Debord était de renverser l'idée communément admise de la liberté de l'étudiant et de son potentiel subversif pour montrer que c'est justement l'illusion de cette liberté et ses prétentions qui le rendent misérable. Sa propre expérience de l'Université, volontairement écourtée, et le dégoût qu'elle lui a inspiré sont probablement à l'origine du mépris définitif qu'il avait pour ce milieu. Il a donc envoyé quelques notes non rédigées. Il m'a écrit : « Pour un début, c'est une façon choquante de prendre les bestiaux de front. » Puis un conseil précieux, « le style devrait être froid et impassible. »[6]

MEH : *Comment s'est déroulée la rédaction du texte ? Cela s'est fait très vite je crois, quelques semaines tout au plus ? Qui d'autre a collaboré à la rédaction et aux corrections ?*

MK : J'ai alors rédigé une dizaine de pages dont j'ai d'abord voulu discuter avec Paris. Je faisais donc l'aller-retour. Ensuite, j'ai discuté avec le groupe de l'AFGES, notamment Joubert, André Schneider, Christine Ballivet et si je me souviens bien, Bruno Vayr-Piova.[7] On discutait et ensuite j'écrivais, soit à Paris, soit à Strasbourg. Le groupe de l'AFGES a proposé quelques apports, quelques corrections, quelques formules, mais aucune objection.

Plus j'avançais, plus je voyais la structure du texte. Un plan en trois parties a finalement été retenu. D'abord l'étudiant, sa misère, ses misères en fait... La question n'était pas tant de faire ou non des études que de « se prendre pour » un étudiant, comme un être qui par sa culture globalement au-dessus de la moyenne, par sa vie en-dehors du travail, peut se donner l'illusion qu'il est libre, qu'il fait partie d'un groupe social à part, délié de toute contrainte. Ce qui est visé dans ce pamphlet, c'est le fantasme de l'étudiant intellectuel bohème. La première partie était la plus offensive, la plus difficile aussi. Je n'avais pas de textes de référence, tout était à imaginer. Je me suis donc appuyé sur ce que nous voyions et dont nous nous moquions en permanence, les étudiants de Strasbourg, qui étaient pour la plupart des « ploucs » qui se prenaient pour des intellos. Toute la violence de cette première partie, qui est sans aucun doute la vraie cause du scandale, vient justement du fait qu'elle s'appuyait sur la réalité de la vie étudiante à Strasbourg, et s'attaquait à toutes les institutions, universitaires, religieuses, culturelles, d'une ville de province administrée et dominée par des notables profondément conservateurs.

Après l'état des lieux de la situation de l'étudiant, il fallait aborder les mouvements de contestation de la jeunesse, leurs forces et leurs faiblesses. Lors de mon voyage à Londres quelques semaines auparavant, j'avais rassemblé plusieurs publications américaines ou anglaises parmi les plus radicales de l'époque. J'avais aussi à l'esprit les discussions que j'ai eues avec Chris Gray et Charles Radcliffe au cours de ce séjour. Il fallait démythifier la conception dominante, qui fait de la révolte des jeunes un fait quasi biologique, pour la rapporter à ses racines historiques et la rattacher aux autres mouvements de contestation qui commençaient à se manifester un peu partout dans le monde. J'ai ainsi pu faire la critique des Blousons Noirs, une thématique déjà présente dans l'*IS*, des Provos d'Amsterdam, qui se réclamaient à la fois des Blousons Noirs et de l'anarchie, mais qui étaient dirigés par des gens suspects à nos yeux – comme l'artiste Constant et Bernhard De Vries, qui venait d'être élu à la mairie d'Amsterdam. A cause de la guerre du Vietnam, la contestation de la jeunesse américaine, notamment dans les universités californiennes, étaient beaucoup plus avancée qu'en France, où la tradition stalino-trotskyste restait dominante parmi les étudiants politisés. Toutefois, les plus radicaux étaient attirés par les modèles vietnamiens ou chinois. C'est cette confusion que la *Misère* critique, de même que le mode de vie hippie et l'idéologie de la « drogue qui libère ». La conclusion était que les protestations de la jeunesse, aussi massives soient-elles, n'aboutissaient jamais à une critique globale du système, qu'elles restaient dans la lutte contre les symptômes, sans s'attaquer aux causes.

La troisième partie tente d'esquisser les perspectives de la révolution : les révoltes de la jeunesse ne peuvent devenir révolutionnaires que si elles s'unissent aux luttes des travailleurs. Comme exemple de cette union possible, je cite les mouvements révolutionnaires japonais, Zengakuren et la Ligue des jeunes travailleurs marxistes, qui étaient les tentatives les plus conséquentes à l'époque, du moins de ce que nous en savions.[8] C'est comme ça que le pamphlet s'est mis en place. Il y a eu quelques corrections, des termes ou quelques notions à corriger ou à définir, des ajouts dans la première partie. Pour la deuxième et la troisième partie, il y a eu très peu de discussions. L'écriture était facile pour moi et ça n'a pas pris autant de temps que la première partie. Tout ça s'est fait en l'espace de moins de deux mois.

MEH : *Quelles furent certaines des principales influences pour ce texte ?*

MK : Il n'y avait pas seulement les lectures mais aussi l'attitude très moqueuse de notre groupe, qui avait fait dès le début le ciment de notre amitié, par rapport à la majorité, à la masse des étudiants qui étaient issus de bleds alsaciens où il y avait encore beaucoup de retards, notamment du côté de la religion… Il y avait aussi notre hostilité envers la plupart des enseignants, majoritairement conservateurs et croyants, ensuite notre tract contre Moles. C'est tout cela qui avait nourri le texte. Ensuite, pour l'analyse, les deux livres sur la fin de l'université de Georges Gusdorf, qui avait été mon professeur en 1964, ont joué un rôle. Ces deux ouvrages, *Pourquoi des professeurs ?* et *l'Université en question,* faisaient une critique pertinente mais bien entendu très élitiste et réactionnaire de la « démocratisation » de l'enseignement, notamment de l'enseignement des sciences sociales qui commençait à peine à émerger. Gusdorf avait sûrement dû lire Schopenhauer, chez qui on trouve ce mépris des professeurs d'Université et cette critique du savoir institué. Quand Gusdorf pose la question « Pourquoi des professeurs ? », il suppose que l'on peut acquérir le savoir autrement et pense à un savoir aristocratique, qui trouve sa fin en soi et non dans la formation de futurs cadres de l'économie et de l'administration. Une formule un peu cassante de *la Misère* reprend ce mépris des enseignants, à l'image du mépris pour les étudiants.

MEH : *Comment le texte a-t-il été finalisé ?*

MK : Je l'ai relu avec le groupe de Paris, ensuite à Strasbourg avec les gens de l'AFGES, et il a été adopté. Garnault a assisté à quelques réunions finales quand il est revenu à Strasbourg. Dans le groupe de l'AFGES, il y avait quelques déconneurs qui ont proposé les formules du type : « la ménopause de l'esprit », je crois que ça vient de Joubert, et Roby Grunenwald, « quand on ne lui pisse pas dans la raie ».[9] A Paris aussi, ça a été des parties de rigolade pour trouver les bonnes formules, surtout pour la première partie, la plus pamphlétaire. Ce texte a été écrit dans une grande joie.

MEH : *Comment est venue l'idée du titre ?*

MK : Ce sont les titres des listes bibliographiques d'ouvrages du XVIIIe siècle que je consultais, soit à la Bibiliothèque Nationale soit à la bibliothèque de Strasbourg, qui m'ont donné cette idée. J'ai pensé que le titre devait être aussi long que ceux de l'époque, un titre qui annonce la couleur, sans aucune ambiguïté possible. Après discussion, on a trouvé sa forme définitive : *De la Misère en milieu étudiant considérée sous ses aspects économique, politique, sexuel et notamment intellectuel.* Le titre transforme toutes les prétentions de l'étudiant en misères, et évidemment, sa prétention intellectuelle est la plus grande.

MEH : *Avais-tu conscience des répercussions que ce texte pourrait avoir ?*

MK : Pour moi comme pour les autres, c'était un texte important dans la mesure où il allait, pour la première fois, être distribué directement au public concerné. Il avait donc des chances d'être entendu, mais ni moi, ni personne n'avions idée de ce que cela allait donner. Il y a toujours les concours de circonstances, le hasard aussi, qui font qu'à un moment donné, les choses peuvent prendre ou non. On ne pouvait pas imaginer que cela allait provoquer ce scandale inédit, puisque depuis des années, des gauchistes parlaient des contestations étudiantes sans intéresser grand monde. Je pense qu'un tel texte diffusé à Paris n'aurait jamais eu l'écho qu'il allait avoir à Strasbourg. Il a fallu que la presse locale s'en occupe et crie au scandale pour que cela devienne scandaleux et oblige les autorités à prendre des mesures répressives qui, à mon avis, n'étaient pas leur intention première.

Le scandale de Strasbourg

MEH : La Misère *est rapidement imprimé à près de 10.000 exemplaires. Comment as-tu trouvé un imprimeur et géré la logistique ?*

MK : On a trouvé un petit imprimeur, Weibel, qui s'est chargé de la mise en page. J'allais chez l'imprimeur pour corriger les épreuves et suivre la progression de l'impression. Nous avions décidé de faire un tirage de 10.000 exemplaires. Le résultat était beau. L'imprimeur avait fait un excellent travail, très professionnel : une belle brochure de 32 pages, parachevée d'une belle couverture cartonnée vert câpre avec de beaux caractères, pour les 1.000 premiers exemplaires, qui rappelait fortuitement la couverture de la première édition allemande du *Manifeste du parti communiste...* C'était une vraie impression, alors que la plupart des publications de l'époque étaient ronéotypées. Evidemment, c'était une référence à la revue de l'IS, mais là, elle allait être distribuée et non vendue. Le texte est au nom de l'AFGES ; le bureau de l'AFGES était donc engagé juridiquement. La brochure était prête fin octobre. La rentrée universitaire, grand évènement de la ville de Strasbourg, me paraissait la meilleure occasion pour la diffuser.

MEH : *Peux-tu justement décrire la distribution du texte, au cours de la cérémonie marquant le début de l'année universitaire 1966-1967 ?*

MK : Depuis 1919, la rentrée universitaire solennelle avait lieu le 22 novembre, date de la réouverture de l'Université française de Strasbourg après la défaite allemande. Tous les ans, les notables, les autorités, les personnalités de Strasbourg y assistaient. Le gros de la distribution devait se faire après la cérémonie d'inauguration auprès des étudiants devant les restos U.

L'ouverture de la salle devait avoir lieu vers 9h30 ou 10h00. Nous quatre, Edith, Théo, Garnault et moi, ainsi que quelques membres de l'AFGES sommes entrés une heure avant dans la salle. Certains d'entre eux avaient refusé de distribuer la brochure le jour de la rentrée, notamment Schneider, par peur de sanctions proprement universitaires de la part du rectorat ou du doyen, et n'ont donc pas participé à l'opération. Nous avons déposé un exemplaire sur chaque fauteuil et sommes restés à attendre dans le hall. Puis on a commencé à voir les personnalités entrer. Ils prenaient leur siège, trouvaient le livre, et le mettait sur leurs genoux. Comme c'était un beau livre, ils n'ont pas osé le jeter. Ensuite la cérémonie a eu lieu, deux ou trois heures. Enfin les gens sont sortis, chacun avec sa brochure, tous en tenue officielle, les militaires en uniforme, les religieux en soutane et les professeurs en toge… C'était un moment unique et jouissant de voir tous ces bourgeois de Strasbourg tenir la *Misère* sur leur ventre sans imaginer ce qu'il y avait dedans ! Dommage qu'aucune photo ne l'ait immortalisé… Deux ans plus tard, Bayen, le recteur de l'Université, n'a d'ailleurs pu s'empêcher de rappeler à ses auditeurs cet épisode lors de son discours inaugural de la rentrée 1968.[10] Ensuite, on a généreusement distribué la brochure devant les restos U, notamment à la *Gallia*, le plus fréquenté.

MEH : *Les journaux locaux s'insurgent de cette action, et même* Le Monde *parle de toi ! Comment se déroulent les quelques semaines qui suivent la parution du texte ?*

MK : Les premiers bruits sont venus de la conférence de presse que l'AFGES avait convoquée le lendemain de la distribution, et où il n'y avait que trois journalistes. J'avais préparé des notes et c'est Schneider, au nom de l'AFGES, qui a pris la parole : « Nous avons pris le pouvoir, en tant qu'une des tendances de l'UNEF, pour critiquer le monde et montrer la place de l'étudiant dans la société moderne. Le syndicalisme étudiant n'est déjà qu'une caricature du syndicalisme ouvrier et ce n'est pas du tout dans ce sens-là que la brochure est conçue mais dans le sens d'une critique totale de la société. L'AFGES, institution reconnue et qui dispose de moyens, a servi de plateforme et de tribune pour diffuser nos idées. »[11] J'ai ensuite pris la parole pour expliquer ce qu'était vraiment l'Internationale Situationniste. Dès le lendemain, dans les journaux, on criait au scandale. *Les Dernières nouvelles d'Alsace,* ensuite, *Le Nouvel Alsacien.* Les premiers journalistes étaient un peu réservés. Mais très vite, les autres journaux ont commencé à s'exciter mutuellement. Ils ont commencé à attaquer, à traiter les auteurs de «

farfelus », de « fous », de « beatniks ». Ce qui a vraiment soulevé la tempête, c'était quelques-unes des phrases les plus provocatrices de la première partie. Le reste était à peine évoqué. Finalement, ce sont les médias qui, en criant au scandale, ont fait une publicité monstre. Une sorte de « buzz » avant la lettre. Les journaux nationaux, notamment *France-Soir*, se sont sentis obligés d'en faire écho et ceux de l'extrême-droite ont sauté sur l'occasion pour pourfendre l'UNEF et la gauche.

Les journalistes avaient vaguement compris que les idées défendues dans le livre étaient celles de l'IS; ils ont donc commencé à chercher des articles sur le groupe mais personne n'est allé regarder de plus près la revue. Ils ont tous repris l'expression « Internationale occulte » employée dans l'article du *Figaro littéraire* et ont essayé de nous cataloguer.[12] Ils parlaient de débauche sexuelle, de vol de l'argent des syndicats, faisaient essentiellement des condamnations morales pour scandaliser leurs lecteurs. Ce qui a le plus mis tous ces gens hors d'eux, ça a été le choc des premières phrases, la charge grossière contre la religion et les profs, l'apologie du vol des livres, en somme le blasphème de tout ce qui faisait l'institution universitaire. Ce sont donc les journalistes réactionnaires qui ont fait la première « publicité » de la brochure et en ont fait un objet journalistique vendeur en France et à l'étranger…

Il y avait un paquet de cent exemplaires pour Paris. Debord m'a envoyé un listing de tout le service de presse de l'*IS*, abonnés et amis, pour leur envoyer un, cinq, ou dix exemplaires à chacun. Nous devions résoudre un certain nombre de problèmes qui se sont très vite posés. D'abord, ceux de la presse, car les journalistes ont commencé à affluer. Qui allait répondre ? Debord a un peu paniqué et a dit qu'il fallait établir une distinction radicale entre ce qu'est l'IS et les autres. Nous avons convenu que je représenterais l'IS et que je sois toujours accompagné d'un responsable AFGES, en l'occurrence Schneider, le président. Nous recevions les journalistes ensemble.

MEH : *Comment se sont déroulés les entretiens avec les journalistes ?*

MK : Il s'agissait de rétablir les faits et expliquer ce qu'était l'IS. J'ai parlé sans retenue, et le scandale aidant, comme les journalistes devaient rivaliser d'informations, on m'a laissé parler et écouté avec attention. Tous les jours, il fallait répondre à de nouveaux journalistes. Suite à quelques articles publiés dans la presse italienne, des étudiants contestataires de Turin sont arrivés, puis une équipe de la RAI. Les étudiants Luisella Passerini et Mario Perniola nous ont décrit le mouvement d'agitation qu'il y avait à Turin à ce moment-là, en opposition avec les lignes du Parti Communiste italien, un des plus importants d'Europe, et du togliatisme.[13] Perniola venait de publier un texte favorable à l'IS mais c'était la première fois que nous prenions connaissance de l'existence de groupes contestataires italiens. Après une longue discussion, ils ont pris avec eux beaucoup d'exemplaires de la *Misère* et nous ont dit : « On va essayer de diffuser ces idées-là, mais il faudra qu'on discute encore. » Je suis donc resté en correspondance avec Luisella Passerini, qui va être l'une des traductrices de la *Misère*. Et, ce qui nous a à la fois étonnés et réjouis, Giangiacomo Feltrinelli, un ancien stalinien en dissidence, un peu l'équivalent de Maspéro en France, a accepté, en mai 1967, de publier cette traduction.[14]

Le journaliste de la RAI venu à Strasbourg était un ancien stalinien en rupture de ban d'une quarantaine d'années content de trouver quelqu'un qui pourrait le venger. J'ai discuté avec lui et il m'a dit : « J'ai lu le texte. Il m'a beaucoup intéressé et même ému. J'y ai retrouvé des idées que j'avais quand j'étais au Parti. Vous avez tout à fait raison de dire que la destruction du stalinisme est le premier pas nécessaire pour le nouveau départ d'une révolution prolétarienne. » Il m'a demandé de m'expliquer en détail sur le contenu de cette brochure et sur ma conception de la révolution pendant qu'il me filmait. Ensuite, il a interviewé d'autres étudiants. J'ai parlé comme devant une assemblée et l'interview a été diffusée intégralement à la télévision italienne le jour de Noël, un 25 décembre ! Cela arrangeait peut-être aussi la démocratie chrétienne que l'on tape sur les staliniens, très puissants en Italie. C'est ce jour-là que Gianfranco Sanguinetti, alors âgé de 17 ans, est devenu situationniste.[15] J'ai aussi retrouvé une petite lettre de Perniola disant qu'il avait vu l'émission, qu'elle était très bien, n'avait pas été coupée, et restituait toutes les idées. Je ne l'ai jamais vue…

Une quarantaine d'enseignants et diverses corporations étudiantes ont alors porté plainte. Ils ont pris des avocats et ont demandé la mise sous séquestre du bureau de l'AFGES, ce qui a été accepté par le tribunal. Les attendus du juge Llabador de la mise sous séquestre sont un extraordinaire morceau de littérature pour définir nos actes et nos intentions. C'est l'un des textes les plus lucides sur ce qu'on était et ce qu'on voulait.[16] Par ailleurs, le recteur Bayen, qui venait d'un autre monde, dépassé par les événements et ne trouvant pas de prétexte pour sévir, a tenu le discours rétrograde des journalistes les plus idiots en déclarant que les auteurs du texte et les organisateurs de l'événement relevaient de la psychiatrie, qu'il fallait les enfermer dans un hôpital de fous.[17] Si on était en URSS, c'est effectivement là qu'on se serait sûrement retrouvés…

Vers décembre déjà, ma situation a commencé à devenir un peu compliquée, notamment après l'article de *L'Express*, où on me dénomme MK, et me présente comme l' « éminence grise » de tout le scandale.[18] Le journaliste de *L'Express* était venu accompagné d'un photographe qui nous a pris en photo à notre insu. C'est cette photo qui va être reproduite dans le *Times*, où j'apparais avec Schneider.[19] On s'est dit que ça risquait de m'exposer à une expulsion du territoire. C'est à ce moment-là, que le groupe de Paris, et notamment Debord, a dit : Il faut que Mustapha se replie à Paris.

À la mi-janvier 1967, s'est tenue la conférence générale de l'UNEF à Paris. Le groupe de Strasbourg est venu. J'y ai assisté et j'ai rédigé avec eux une motion demandant la dissolution de l'UNEF.[20] Trois associations ont voté pour la dissolution. C'est le début de notre relation avec le groupe de Nantes et avec Yvon Chotard qui va faire de l'agitation à Nantes les années suivantes. Un deuxième tirage de la *Misère* a été distribué dans toute la France[21] puis reproduit un peu partout. Dans les lettres que nous recevions, certains groupes nous informaient de leurs propres activités et projets. De l'autre côté, très vite, les staliniens, les cathos, et d'autres ont commencé à faire des démarches pour stopper le scandale et surtout arracher l'association à ce groupe d' « anarchistes débridés » décrits comme « farfelus » et « irresponsables »…

Vers Mai 68

MEH : La Misère *s'achève sur la célèbre phrase : « Les révolutions prolétariennes seront des fêtes ou ne seront pas, car la vie qu'elles annoncent sera elle-même créée sous le signe de la fête. Le jeu est la rationalité ultime de cette fête, vivre sans temps mort, jouir sans entraves sont les seules règles qu'il pourra reconnaître. » Le slogan « vivre sans temps mort, jouir sans entraves » sera repris en Mai 68.*

Parlons donc de la trajectoire qui va de Strasbourg à Nanterre. René Riesel fut, je crois, très influencé par la Misère. *Le texte est rapidement distribué à Nanterre par le groupe des « Enragés »…*

MK : On peut dire qu'avec les Enragés, mais aussi d'autres groupes radicaux, la *Misère* a trouvé les lecteurs qu'elle souhaitait avoir, c'est-à-dire des individus et des groupes capables de traduire en actes sa critique théorique. Toute l'année 67 et le début de l'année 68, nous avons ainsi multiplié nos contacts avec les individus et les groupes qui adhéraient aux thèses de la *Misère*, et ont activement participé à sa diffusion. C'était essentiellement des anarchistes déçus et hostiles à la direction de la Fédération Anarchiste, et qui ont pris parti pour l'IS dans sa polémique contre le *Monde Libertaire*, devenu la propriété de Maurice et Suzy Joyeux.[22] La révolution de mai 68 a donc été l'aboutissement imprévisible de tous ces mouvements de contestation qui la précédaient et dont le scandale de la *Misère* a joué le rôle de catalyseur.

MEH : *La Misère atteint ensuite la Sorbonne, et l'on dit souvent qu'elle fut l'étincelle qui alluma le brasier de Mai 68. Qu'en penses-tu ?*

MK : La *Misère*, par son style et le scandale qu'a suscité sa publication, ont permis une plus large diffusion des thèses situationnistes, mais la phrase de l'IS « Nos idées sont dans toutes les têtes » n'est pas un simple slogan. Les Enragés, comme d'autres, se sont approprié les thèses de la *Misère* parce qu'ils s'y reconnaissaient. Ils ont alors imaginé des actions subversives totalement autonomes de l'IS, qui ont à leur tour séduit de nombreux étudiants. A l'époque, la plupart des étudiants contestataires, en dehors des groupuscules politiques, luttaient pour la libération des cités universitaires et leurs revendications ne dépassaient pas les murs de l'Université.

Dès janvier 68, les Enragés ont mis la barre très haut : destruction des universités comme un premier pas vers une révolution de toute la société, d'autant que Nanterre était justement le symbole de cette « nouvelle » Université modernisée. Par ses positions à la fois provocatrices et en rupture, le groupe se détachait de la tendance dominante du moment, notamment parmi les anarchistes et les gauchistes. L'affiche *En attendant la cybernétique, les flics*, après que le doyen Grappin a appelé la police à l'Université suite à une de leurs actions ; leurs slogans bombés sur les murs de Nanterre, « Ne travaillez jamais », « Prenez vos désirs pour la réalité », « Les syndicats sont des bordels » ; leur chanson « La Grapignole », étaient d'inspiration situ, mais l'initiative venait des Enragés. On n'a jamais été impliqués et on suivait ça de loin. Personne ne savait ce qu'allait devenir le mouvement de Nanterre. C'est grâce à eux, à leur radicalité, à leur imagination que le mouvement est très vite devenu insurrectionnel.

Nous, nous n'étions que trois à Paris, Debord, Viénet et moi. Vaneigem venait de temps en temps. Nous travaillions à la distribution du numéro 11, nous étions en contact avec énormément de gens après le scandale de la *Misère*, à travers la France et un peu en Europe. Nous soutenions donc les gens de Nanterre et d'autres, à Nantes, à Lyon, nous discutions avec eux de ce qu'ils faisaient ou bien nous leur fournissions des exemplaires de la *Misère* quand ils voulaient les distribuer. Mais l'essentiel, ils le faisaient eux-mêmes.

MEH : *On oublie souvent que* La Misère *est un texte qui prône non seulement la révolution politique mais également culturelle. Par exemple, on peut y lire : « trente ans après Wilhelm Reich, cet excellent éducateur de la jeunesse, les étudiants continuent d'avoir les comportements érotico-amoureux les plus traditionnels, reproduisant les rapports généraux de la société de classes dans leurs rapports intersexuels. » Dans quelle mesure* la Misère *anticipe-t-elle la révolution des mœurs à la fin des années 60 et dans les années 70 ?*

MK : On disait déjà avant le soulèvement de mai que tout ce qui ne tue pas le pouvoir le rend plus fort. Et de fait, il s'est rendu plus fort en s'emparant des armes qui étaient dirigées contre lui, et en récupérant une minorité de « soixante-huitards », notamment parmi la secte des maolâtres, pour les employer dans divers secteurs du spectacle à l'œuvre. La libération des mœurs et ce que tu appelles la « révolution culturelle » ont naturellement découlé de la participation massive des individus au mouvement de mai 68.

Mais il a fallu moins d'une décennie à la grande entreprise de récupération pour populariser le mode de vie et les valeurs d'une minorité subversive, la légitimer, et même l'ériger en modèle. L' « amère victoire » de cette subversion coïncide avec l'intégration par le capitalisme et son « nouvel esprit » de ce qu'un sociologue appelle la « critique artiste », et qui n'est en fait ni « critique » ni « artiste ». Chaque étape de cette intégration s'est accompagnée d'une idéologie et d'un nouveau marché de « produits culturels », qui permettent au système de surmonter ses propres retards en vampirisant ce qu'il y a de plus vivant et d'inédit dans le mouvement révolutionnaire. Au bout d'un demi-siècle, la permissivité, la licence, l'impératif de jouissance, l'interdit d'interdire sont devenus la nouvelle norme, consacrée par la loi, qui pèse sur les millions d'individus séparés qui peuplent le monde dit occidental.

Circulations : autour des traductions et des rééditions

MEH : La Misère *connaît un succès énorme avec 250.000 à 300.000 exemplaires imprimés avant 1970.*[23] *En 1976, l'éditeur Gérard Lebovici entreprend une réédition controversée du texte chez Champ Libre. Dans une lettre datée du 12 octobre 1976, tu lui écris « Ce texte n'est point fait pour la forme commerciale officielle que vous souhaitez lui donner [...] il faut le laisser continuer son chemin à travers les nombreuses éditions sauvages ».*[24] *Peux-tu nous en dire davantage sur la nécessité pour* la Misère *de continuer de circuler sans entraves ?*

MK : Tout ce que je peux dire, c'est que de ces centaines de milliers d'exemplaires qui circulent, je n'ai jamais touché un centime de droits d'auteur et c'était bien le but. J'ai autorisé Sulliver lors des grèves de 1995 à rééditer le texte à la condition de le vendre au prix de revient.[25] Je m'étais opposé à la réédition faite par Champ Libre en 1976 et avec l'appui de quelques amis, j'ai essayé de la torpiller en écrivant un petit texte pour répondre à l'insolence hautaine de Lebovici, qui s'exprimait par la plume de Debord.[26]

Une autre tentative a été subrepticement menée par la veuve de celui-ci en essayant d'inclure la *Misère* dans les *Œuvres Complètes* de Guy Debord publiées par

Gallimard en 2006. Alerté à temps, j'ai pu stopper l'opération grâce au bon sens de François Gallimard, habitué qu'il est à ce type de folles prétentions.

La dernière édition commerciale en date est celle d'une petite maison d'édition protestante, la seule à ma connaissance réalisée par des religieux...[27] L'auteur de la préface[28] a même la témérité de revendiquer la *Misère* à travers Daniel Joubert, en faisant mine d'oublier que celui-ci, dans son abjuration, l'avait, lui et ses semblables, définitivement traîné dans la fange !

MEH : *L'édition originale de la Misère comprend la mention « ce texte peut être librement reproduit même sans indication d'origine ». On trouve donc assez rapidement des contrefaçons françaises (1967), belges (1968) et suisses (1974). Le texte est également rapidement adapté en anglais (1967) par Donald Nicholson-Smith, puis traduit en espagnol, allemand, portugais, italien, néerlandais, danois, suédois, serbo-croate, chinois... et plus récemment en russe ou en coréen. Certaines traductions ou éditions t'ont-elles particulièrement marqué ? Je pense par exemple à l'édition chinoise éditée par René Viénet et parue à Hong-Kong en 1972...*

MK : La *Misère* a eu une vie autonome après sa première publication et j'ai très peu suivi l'histoire de sa diffusion et de ses traductions, sauf quand j'en connaissais personnellement les auteurs. Outre la première traduction/adaptation anglaise réalisée par d'anciens camarades,[29] la plus ancienne traduction est, comme je l'ai déjà dit, la version italienne réalisée par de semi-sympathisants de l'IS que j'ai connus personnellement.[30] A la fin des années 60, j'ai aussi rencontré une jeune femme du groupe madrilène Acratas qui nous a dit que son groupe en avait diffusé une version espagnole.[31] Enfin, j'ai connu Pierre Gallissaires, traducteur bien connu, qui a publié une des traductions allemandes de la *Misère* dans les années 70.[32]

La Misère aujourd'hui

MEH : *En 2021,* la Misère *continue d'être réimprimé, presque toujours de manière sauvage. On recense aujourd'hui plus d'une centaine d'éditions dans au moins dix-huit langues. Pourquoi, cinquante-cinq ans plus tard, ce texte continue-t-il d'être aussi influent ?*

MK : Je peux avancer deux hypothèses : l'une relève de l'histoire de l'édition, l'autre de l'histoire tout court.

Après le succès qu'elle a rencontré un peu partout, la *Misère*, sans publicité volontaire ni moyens spécifiques de diffusion, est devenue en quelque sorte un texte classique de la subversion, que les petits éditeurs dans chaque pays trouvent bon de mettre sur le marché, comme une curiosité éditoriale, liée d'abord à un scandale universitaire puis à un groupe qui a gagné de la célébrité parmi les avant-gardes culturelles et enfin à un mouvement révolutionnaire aujourd'hui muséifié.

La seconde hypothèse, qui m'intéresse bien plus, est l'écho que peut encore aujourd'hui rencontrer ce texte de par le monde chez des groupes ou des individus en quête de moyens pour penser et combattre le monde où ils vivent. La notion de « misère » demeure une idée très forte, qui à elle-seule résume tous les malheurs des hommes à l'ère du spectacle marchand qui domine toujours. La *Misère* est le miroir devant lequel chacun peut reconnaître sa condition misérable et s'écrier « Mais qu'est-ce qu'on est en train de faire de moi et qu'est-ce que je fous là ? ». Ce sont ceux qui ont refusé de se résigner à rester le monstre qu'ils voyaient dans ce miroir qui ont fait mai 68, comme ce sont ceux qui clament « On veut vivre et non survivre ! » qui se soulèvent aujourd'hui de par le monde. Dans leur misère la plus grande existe le germe de la vie, au lieu que, dans sa puissance écrasante, le monde de la marchandise ne porte que le germe de la mort, dans le grand hypermarché des « droits » jetés en pâture pour pérenniser la survie.

MEH : *Que voudrais-tu dire aux étudiants qui aujourd'hui lisent* la Misère *et se trouvent en adéquation avec ses thèses ?*

MK : Rien, surtout ! Les étudiants décrits et moqués en 1966 n'existent plus. De toutes leurs misères, seule la misère économique a prospéré et cette partie de la société, dont l'avenir était garanti autrefois par le système économique, s'est à la fois démographiquement multipliée et dissoute dans la grande masse des travailleurs dits précaires. Elle ne mérite plus aujourd'hui le mépris dont l'accablait la *Misère*.

Si l'on devait écrire une *Misère* aujourd'hui, ce ne seraient sûrement pas les étudiants qui en seraient l'objet. D'autres acteurs, souvent moins pauvres, plus prétentieux et plus intégrés (des étudiants qui ont réussi ?) sont venus prendre leur place de candidats au mépris : le monde de ladite « contre-culture », de l' « alternatif », devenu après un long détour une des idéologies dominantes de notre Temps. Idéologie qui entretient l'illusion qu'il serait possible de vivre « autrement » et « à côté » du monde tel qu'il est en s'épargnant l'inévitable entreprise de sa démolition.

Notes

1   Voir lettre du mercredi 9 juin 1965 in Guy Debord, *Correspondance, volume 3 : janvier 1965 - décembre 1968* (Paris : Librairie Arthème Fayard, 2003), 39-40.

2   André Bertrand est l'auteur de *Le retour de la colonne Durutti*, comics détourné qui annonce la parution de *La misère en milieu étudiant*.

3   Unique abonné américain de la revue, il avait déjà été sollicité pour la traduction du *Déclin et la chute de l'économie spectaculaire-marchande* sur la révolte de Watts.

4   Néo-strasbourgeois était une expression utilisée par Debord pour caractériser les étudiants de Strasbourg qui, s'ils participent au scandale de *La Misère*, ne sont pas membres à part entière de l'IS.

5   Voir lettre du mercredi 10 août 1966 in Guy Debord, *Correspondance, vol. 3*, 158.

6   Voir lettre du vendredi 9 septembre 1966 in Guy Debord, *Correspondance, vol. 3*, 161-162.

7   Schneider était Président du Bureau de l'AFGES, Vayr-Piova en était le vice-président.

8   La traduction chinoise de La Misère chez Champ Libre, qui a été produite par René Viénet, supprimera cette référence aux Zengakuren.

9   Membre de l'AFGES et étudiant en médecine.

10 « Le mouvement de contestation qui a surpris la France entière ne nous a pas entièrement étonnés. Nous avions eu un avertissement par l'agitation de quelques situationnistes qui s'étaient assurés en 1966 des postes clé à la Mutuelle des étudiants et l'Association des étudiants de Strasbourg. Vous vous souvenez qu'à la séance de rentrée de 1966, les situationnistes avaient déposé sans autorisation des brochures sur les chaises qui allaient être occupées par nos invités : *De la misère en milieu étudiant…* ». André Bertrand et André Schneider, *Le scandale de Strasbourg mis à nu par ses célibataires, même* (Montreuil : L'Insomniaque, 2018), 206.

11 C'est peu ou prou ce qu'annonce le « Communiqué du dernier Bureau de l'AFGES » du 23 novembre 1966. Pour une reproduction mot à mot dudit communiqué, voir André Bertrand et André Schneider, *Le scandale de Strasbourg mis à nu par ses célibataires, même* (Montreuil : L'Insomniaque, 2018), 298.

12 Dominique Jamet, « La prise de pouvoir des 'situationnistes' à Strasbourg », *Le Figaro littéraire* (jeudi 1er décembre 1966), 11.

13 Palmiro Togliatti fut l'un des fondateurs du Parti Communiste italien, qu'il dirigea (hormis une brève interruption) de 1927 jusqu'à son décès en 1964. Devenu citoyen soviétique en 1930, il fut proche de l'URSS.

14 *Della miseria nell'ambiente studentesco* (Milan : Feltrinelli, 1967). Anna Bravo, Giovanni Butrico, Daniela Marin et Luisella Passerini collaborent à la traduction et corédigent la préface.

15 Gianfranco Sanguinetti ne devient membre officiel de l'Internationale Situationniste que quelques années plus tard. Il sera le cofondateur de la section italienne de l'Internationale Situationniste en janvier 1969.

16 Ordonnance de référé rendue le 13 décembre 1966 par le Tribunal de Grande Instance de Strasbourg, présidé par le Juge Llabador. Certaines éditions de *La Misère*

reproduisent des extraits du texte (par exemple, en quatrième de couverture de l'édition Champ Libre en 1976).

17 « Ces étudiants insultent leurs professeurs. Ils relèvent de la maison de fous. » Citation du recteur M. Bayen par Jacques Clauvel dans *L'Aurore* du 26 novembre 1966.

18 Jean Girbas, « A Strasbourg, les étudiants découvrent la démocratie », *L'Express* 807 (5-11 décembre 1966), 110-111.

19 Cette photographie est reproduite dans André Bertrand et André Schneider, *Le scandale de Strasbourg mis à nu par ses célibataires, même* (Montreuil : L'Insomniaque, 2018), 300-301.

20 « Association Fédérative Générale des Etudiants de Strasbourg. Projet de motion en vue de l'Assemblée Générale de l'UNEF des 14-15 janvier 1967 ». Reproduit en Annexe dans André Bertrand et André Schneider, *Le scandale de Strasbourg mis à nu par ses célibataires, même* (Montreuil : L'Insomniaque, 2018), 300-301.

21 *De la misère en milieu étudiant, considérée sous ses aspects économique, politique, psychologique, sexuel et notamment intellectuel et de quelques moyens pour y remédier* (Paris : Internationale Situationniste, 1967), 20e mille, sans la faute à « psychologique ». Supplément à la revue Internationale Situationniste, Boite Postale 307-03, Paris.

22 Pour un compte-rendu détaillé, voir Miguel Amorós, *Les Situationnistes et l'anarchie* (Villasavary : Editions de la Roue, 2012).

23 « La brochure *De la misère en milieu étudiant*, à considérer sa diffusion dans plusieurs pays, a atteint un tirage total que l'on peut évaluer entre 250 000 et 300 000 exemplaires. Sur ce nombre environ 70 000 exemplaires ont été directement édités par l'IS ; le reste a été publié par des groupes révolutionnaires indépendants, des éditeurs, ou des journaux extrémistes. » Internationale Situationniste, *Internationale Situationniste* 12 (1969), 103.

24 *Champ Libre, Correspondance, vol. 1* (Paris : Champ Libre, 1978), 31.

25 *De la misère en milieu étudiant, considérée sous ses aspects économique, politique, psychologique, sexuel et notamment intellectuel et de quelques moyens pour y remédier* (Aix-en-Provence : Sulliver, 30 novembre 1995).

26 Mustapha Khayati, « A propos de la réédition de *La Misère en milieu étudiant*. » *Champ Libre, Correspondance vol. 1* (Paris : Champ Libre, 1978), 34-37.

27 *De la misère en milieu étudiant, considérée sous ses aspects économique, politique, psychologique, sexuel et notamment intellectuel et de quelques moyens pour y remédier* (Maisons-Laffitte : Éditions Ampélos, 2018).

28 Il s'agit de Jean Baubérot.

29 *Ten days that shook the university : the situationists at Strasbourg* (Londres : BCM / Situationist International, 1967).

30 *Voir note 14.*

31 Nous n'avons pas pu retrouver la trace de cette édition.

32 *Über das Elend im Studentenmilieu* (Hambourg : Nautilus, 1977).

On the Poverty of Student Life
The Black and Red Edition

Allan Antliff

My introduction to *On the Poverty of Student Life* came by way of a 1973 English-language edition published in Detroit by Black & Red Press. I picked it up at an anarchist bookstore in Montreal sometime in the late 1970s. Cofounded by American radicals Lorraine and Fredy Perlman, Black & Red played an important role in the dissemination of Situationist ideas in North America. The Perlmans were first introduced to the Situationist International (SI) in 1968. That April, Fredy Perlman had given a three-week lecture course on economic theory at the Institut Universitaire d'Études Européennes in Turin, Italy[1] before traveling to Paris, where he got "caught up in the tumultuous events of May."[2]

I was fortunate to have the chance to hear Lorraine Perlman's perspective on these events, after a long correspondence beginning in the late 1990s. She remembers, "During these action-filled weeks there was little time for reading, but Fredy learned about ideas and histories which influenced him in the decade that followed: the texts of the SI, anarchism and the Spanish Revolution, the council communists."[3] He returned to the United States in July with publications from Paris, notably *Ten Days that Shook the University–The Situationists at Strasbourg*, the first English-language edition (1967) of *On the Poverty of Student Life*. Produced by Donald Nicholson-Smith and T.J. Clark of the SI, it included an introductory text concerning events at Strasbourg University and a *détourned* postscript outlining the pamphlet's relevance for revolutionary prospects in Britain. "As a document of an unusual radical action," Lorraine Perlman recalls, "it stimulated us enormously. The pamphlet's title is a provocation and the immediate insight it communicates makes a reader complicitly part of the rebel camp."[4]

"Of Student Poverty." *Black & Red* 3 (November 1968): 49–57.

Number 4   Christmas 1968

"It is Not Enough for Thought to Seek its Realization in Practice: Practice Must Seek its Theory."
Black & Red 4 (December 1968): 47–53.

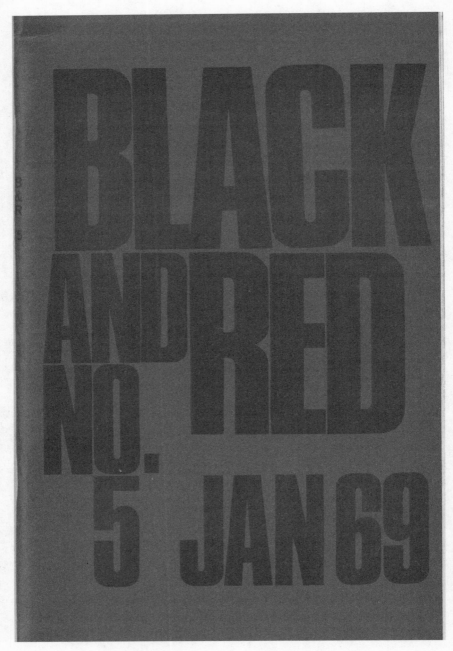

"To Create at Long Last a Situation which Goes Beyond the Point of No Return."
Black & Red 5 (January 1969): 50–57.

"If You Make a Social Revolution, Do It for Fun!" *Black & Red* 6 (March 1969): 79–84.

In the autumn of 1968, the couple serialized the British pamphlet in *Black & Red*,[5] a short-lived journal they copublished with student and activist collaborators[6] at Western in Kalamazoo, where Fredy Perlman was an assistant professor (1966–1968).[7] The project was unabashedly anti-authoritarian:

> BLACK—against the social hierarchy of masters and slaves. RED—against the division of society into pimps and prostitutes. BLACK—against all masters: the state, its army, its police; the corporations, their owners, their managers. RED—against all pimps: the job pimps who force workers to sell their labor; the knowledge pimps who teach students to sell their minds. BLACK—for the destruction of a political system in which society's power, appropriated by the State, oppresses society. RED—for the destruction of an economic system in which men's labor, transformed into Capital, exploits the laborers. BLACK—for the end of violence: the end of armies and the police. RED—for the end of exploitation: the end of ownership of society's productive forces. BLACK—for the oppressed who alienate their power. RED—for the exploited who alienate their labor. BLACK—for everyone to make the decisions which affect him, without orders, without leaders, without cops. RED—for everyone to create the environment in which he lives, without specialists, without experts, without supervisors. BLACK—for the night when everything is possible. RED—for the fire which will light a new way. BLACK—for the reappropriation of power by all communities. RED—for the reappropriation of labor by all creators.[8]

"In the fall of 1968," Lorraine Perlman recollects, "we were living in Kalamazoo and had started a monthly publication called *Black & Red*. In the third issue (November 1968) we began printing a translation of *On the Poverty of Student Life*. We did not need to translate it ourselves because it already existed in a British pamphlet."[9] The three sections comprising *On the Poverty of Student Life* reproduced in *Black & Red* are: no. 3 (November 1968)—"To Make Shame More Shameful Still by Making It Public"; no. 4 (December 1968)—"It is Not Enough for Thought to Seek Its Realization in Practice: Practice Must Seek Its Theory"; and no. 5 (January 1969)—"To Create at Long Last a Situation Which Goes Beyond the Point of No Return." No. 6 (March 1969) featured the British pamphlet's postscript, "If You Make a Social Revolution, Do It for Fun."[10] The decision to publish *On the Poverty of Student Life* serially not only reflected the tenor of the period (1968–1969), when student-led revolts were surging globally: the pamphlet was integral to the journal's stated purpose. Taking their cue from *On the Poverty of Student Life*, the collective's "present field of action" was "the student milieu," a "new front in the world anti-capitalist struggle."[11] Conceived as "an organic link between the theory-action of the world revolutionary movement and the action-theory of the new revolutionary front," the journal's ultimate aim was "to create at long last a situation which goes beyond the point of no return (International Situationist)."[12]

In keeping with this goal, *Black & Red*'s inaugural issue led off with "Revolt in France: Repression Unveiled." Compiled from interviews with two members of Nanterre University's March 22nd Movement,[13] the article aligned the revolt in France with recent unrest at Columbia University from April to May 1968. In both cases, students were fighting against "the transformation of the university into a knowledge factory" in the service of capitalism.[14] Occupying administrative buildings, as students had done at Nanterre and Columbia, revealed "the so-called neutral knowledge of the university (which is bourgeois knowledge) and the police" were seamless components of the same system. Thanks to direct action, the integral relationships linking universities to state apparatuses had been rendered self-evident.[15] In the next article, "Anything Can Happen," Fredy Perlman argued "common sense" declarations about the impossibility of people rising up against hierarchical institutions and economic inequality were belied by the fact that "millions of students all over the world—in Tokyo, Turin, Belgrade, Berkeley, Rome, Rio, Warsaw, New York, Paris—are fighting for power to control and decide about the social and material conditions in which they live."[16] Social scientists asserting people were naturally disposed towards the status quo were myth-making adjuncts to the brute force of state repression.[17] As recent events in France had demonstrated, "ANYTHING IS POSSIBLE."[18] This set the tone for subsequent issues, which analyzed student militancy in Mexico City, West Berlin, Belgrade, New York, and Chicago, as well as curricular-administrative machinations at Western Michigan University (and a critique concerning the local chapter of Students for a Democratic Society).[19] The final issue (no. 6 ½) discussed the expulsion of one of *Black & Red*'s collaborators from Western Michigan University on the grounds that she was an "outside agitator."[20] By then, Kalamazoo's "*Black & Red* gang" had dispersed and the Perlmans were in Detroit.[21]

In Detroit they cofounded a printing co-op and began Black & Red Press in fall 1969. An early endeavor was to translate and copublish the first English-language edition of *The Society of the Spectacle* (1970) and, that same year, an excerpt from Raoul Vaneigem's *The Revolution of Everyday Life*.[22] Beautifully produced and illustrated, *The Society of the Spectacle* circulated widely through numerous editions.[23] A few years later, the Perlmans published *On the Poverty of Student Life* (1973). The pamphlet opens with a short explanatory text relating the circumstances of its original publication in 1966 by members of the SI and students at the University of Strasbourg, noting [citing from the British edition], "The front cover is a collage depicting the pamphlet's 'wide diffusion in both student circles and among the general public, by the local, national, international, and foreign press.'"[24] The back cover reproduces the "summation of the judge, Strasbourg, 1966" condemning the spread of "noxious" theories of a "basically anarchist character" at the expense of Strasbourg University's student union.[25]

On the Poverty of Student Life. Detroit: Black & Red, 1973. Front wrapper.

The accused have never denied the charge of misusing the funds of the student union. Indeed, they openly admit to having made the union pay some $1500 for the printing and distribution of 10,000 pamphlets, not to mention the cost of other literature inspired by "Internationale Situationniste". These publications express ideas and aspirations which, to put it mildly, have nothing to do with the aims of a student union. One has only to read what the accused have written, for it is obvious that these five students, scarcely more than adolescents, lacking all experience of real life, their minds confused by ill-digested philosophical, social, political and economic theories, and perplexed by the drab monotony of their everyday life, make the empty, arrogant, and pathetic claim to pass definitive judgements, sinking to outright abuse, on their fellow-students, their teachers, God, religion, the clergy, the governments and political systems of the whole world. Rejecting all morality and restraint, these cynics do not hesitate to commend theft, the destruction of scholarship, the abolition of work, total subversion, and a world-wide proletarian revolution with "unlicensed pleasure" as its only goal.

In view of their basically anarchist character, these theories and propaganda are eminently noxious. Their wide diffusion in both student circles and among the general public, by the local, national and foreign press, are a threat to the morality, the studies, the reputation and thus the very future of the students of the University of Strasbourg.

—*Summation of the judge, Strasbourg, 1966.*

On the Poverty of Student Life. Detroit: Black & Red, 1973. Rear wrapper.

Lorraine Perlman recalls they initially distributed copies for free "to people who ordered Black & Red books and pamphlets."[26]

In 2000, she published a new translation based on the Champ Libre imprint (Paris 1976) with a cover depicting Greco-Roman ruins designed by "a Detroit comrade," Ralph Franklin.[27] Why? Because "the ambitious project of the activists who scammed the University of Strasbourg in order to expose humiliations of the university experience as well as the materialist goals of the university institution is still admired today."[28]

On the Poverty of Student Life. Detroit: Black & Red, 2000.

Notes

1   Lorraine Perlman, *Having Little, Being Much: A Chronicle of Fredy Perlman's Fifty Years* (Detroit: Black & Red, 1989), 46.

2   Perlman, *Having Little*, 46.

3   Perlman, *Having Little*, 48.

4   Lorraine Perlman, email message to Allan Antliff, September 27, 2021.

5   In total, seven issues were published. The last issue (no. 6 ½) appeared in August 1969.

6   The nucleus was comprised of the Perlmans, Western Michigan University students Bob Maier and Linda Lanphear, German exchange student Ursula Kneisel, and French activist Roger Grégoire, who met Fredy Perlman during the May events in Paris.

7   The appointment was for two years and was not renewed. See Perlman, *Having Little*, 42.

8   See "Black & Red," *Black & Red* 1 (September 1968): back cover.

9   Perlman, email message to Antliff, September 27, 2021.

10   The British source was noted, as was the pamphlet's initial publication date of 1966.

11   "Purpose of *Black & Red*," *Black & Red* 3 (November 1968): 64. The statement was preceded by the first excerpt from *On the Poverty of Student Life*.

12   "Purpose of *Black & Red*."

13   Named after the date students occupied Nanterre University's administrative offices, March 22nd Movement activists propelled subsequent events at Nanterre.

14   Two Members of the March 22nd Movement, "Revolt in France: Repression Unveiled," *Black & Red* 1 (September 1968): 1.

15   Two Members of the March 22nd Movement, "Revolt in France": 2.

16   Fredy Perlman, "Anything is Possible," *Black & Red* 1 (September 1968): 11–12.

17   Perlman, "Anything is Possible": 17–22.

18   Perlman, "Anything is Possible": 24.

19   Convened in 1962 as an autonomous student organization, SDS chapters spread rapidly through US universities and colleges as opposition to the US war in Vietnam grew. It disintegrated in the late 1960s.

20   The student was Linda Lanphear. See *Black & Red* 6 1/2 (Fall 1969). Fredy Perlman produced this issue in Detroit. [See Perlman, *Having Little*, 59.]

21   There were expectations that collaborations might continue, as Grégoire and Lanphear had departed for Paris with the intention of continuing involvement with *Black & Red* projects. However, once there, they broke with the Perlmans in an effort to prove themselves worthy of joining the French SI. Lorraine Perlman discusses the farcical outcome in *Having Little*, 71–73.

22   The first edition of *The Society of the Spectacle* was copublished by *Black & Red* and the leftist journal *Radical America*. The translation was a cooperative effort involving the Perlmans, Don Campbell, Judy Campbell, Hannah Ziegellaub, and Jon Supak. The seventy-page pamphlet excerpted from *The Revolution of Everyday Life* was translated by Supak and Marilyn Keydal. See Danielle Aubert, *The Detroit Printing Co-op: The*

Politics of the Joy of Printing (Los Angeles: Inventory Press, 2020), 134, 144.

23 Aubert, *The Detroit Printing Co-op*, 134.

24 Situationist International, *On the Poverty of Student Life: Ten Days That Shook the University* (Detroit: Black & Red, 1973). See preface, n.p.

25 See back cover of Black & Red's 1973 reprint of SI's *On the Poverty of Student Life*.

26 Perlman, email message to Antliff, September 27, 2021.

27 Perlman, email message to Antliff, September 27, 2021. Translation by Lorraine Perlman. See *On the Poverty of Student Life* (Detroit: Black & Red, 2000).

28 Lorraine Perlman, email message to Allan Antliff, October 2, 2021.

II
On the Poverty of Student Life

Ten Days that Shook the University
A Note on an Adaptation

In the wake of the "Strasbourg scandal" of November and December 1966, the Situationist International decided to produce an English-language edition of the pamphlet *De la misère en milieu étudiant*. After a general discussion the task of translation fell to T.J. (Tim) Clark and me, two English members residing in Paris. Tim and I felt that a literal translation would be less useful to the Situationist project than one that was freely adapted to make it more readily accessible to an anglophone (chiefly British) readership. For that reason too, we wanted to add "framing" matter. This approach was agreed upon. We consulted with other members over points of translation, notably with Mustapha Khayati, the chief author of the original French text.

Our translation and the framing material—a one-page presentation and the afterword, "Postscript: If You Make a Social Revolution, Do It for Fun"—were composed by Tim and me in Paris, while the physical production of the pamphlet was handled by two Situationists in London, namely Chris Gray and Charlie Radcliffe. At some point in early 1967 we crossed the Channel briefly, if memory serves, and I remember working with our comrades on the translations of the panels of André Bertrand's *Le retour de la colonne Durutti* that were used for the front and back covers of *Ten Days* and to illustrate the text.

A title page follows the introductory note and precedes the translation. The original title is rendered there as *On the Poverty of Student Life Considered in Its Economic, Political, Psychological, Sexual, and Particularly Intellectual Aspects, and a Modest Proposal for Its Remedy*. The mild *détournement* of Dean Swift is not implicit in the French and was generally abandoned by subsequent English versions of the "Strasbourg pamphlet." This is a good example of the way in which our translation was in no way strict. On the contrary, it was conceived deliberately as a *texte de combat* rather than a rigorous rendering of the original French. A close representation of that original must be sought elsewhere.

Ten Days That Shook the University was printed by Equity Printers Ltd., 1 Regent Square, London WC1. Neither Tim nor I can remember the size of the print run. It was never reprinted, though it has been much reproduced, of course, in part or in whole.

Donald Nicholson-Smith
August 2021

On the Poverty of Student Life

Ten Days That Shook the University (1967)

Donald Nicholson-Smith and T.J. Clark

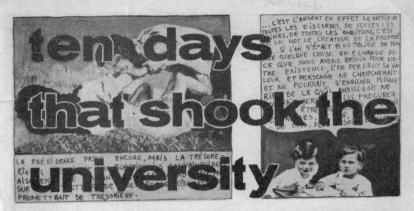

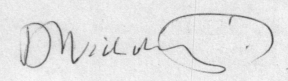

In November 1966, Strasbourg University was the scene of a preliminary skirmish between modern capitalism and the new revolutionary forces which it is beginning to engender.

For the first time, a few students abandoned pseudo-revolt and found their way to a coherent radical activity of a kind which has everywhere been repressed by reformism. This small group got itself elected, amidst the apathy of Strasbourg's 16,000 students, to the committee of the left-wing students' union. Once in this position of power, they began to put union funds to good use. They founded a Society for the Rehabilitation of Karl Marx and Ravachol. They plastered the walls of the city with a Marxist comic-strip, "The Return of the Durutti Column". They proclaimed their intention to dissolve the union once and for all. Worst of all, they enlisted the aid of the notorious Situationist International, and ran off ten thousand copies of a lengthy pamphlet which poured shit on student life and loves (and a few other things). When this was handed out at the official ceremony marking the beginning of the academic year, only de Gaulle was unaffected. The press—local, national and international—had a field-day. It took three weeks for the local Party of Order—from right-wing students to the official left, via Alsatian mill-owners—to eject these fanatics. The union was closed by a court order on the 14th of December. The judge's summing-up was disarmingly lucid:

> *The accused have never denied the charge of misusing the funds of the students' union. Indeed, they openly admit to having made the union pay some £500 for the printing and distribution of 10,000 pamphlets, not to mention the cost of other literature inspired by "Internationale Situationniste". These publications express ideas and aspirations which, to put it mildly, have nothing to do with the aims of a student union. One has only to read what the accused have written, for it to be obvious that these five students, scarcely more than adolescents, lacking all experience of real life, their minds confused by ill-digested philosophical, social, political and economic theories, and perplexed by the drab monotony of their everyday life, make the empty, arrogant and pathetic claim to pass definitive judgements, sinking to outright abuse, on their fellow-students, their teachers, God, religion, the clergy, the governments and political systems of the whole world. Rejecting all morality and restraint, these cynics do not hesitate to commend theft, the destruction of scholarship, the abolition of work, total subversion and a world-wide proletarian revolution with "unlicensed pleasure" as its only goal.*
>
> *In view of their basically anarchist character, these theories and propaganda are eminently noxious. Their wide diffusion in both student circles and among the general public, by the local, national and foreign press, are a threat to the morality, the studies, the reputation and thus the very future of the students of the University of Strasbourg.*

What follows is a translation of the infamous pamphlet in question. It has already been translated into Swedish and Italian, and is at present being translated into Dutch, German and Spanish. At the end we have added a few remarks on the importance of situationist activity in Strasbourg, and its relevance to the (very different) English situation.

OF STUDENT POVERTY

Considered in its economic, political, psychological, sexual and, particularly intellectual aspects, and a modest proposal for its remedy

To make shame more shameful by giving it publicity

We might very well say, and no-one would disagree with us, that the student is the most universally despised creature in France, apart from the priest and the policeman. Naturally he is usually attacked from the wrong point of view, with specious reasons derived from the ruling ideology. He may be worth the contempt of a true revolutionary, yet a revolutionary critique of the student situation is currently taboo on the official Left. The licensed and impotent opponents of capitalism repress the obvious—that what is wrong with the students is also what is wrong with them. They convert their unconscious contempt into a blind enthusiasm. The radical intelligentsia (from *Les Temps Modernes* to *L'Express*) prostrates itself before the so-called "rise of the student" and the declining bureaucracies of the Left (from the "Communist" party to the Stalinist National Union of Students) bids noisily for his moral and material support.

There are reasons for this sudden enthusiasm, but they are all *provided* by the present form of capitalism, in its overdeveloped state. We shall use this pamphlet for denunciation. We shall expose these reasons one by one, on the principle that the end of alienation is only reached by the straight and narrow path of alienation itself.

Up to now, studies of student life have ignored the essential issue. The surveys and analyses have all been psychological or sociological or economic: in other words, academic exercises, content with the false categories of one specialization or another. None of them can achieve what is most needed—a view of modern society as a whole. Fourier denounced their error long ago as the attempt to apply scientific laws to the basic assumptions of the science (*"porter régulièrement sur les questions primordiales"*). Everything is said about our society except what it *is*, and the nature of its two basic principles—the commodity and the spectacle. The fetishism of facts masks the essential category, and the details consign the totality to oblivion.

Modern capitalism and its spectacle allot everyone a specific role in a general passivity. The student is no exception to the rule. He has a provisional part to play, a rehearsal for his final role as an element in market society as conservative as the rest. Being a student is a form of initiation. An initiation which echoes the rites of more primitive societies with bizarre precision. It goes on outside of history, cut off from social reality. The student leads a double life, poised between his present status and his future role. The two are absolutely separate, and the journey from one to the other is a mechanical event "in the future". Meanwhile, he basks in a schizophrenic consciousness, withdrawing into his initiation group to hide from that future. Protected from history, the present is a mystic trance.

At least in consciousness, the student can exist apart from the official truths of "economic life". But for very simple reasons: looked at economically, student life is a hard one. In our "society of abundance", he is still a pauper. 80% of students come from income groups well above the working class, yet 90% have less money than the meanest labourer. Student poverty is an anachronism, a throw-back from an earlier age of capitalism; it does not share in the *new* poverties of the spectacular societies; it has yet to attain the new poverty of the new proletariat. Nowadays the teenager shuffles off the moral prejudices and authority of the family to become part of the market even before he is adolescent: at fifteen he has all the delights of being directly exploited. In contrast the student covets his protracted infancy as an irresponsible and docile paradise. Adolescence and its crises may bring occasional brushes with his family, but in essence he is not troublesome: he agrees to be treated as a baby by the institutions which provide his education[1]. There is no "student problem". Student passivity is only the most obvious symptom of a general state of affairs, for each sector of social life has been subdued by a similar imperialism.

Our social thinkers have a bad conscience about the student problem, but only because the real problem is the poverty and servitude of all. But we have different reasons to despise the student and all his works. What is unforgivable is not so much his actual misery but his complaisance in the face of the misery of others. For him there is only one real alienation: his own. He is a full-time and happy consumer of that commodity, hoping to arouse at least our pity, since he cannot claim our interest. By the logic of modern capitalism, most students can only become mere *petits cadres* (with the same function in neo-capitalism as the skilled worker had in the nineteenth-century economy). The student really knows how miserable will be that golden future which is supposed to make up for the shameful poverty of the present. In the face of that knowledge, he prefers to dote on the present and invent an imaginary prestige for himself. After all, there will be no magical compensation for present drabness: tomorrow will be like yesterday, lighting these fools the way to dusty death. Not unnaturally he takes refuge in an unreal present.

The student is a stoical slave: the more chains authority heaps upon him, the freer he is in phantasy. He shares with his new family, the University, a belief in a curious kind of autonomy. Real independence, apparently, lies in a direct subservience to the two most powerful systems of social control: the family and the State. He is their well-behaved and grateful child, and like the submissive child he is over-eager to please. He celebrates all the values and mystifications of the system, devouring them with all the anxiety of the infant at the breast. Once, the old illusions had to be imposed on an aristocracy of labour; the *petits cadres*-to-be ingest them willingly under the guise of culture.

There are various forms of compensation for poverty. The total poverty of ancient societies produced the grandiose compensation of religion. The student's poverty by contrast is a marginal phenomenon, and he casts around for compensations among the most down-at-heel images of the ruling class. He is a bore who repairs the old jokes of an alienated culture. Even as an ideologist, he is always out of date. One and all, his latest enthusiasms were ridiculous thirty years ago.

Once upon a time the universities were respected; the student persists in the belief that he is lucky to be there. But he arrived too late. The bygone excellence of bourgeois culture[2] has vanished. A mechanically produced specialist is now the goal of the "educational system". A modern economic system demands mass production of students who are not educated and have been rendered incapable

[1] If ever they stop screwing his arse off, it's only to come round and kick him in the balls.

[2] By this we mean the culture of a Hegel or of the *encyclopédistes*, rather than the Sorbonne and the Ecole Normale Supérieure.

of thinking. Hence the decline of the universities and the automatic nullity of the student once he enters its portals. The university has become a society for the propagation of ignorance; "high culture" has taken on the rhythm of the production line; *without exception,* university teachers are cretins, men who would get the bird from any audience of schoolboys. But all this hardly matters: the important thing is to go on listening respectfully. In time, if critical thinking is repressed with enough conscientiousness, the student will come to partake of the wafer of knowledge, the professor will tell him the final truths of the world. Till then—a menopause of the spirit. As a matter of course the future revolutionary society will condemn the doings of lecture theatre and faculty as mere *noise*— socially undesirable. The student is already a very bad joke.

The student is blind to the obvious—that even his closed world is changing. The "crisis of the university"—that detail of a more general crisis of modern capitalism—is the latest fodder for the deaf-mute dialogue of the specialists. This "crisis" is simple to understand: the difficulties of a specialised sector which is adjusting (too late) to a general change in the relations of production. There was once a vision—if an ideological one—of a liberal bourgeois university. But as its social base disappeared, the vision became banality. In the age of free-trade capitalism, when the "liberal" state left it its marginal freedoms, the university *could* still think of itself as an independent power. Of course it was a pure and narrow product of that society's needs—particularly the need to give the privileged minority an adequate general culture before they rejoined the ruling class (not that going up to university was straying very far from class confines). But the bitterness of the nostalgic don [1] is understandable: better, after all, to be the blood-hound of the *haute bourgeoisie* than sheepdog to the world's white-collars. Better to stand guard on privilege than harry the flock into their allotted factories and bureaux, according to the whims of the "planned economy". The university is becoming, fairly smoothly, the honest broker of technocracy and its spectacle. In the process, the purists of the academic Right become a pitiful sideshow, purveying their "universal" cultural goods to a bewildered audience of specialists.

More serious, and thus more dangerous, are the modernists of the Left and the Students' Union, with their talk of a "reform of University structure" and a "reinsertion of the University into social and economic life", i.e., its adaptation to the needs of modern capitalism. The one-time suppliers of general culture to the ruling classes, though still guarding their old prestige, must be converted into the forcing-house of a new labour aristocracy. Far from contesting the historical process which subordinates one of the last relatively autonomous social groups to the demands of the market, the progressives complain of delays and inefficiency in its completion. They are the standard-bearers of the cybernetic university of the future (which has already reared its ugly head in some unlikely quarters). And they are the enemy: the fight against the market, which is starting again in earnest, means the fight against its latest lackeys.

As for the student, this struggle is fought out entirely over his head, somewhere in the heavenly realm of his masters. The whole of his life is beyond his control, and for all he sees of the world he might as well be on another planet. His acute economic poverty condemns him to a paltry form of *survival*. But, being a complacent creature, he parades his very ordinary indigence as if it were an original life-style: self-indulgently, he affects to be a Bohemian. The Bohemian solution is hardly viable at the best of times, and the notion that it could be achieved without a complete and final break with the university milieu is quite ludicrous. But the student Bohemian (and every student likes to pretend that he is a Bohemian at heart) clings to his false and degraded version of individual revolt. He is so "eccentric" that he continues—thirty years after Reich's excellent

---

[1] No-one dares any longer to speak in the name of nineteenth century liberalism; so they reminisce about the "free" and "popular" universities of the middle ages—that "democracy of unfreedom".

lessons—to entertain the most traditional forms of erotic behaviour, reproducing at this level the general relations of class society. Where sex is concerned, we have learnt better tricks from elderly provincial ladies. His rent-a-crowd militancy for the latest good cause is an aspect of his real impotence.

The student's old-fashioned poverty, however, does put him at a potential advantage—if only he could see it. He does have marginal freedoms, a small area of liberty which as yet escapes the totalitarian control of the spectacle. His flexible working-hours permit him adventure and experiment. But he is a sucker for punishment, and freedom scares him to death: he feels safer in the straight-jacketed space-time of lecture hall and weekly "essay". He is quite happy with this open prison organised for his "benefit", and, though not constrained, as are most people, to separate work and leisure, he does so of his own accord—hypocritically proclaiming all the while his contempt for assiduity and grey men. He embraces every available contradiction and then mutters darkly about the "difficulties of communication" from the uterine warmth of his religious, artistic or political clique.

Driven by his freely-chosen depression, he submits himself to the subsidiary police force of psychiatrists set up by the avant-garde of repression. The university mental health clinics are run by the student mutual organisation, which sees this institution as a grand victory for student unionism and social progress. Like the Aztecs who ran to greet Cortes's sharpshooters, and then wondered what made the thunder and why men fell down, the students flock to the psycho-police stations with their "problems".

The real poverty of his everyday life finds its immediate, phantastic compensation in the opium of cultural commodities. In the cultural spectacle he is allotted his habitual role of the dutiful disciple. Although he is close to the production-point, access to the Sanctuary of Thought is forbidden, and he is obliged to discover "modern culture" as an *admiring spectator*. Art is dead, but the student is necrophiliac. He peeks at the corpse in cine-clubs and theatres, buys its fish-fingers from the cultural supermarket. Consuming unreservedly, he is in his element: he is the living proof of all the platitudes of American market research: a conspicuous consumer, complete with induced irrational preference for Brand X (Camus, for example), and irrational prejudice against Brand Y (Sartre, perhaps).

Impervious to real passions, he seeks titillation in the battles between his anaemic gods, the stars of a vacuous heaven: Althusser — Garaudy — Barthes — Picard — Lefebvre — Lévi-Strauss — Halliday — de Chardin — Brassens .. ; and between their rival theologies, designed like all theologies to mask the real problems by creating false ones: humanism — existentialism — scientism — structuralism — cyberneticism — new criticism — dialectics-of-naturism — metaphilosophism . . .

He thinks he is avant-garde if he has seen the latest Godard or "participated" in the latest happening. He discovers "modernity" as fast as the market can produce its ersatz version of long outmoded (though once important) ideas; for him, every rehash is a cultural revolution. His principal concern is status, and he eagerly snaps up all the paperback editions of important and "difficult" texts with which mass culture has filled the bookstores [1]. Unfortunately, he cannot read, so he devours them with his gaze, and enjoys them vicariously through the gaze of his friends. He is an other-directed *voyeur*.

---

[1] If he had an atom of self-respect or lucidity, he would knock them off. But no: conspicuous consumers always pay!

Our friends had a good laugh about that. "We know that one already, don't we comrades. It'll take more than that to stop us. Let's play poker for the presidency, and don't forget: to the loser the spoils!" (The Return of the Durutti Column)

His favorite reading matter is the *kitsch* press, whose task it is to orchestrate the consumption of cultural nothing-boxes. Docile as ever, the student accepts its commercial *ukases* and makes them the only measuring-rod of his tastes. Typically, he is a compulsive reader of weeklies like *le Nouvel Observateur* and *l'Express* (whose nearest English equivalents are the posh Sundays and *New Society*). He generally feels that *le Monde*—whose style he finds somewhat difficult—is a truly objective newspaper. And it is with such guides that he hopes to gain an understanding of the modern world and become a political initiate!

In France more than anywhere else, the student is passively content to be politicised. In this sphere too, he readily accepts the same alienated, spectacular participation. Seizing upon all the tattered remnants of a Left which was annihilated *more than forty years ago* by "socialist" reformism and Stalinist counter-revolution, he is once more guilty of an amazing ignorance. The Right is well aware of the defeat of the workers' movement, and so are the workers themselves, though more confusedly. But the students continue blithely to organise demonstrations which mobilise students and students only. This is political false consciousness in its virgin state, a fact which naturally makes the universities a happy hunting ground for the manipulators of the declining bureaucratic organisations. For them, it is child's play to programme the student's political options. Occasionally there are deviationary tendencies and cries of "Independence!" but after a period of token resistance the dissidents are reincorporated into a *status quo* which they have never really radically opposed .[1] The "Jeunesses Communistes Révolutionnaires", whose title is a case of ideological falsification gone mad (they are neither young, nor communist, nor revolutionary), have with much

---

[1] Recent "schisms" in both christian and communist organisations have shown, if anything, that *all* these students are united on one fundamental principle: unconditional submission to hierarchical superiors.

The brilliance of this theoretical knowledge called for an appropriate praxis. Gradually they had discovered those with whom wrecking the social machine would be a pitiless game. Thus it was that their palavers with the "Occult International" began. (The Return of the Durutti Column)

brio and accompanying publicity defied the iron hand of the Party . . . but only to rally cheerily to the pontifical battle-cry, "Peace in Vietnam!"

The student prides himself on his opposition to the "archaic" Gaullist régime. But he justifies his criticism by appealing—without realising it—to older and far worse crimes. His radicalism prolongs the life of the different currents of edulcorated Stalinism: Togliatti's, Garaudy's, Krushchov's, Mao's, etc. His youth is synonymous with appalling *naïveté,* and his attitudes are in reality far more archaic than the régime's—the Gaullists do after all understand modern society well enough to administer it.

But the student, sad to say, is not deterred by the odd anachronism. He feels obliged to have general ideas on everything, to unearth a coherent world-view capable of lending meaning to his need for activism and asexual promiscuity. As a result, he falls prey to the last doddering missionary efforts of the churches. He rushes with atavistic ardour to adore the putrescent carcass of God, and cherishes all the stinking detritus of prehistoric religions in the tender belief that they enrich him and his time. Along with their sexual rivals, those elderly provincial ladies, the students form the social category with the highest percentage of admitted adherents to these archaic cults. Everywhere else, the priests have been either beaten off or devoured, but university clerics shamelessly continue to bugger thousands of students in their spiritual shithouses.

We must add in all fairness that there do exist students of a tolerable intellectual level, who without difficulty dominate the controls designed to check the mediocre capacity demanded from the others. They do so for the simple reason that they have understood the system, and so despise it and know themselves to be its enemies. They are in the system for what they can get out of it—particularly grants. Exploiting the contradiction which, for the moment at least, ensures the maintenance of a small sector—"research"—still governed by a liberal-academic rather than a technocratic rationality, they calmly carry the germs of sedition to the highest level: their open contempt for the organisation is the counterpart of a lucidity which enables them to outdo the system's lackeys, intellectually and otherwise. Such students cannot fail to become theorists of the coming revolutionary movèment. For the moment, they make no secret of the fact that what they take so easily from the system shall be used for its overthrow.

The student, if he rebels at all, must first rebel against his studies, though the necessity of this initial move is felt less spontaneously by him than by the worker, who intuitively identifies his work with his total condition. At the same time, since the student is a product of modern society just like Godard or Coca-Cola, his extreme alienation can only be fought through the struggle against this whole society. It is clear that the university can in no circumstances become the battlefield; the student, insofar as he defines himself as such, manufactures a pseudo-value which must become an obstacle to any clear consciousness of the reality of his dispossession. The best criticism of student life is the behaviour of the rest of youth, who have already started to revolt. Their rebellion has become one of the *signs* of a fresh struggle against modern society.

It is not enough for thought to seek its realisation in practice: practice must seek its theory

After years of slumber and permanent counter-revolution, there are signs of a new period of struggle, with youth as the new carriers of revolutionary infection. But the society of the spectacle paints its own picture of itself and its enemies, imposes its own ideological categories on the world and its history. Fear is the very last response. For everything that happens is reassuringly part of the natural order of things. Real historical changes, which show that this society can be *superseded,* are reduced to the status of novelties, processed for mere consumption. The revolt of youth against an imposed and "given" way of life is the first sign of a total subversion. It is the prelude to a period of revolt—the revolt of those who can no longer *live* in our society. Faced with a danger, ideology and its daily machinery perform the usual inversion of reality. An historical process becomes a pseudo-category of some socio-natural science: the Idea of Youth. Youth is in revolt, but this is only the eternal revolt of youth; every generation espouses "good causes", only to forget them when "the young man begins the serious business of production and is given concrete and real social aims". After the social scientists come the journalists with their verbal inflation. The revolt is contained by over-exposure: we are given it to contemplate so that we shall forget to participate. In the spectacle, a revolution becomes a social aberration—in other words a social safety valve—which has its part to play in the smooth working of the system. It reassures because it remains a marginal phenomenon, in the apartheid of the temporary problems of a healthy pluralism (compare and contrast the "woman question" and the "problem of racialism"). In reality, if there is a problem of youth in modern capitalism it is part of the total crisis of that society. It is just that youth feels the crisis most acutely .[1]

Youth and its mock freedoms are the purest products of modern society. Their modernity consists in the choice they are offered and are already making: total integration to neo-capitalism, or the most radical refusal. What is surprising is not that youth is in revolt but that its elders are so soporific. But the reason is history, not biology—the previous generation lived through the defeats and were sold the lies of the long, shameful disintegration of the revolutionary movement.

In itself Youth is a publicity myth, and as part of the new "social dynamism" it is the potential ally of the capitalist mode of production. The illusory primacy of youth began with the economic recovery after the second world war. Capital was able to strike a new bargain with labour: in return for the mass production of a new class of manipulable consumers, the worker was offered a *role* which gave him full membership of the spectacular society. This at least was the ideal social model, though as usual it bore little relation to socio-economic reality

[1] Not only feels it but tries to give it expression.

"Some delinquents, by stealing commodities so that they can give them away, reproduce on a higher level the practice of the gift which dominated ancient societies—a practice which exchange destroyed, by founding social relations on the basis of a feeble rate of development of the productive force. In this they have discovered a form of action perfectly appropriate to a society which defines itself as affluent and which, in some measure, is already transcended by such acts." (The Return of the Durutti Column)

(which lagged behind the consumer ideology). The revolt of youth was the first burst of anger at the persistent realities of the new world—the boredom of every-day existence, the *dead life* which is still the essential product of modern capital-ism, in spite of all its modernizations. A small section of youth is able to refuse that society and its products, but without any idea that this society can be super-seded. They opt for a nihilist present. Yet the destruction of capitalism is once again a real issue, an event in history, a process which has already begun. Dissi-dent youth must achieve the coherence of a critical theory, and the practical organisation of that coherence.

At the most primitive level, the "delinquents" (*blousons noirs*) of the world use violence to express their rejection of society and its sterile options. But their refusal is an abstract one: it gives them no chance of actually escaping the contra-dictions of the system. They are its products—negative, spontaneous, but none the less exploitable. All the experiments of the new social order produce them: they are the first side-effects of the new urbanism; of the disintegration of all values; of the extension of an increasingly boring consumer leisure; of the grow-ing control of every aspect of everyday life by the psycho-humanist police force; and of the economic survival of a family unit which has lost all significance.

The "young thug" despises work but accepts the goods. He wants what the spectacle offers him—but *now*, with no down payment. This is the essential contradiction of the delinquent's existence. He may try for a real freedom in the use of his time, in an individual assertiveness, even in the construction of a kind of community. But the contradition remains, and kills. (On the fringe of society, where poverty reigns, the gang develops its own hierarchy, which can only fulfil itself in a war with other gangs, isolating each group and each individual within the group.) In the end the contradiction proves unbearable. Either the lure of the product world proves too strong, and the hooligan decides to do his honest day's work: to this end a whole sector of production is devoted specifically to his recuperation. Clothes, discs, guitars, scooters, transistors, purple hearts beckon him to the land of the consumer. Or else he is forced to attack the laws of the market itself—either in the primary sense, by stealing, or by a move towards a conscious revolutionary critique of commodity society. For the delinquent only two futures are possible: revolutionary consciousness, or blind obedience on the shop floor.

The *Provos* are the first organisation of delinquency—they have given the delinquent experience its first political form. They are an alliance of two distinct elements: a handful of careerists from the degenerate world of "art", and a mass of beatniks looking for a new activity. The artists contributed the idea of the game, though still dressed up in various threadbare ideological garments. The delinquents had nothing to offer but the violence of their rebellion. From the start the two tendencies hardly mixed: the pre-ideological mass found itself under the Bolshevik "guidance" of the artistic ruling class, who justified and maintained their power by an ideology of provo-democracy. At the moment when the sheer violence of the delinquent had become an *idea*—an attempt to destroy art and go beyond it—the violence was channeled into the crassest neo-artistic reformism. The Provos are an aspect of the last reformism produced by modern capitalism: the reformism of everyday life. Like Bernstein, with his vision of socialism built by tinkering with capitalism, the Provo hierarchy think they can change everyday life by a few well-chosen improvements. What they fail to realise is that the banality of everyday life is not incidental, but *the central mechanism and product of modern capitalism.* To destroy it, nothing less is needed than all-out revolution. The Provos choose the fragmentary and end by accepting the totality.

To give themselves a base, the leaders have concocted the paltry ideology of the provotariat (a politico-artistic salad knocked up from the leftovers of a feast they had never known). The new provotariat is supposed to oppose the passive and "bourgeois" proletariat, still worshipped in obscure Leftist shrines. Because they despair of the fight for a *total* change in society, they despair of the only forces which can bring about that change. The proletariat is the motor of capitalist society, and thus its mortal enemy: everything is designed for its suppression (parties; trade union bureaucracies; the police; the colonization of all aspects of everyday life) because it is the only really menacing force. The Provos hardly try to understand any of this; and without a critique of the system of production, they remain its servants. In the end an anti-union workers demonstration sparked off the real conflict. The Provo base went back to direct violence, leaving their bewildered leaders to denounce "excesses" and appeal to pacifist sentiments. The Provos, who had talked of provoking authority to reveal its repressive character, finished by complaining that they had been provoked by the police. So much for their pallid anarchism.

It is true that the Provo base became revolutionary in practice. But to invent a revolutionary consciousness their first task is to destroy their leaders, to rally the objective revolutionary forces of the proletariat, and to drop the Constants and De Vries of this world (one the favourite artist of the Dutch royal family, the other a failed M.P. and admirer of the English police). There *is* a modern revolution, and one of its bases could be the Provos—but only without their leaders and ideology. If they want to change the world, they must get rid of those who are content to paint it white.

Idle reader, your cry of "What about Berkeley?" escapes us not. True, American society *needs* its students; and by revolting against their studies they have automatically called that society in question. From the start they have seen their revolt against the university hierarchy as a revolt against *the whole hierarchical system,* the dictatorship of the economy and the State. Their refusal to become an integrated part of the commodity economy, to put their specialized studies to their obvious and inevitable use, is a revolutionary gesture. It puts in doubt that whole system of production which alienates activity and its

DANS UNE PAREILLE
SOCIÉTÉ LA SIMPLE
PASSION DU VOL ARRI
VE TOUJOURS À DÉCI
DER LES PLUS INDÉCIS
AUX CHOSES A PRIORI
LES PLUS IMPENSABLES
LES PLUS IMPOSSIBLES.
LA VIE REJOINT LE JEU
LE JEU REJOINT LA VIE
IL FALLAIT DE TOUTES
MANIÈRES ÉTENDRE LEUR
TERRAIN D'EXPÉRIMENTATION
S'EMPARER DE NOUVEAUX
POUVOIRS POUR LUTTER CON
TRE CETTE SOCIÉTÉ
DU POUVOIR.

In a society like this, an outright love of theft inevitably leads even the most indecisive people to do the most unthinkable and impossible things. Life becomes a game and a game becomes life. The least they could do was to extend their field of experiment and seize new powers to fight against this power society. (The Return of the Durutti Column)

products from their creators. For all its confusion and hesitancy, the American student movement has discovered one truth of the new refusal: that a coherent revolutionary alternative can and must be found *within* the "affluent society". The movement is still fixated on two relatively accidental aspects of the American crisis—the negroes and Vietnam—and the mini-groups of the New Left suffer from the fact. There is an authentic whiff of democracy in their chaotic organisation, but what they lack is a genuine subversive content. Without it they continually fall into dangerous contradictions. They may be hostile to the traditional politics of the old parties; but the hostility is futile, and will be recuperated, so long as it is based on ignorance of the political system and naive illusions about the world situation. *Abstract* opposition to their own society produces facile sympathy with its apparent enemies—the so-called Socialist bureaucracies of China and Cuba. A group like Resurgence Youth Movement can in the same breath condemn the State and praise the "Cultural Revolution"—that pseudo-revolt directed by the most elphantine bureaucacy of modern times.

At the same time, these organisations, with their blend of libertarian, political and religious tendencies, are always liable to the obsession with "group dynamics" which leads to the closed world of the sect. The mass consumption of drugs is the expression of a real poverty and a protest against it; but it remains a false search for "freedom" within a world dedicated to repression, a religious critique of a world that has no need for religion, least of all a new one. The beatniks—that right wing of the youth revolt—are the main purveyors of an ideological "refusal" combined with an acceptance of the most fantastic superstitions (Zen, spiritualism, "New Church" mysticism, and the stale porridge of Ghandi-ism and humanism). Worse still, in their search for a revolutionary programme the American students fall into the same bad faith as the Provos, and proclaim themselves "the most exploited class in our society". They must understand one thing: there are no "special" student interests in revolution. Revolution will be made by *all* the victims of encroaching repression and the tyranny of the market.

As for the East, bureaucratic totalitarianism is beginning to produce its own forces of negation. Nowhere is the revolt of youth more violent and more savagely repressed—the rising tide of press denunciation and the new police

"Perhaps they think that responsibilities will cool us down and that we'll stop telling academic mother fuckers to go and get screwed."

"These unionist assholes are bound to take us for an avant-garde version of their own bullshit, for some offbeat repetition of their own impotence."

Lenin: "I couldn't give a fuck about 'Revolutionary Young Communists' either." (The Return of the Durutti Column)

measures against "hooliganism" are proof enough. A section of youth, so the right-minded "socialist" functionaries tell us, have no respect for moral and family order (which still flourishes there in its most detestable bourgeois forms). They prefer "debauchery", despise work and even disobey the party police. The USSR has set up a special ministry to fight the new delinquency.

Alongside this diffuse revolt a more specific opposition is emerging. Groups and clandestine reviews rise and fall with the barometer of police repression. So far the most important has been the publication of the "Open letter to the Polish Workers Party" by the young Poles *Kuron* and *Modzelewski*, which affirmed the necessity of "abolishing the present system of production and social relations" and that to do this "revolution is unavoidable". The Eastern intellectuals have one great task —to make conscious the concrete critical action of the workers of East Berlin, Warsaw and Budapest: the proletarian critique of the dictatorship of the bureaucracy. In the East the problem is not to define the aims of revolution, but to learn how to fight for them. In the West struggle may be easy, but the goals are left obscure or ideological; in the Eastern bureaucracies there are no illusions about what is being fought for: hence the bitterness of the struggle. What is difficult is to devise the forms revolution must take in the immediate future.

In Britain, the revolt of youth found its first expression in the peace movement. It was never a whole-hearted struggle, with the misty non-violence of the Committee of 100 as its most daring programme. At its strongest the Committee could call 300,000 demonstrators on to the streets. It had its finest hour in

Spring 1963 with the "Spies for Peace" scandal. But it had already entered on a definitive decline: for want of a theory the unilateralists fell among the traditional Left or were recuperated by the Pacifist conscience. What is left is the enduring (quintessentially English) archaisms in the control of everyday life, and the accelerating decomposition of the old secular values. These could still produce a total critique of the new life; but the revolt of youth needs allies. The British working class remains one of the most militant in the world. Its struggles—the shop stewards movement and the growing tempo and bitterness of wildcat strikes—will be a permanent sore on an equally permanent capitalism until it regains its revolutionary perspective, and seeks common cause with the *new* opposition. The *débâcle* of Labourism makes that alliance all the more possible and all the more necessary. If it came about, the explosion could destroy the old society—the Amsterdam riots would be child's play in comparison. Without it, both sides of the revolution can only be stillborn: practical needs will find no genuine revolutionary form, and rebellious discharge will ignore the only forces that drive and can therefore destroy modern capitalism.

Japan is the only industrialised country where this fusion of student youth and working class militants has already taken place.

Zengakuren, the organisation of revolutionary students, and the *League of Young Marxist Workers* joined to form the backbone of the *Communist Revolutionary League* [1]. The movement is already setting and solving the new problems of revolutionary organisation. Without illusions, it fights both western capitalism and the bureaucracies of the so-called socialist states. Without hierarchies, it groups together several thousand students and workers on a democratic basis, and aims at the participation of every member in all the activities of the organisation.

They are the first to carry the struggle on to the streets, holding fast to a real revolutionary programme, and with a mass participation. Thousands of workers and students have waged a violent struggle with the Japanese police. In many ways the C.R.L. lacks a complete and concrete theory of the two systems it fights with such ferocity. It has not yet defined the precise nature of bureaucratic exploitation, and it has hardly formulated the character of modern capitalism, the critique of everyday life and the critique of the spectacle. The Communist Revolutionary League is still fundamentally an avant-garde *political* organisation, the heir of the best features of the classic proletarian movement. But it is at present the most important group in the world—and should henceforth be one of the poles of discussion and a rallying point for the new proletarian critique.

---

[1] KAIHOSHA c/o Dairyuso, 3 Nakanoekimae, Nakanoku, TOKYO, JAPAN.
ZENGAKUREN Hirota Building 2-10 Kandajimbo cho, Chiyoda-Ku, TOKYO, JAPAN.

At long last to create a situation which makes all turning back impossible

"To be avant-garde means to keep abreast of reality" (*Internationale Situationniste* 8). A radical critique of the modern world must have the totality as its object and objective. Its searchlight must reveal the world's real past, its present existence and the prospects for its transformation *as an indivisible whole*. If we are to reach the whole truth about the modern world—and *a fortiori* if we are to formulate the project of its total subversion—we must be able to expose its *hidden history;* in concrete terms this means subjecting the history of the international revolutionary movement, as set in motion over a century ago by the western proletariat, to a demystified and critical scrutiny. "This movement against the total organisation of the old world came to a stop long ago" (*Internationale Situationniste* 7). *It failed.* Its last historical appearance was in the Spanish social revolution, crushed in the Barcelona "May Days" of 1937. Yet its so-called "victories" and "defeats", if judged in the light of their historical consequences, tend to confirm Liebknecht's remark, the day before his assassination, that "some defeats are really victories, while some victories are more shameful than any defeat". Thus the first great "failure" of workers' power, the Paris Commune, is in fact its first great *success,* whereby the primitive proletariat proclaimed its historical capacity to organise all aspects of social life *freely.* And the Bolshevik revolution, hailed as the proletariat's first great triumph, turns out in the last analysis to be its most disastrous defeat.

The installation of the Bolshevik order coincides with the crushing of the Spartakists by the German "Social-Democrats". The joint victory of Bolshevism and reformism constitutes a unity masked by an apparent incompatibility, for the Bolshevik order too, as it transpired, was to be a variation on the old theme. The effects of the Russian counter-revolution were, internally, the institution and development of a new mode of exploitation, bureaucratic state capitalism, and externally, the growth of the "Communist" International, whose spreading branches served the unique purpose of defending and reproducing the rotten trunk. Capitalism, under its bourgeois and bureaucratic guises, won a new lease of life—over the dead bodies of the sailors of Kronstadt, the Ukrainian peasants, and the workers of Berlin, Kiel, Turin, Shanghai, and Barcelona.

The third International, apparently created by the Bolsheviks to combat the degenerate reformism of its predecessor, and to unite the avant-garde of the proletariat in "revolutionary communist parties", was too closely linked to the interests of its founders ever to serve an authentic socialist revolution. Despite all its polemics, the third International was a chip off the old block. The Russian model was rapidly imposed on the Western workers' organisations, and the evolution of both was thenceforward one and the same thing. The totalitarian dictatorship of the bureaucratic class over the Russian proletariat found its echo

"What's your scene, man?"
"Reification."
"Yeah? I guess that means pretty hard work with big books and piles of paper on a big table."
"Nope. I drift. Mostly I just drift." (The Return of the Durutti Column)

in the subjection of the great mass of workers in other countries to castes of trade union and political functionaries, with their own private interests in repression. While the Stalinist monster haunted the working-class consciousness, old-fashioned capitalism was becoming bureaucratized and overdeveloped, resolving its famous internal contradictions and proudly claiming this victory to be decisive. Today, though the unity is obscured by apparent variations and oppositions, a *single social form* is coming to dominate the world—this modern world which it proposes to govern with the principles of a world long dead and gone. The tradition of the dead generations still weighs like a nightmare on the minds of the living.

Opposition to the world offered from within—and in its own terms—by supposedly revolutionary organisations, can only be spurious. Such opposition, depending on the worst mystifications and calling on more or less reified ideologies, helps consolidate the social order. Trade unions and political parties created by the working class as tools of its emancipation are now no more than the "checks and balances" of the system. Their leaders have made these organisations their private property; their stepping stone to a role within the ruling class. The party programme or the trade union statute may contain vestiges of revolutionary phraseology, but their practice is everywhere reformist—and doubly so now that official capitalist ideology mouths the same reformist slogans. Where the unions have seized power—in countries more backward than Russia in 1917— the Stalinist model of counter-revolutionary totalitarianism has been faithfully reproduced.[1] Elsewhere, they have become a static complement to the self-regulation of managerial capitalism.[2] The official organisations have become the best guarantee of repression—without this "opposition" the humanist-democratic facade of the system would collapse and its essential violence would be laid bare. In the struggle with the militant proletariat, these organisations are the unfailing defenders of the bureaucratic counter-revolution, and the docile creatures of its foreign policy. They are the bearers of the most blatant falsehood in a world of lies, working diligently for the perennial and universal dictatorship of the State and the Economy. As the situationists put it, "a universally dominant social system, tending toward totalitarian self-regulation, is apparently being resisted—but only apparently—by false forms of opposition which remain trapped on the battlefield ordained by the system itself. Such illusory resistance can only serve to reinforce what it pretends to attack. Bureaucratic pseudo-socialism is only the most grandiose of these guises of the old world of hierarchy and alienated labour".

As for student unionism, it is nothing but the travesty of a travesty, the useless burlesque of a trade unionism itself long totally degenerate.

The principal platitude of all future revolutionary organisation must be the theoretical and practical denunciation of Stalinism in all its forms. In France at least, where economic backwardness has slowed down the consciousness of crisis, the only possible road is over the ruins of Stalinism. It must become the *delenda est Carthago* of the last revolution of prehistory.

Revolution must break with its past, and derive all its poetry from the future. Little groups of "militants" who claim to represent the authentic Bolshevik heritage are voices from beyond the grave. These angels come to avenge the "betrayal" of the October Revolution will always support the defence of the USSR—if only "in the last instance". The "under-developed" nations are their promised land. They can scarcely sustain their illusions outside this context, where their objective role is to buttress theoretical underdevelopment. They struggle for the dead body of "Trotsky", invent a thousand variations on the same ideological theme, and end up with the same brand of practical and theoretical impotence. Forty years of counter-revolution separate these groups from the Revolution; since this is not 1920 they can only be wrong (and they were already wrong in 1920).

Consider the fate of an ultra-Leftist group like *Socialisme ou Barbarie,* where after the departure of a "traditional Marxist" faction (the impotent *Pouvoir Ouvrier*) a core of revolutionary "modernists" under Cardan disintegrated and disappeared within 18 months. While the old categories are no longer revolutionary, a rejection of Marxism à la Cardan is no substitute for the reinvention of a total critique. The Scylla and Charybdis of present revolutionary action are the museum of revolutionary prehistory and the modernism of the system itself.

As for the various anarchist groups, they possess nothing beyond a pathetic and ideological faith in this label. They justify every kind of self-contradiction in liberal terms: freedom of speech, of opinion, and other such bric-a-brac. Since they tolerate each other, they would tolerate anything.

---

[1] These countries have been industrialised on classic lines: primitive accumulation at the expense of the peasantry, accelerated by bureaucratic terror.

[2] For 45 years the French "Communist" Party has not taken a single step towards the conquest of power. The same situation applies in all advanced nations which have not fallen under the heel of the so-called Red Army.

MES PRINCIPES ET MES GOÛTS FIRENT MON BONHEUR DEPUIS MON ENFANCE. ILS FURENT TOUJOURS L'UNIQUE BASE DE MA CONDUITE ET DE MES ACTIONS : PEUT-ÊTRE IRAI-JE PLUS LOIN, JE SENS QUE C'EST POSSIBLE. MAIS POUR REVENIR, NON. J'AI TROP D'HORREUR POUR LES PRÉJUGÉS DES HOMMES, JE HAIS TROP LEUR CIVILISATIONS, LEURS VERTUS ET LEURS DIEUX, POUR Y JAMAIS SACRIFIER MES PENCHANTS.

RAVACHOL JULES, DIT KOENIGSTEIN FRANCISQUE, NÉ LE 11 OCTOBRE 1854 TAILLE 1m 666 ; PROFESSION: TEINTURIER RELATIONS: RÉVOLUTIONNAIRES, CAUSE DE LA DÉTENTION: DESTRUCTION D' IMMEUBLES ET DÉTENTION D'ENGINS EXPLOSIFS

"Since I was a child my happiness has sprung from my principles and my tastes. They were always the sole source of my attitude and my actions: perhaps I will go still further. I'm sure it's possible. But to go back, no. Men's prejudices fill me with too much horror; I hate their civilisations, their virtues and their gods too intensely ever to sacrifice anything to them."

Jules Ravachol, known as Francisque Koenigstein, born the 11th October 1854. Height: 1 metre 66. Profession: dyer. Frequents revolutionary circles. Reasons for detention: destruction of buildings and possession of bombs. (The Return of the Durutti Column)

The predominant social system, which flatters itself on its modernisation and its permanence, must now be confronted with a worthy enemy: the equally modern negative forces which it produces. Let the dead bury their dead. The advance of history has a practical demystifying effect—it helps exorcise the ghosts which haunt the revolutionary consciousness. Thus the revolution of everyday life comes face to face with the enormity of its task. The revolutionary project must be reinvented, as much as the life it announces. If the project is still essentially *the abolition of class society*, it is because the material conditions upon which revolution was based are still with us. But revolution must be conceived with a new coherence and a new radicalism, starting with a clear grasp of the failure of those who first began it. Otherwise its *fragmentary* realisation will bring about only a new division of society.

The fight between the powers-that-be and the new proletariat can only be in terms of the totality. And for this reason the future revolutionary movement must be purged of any tendency to reproduce within itself the alienation produced by the commodity system[1]; it must be the *living* critique of that system and the negation of it, carrying all the elements essential for its transcendence.

[1] Whose defining characteristic is the dominance of work *qua* commodity. Cf. in English our pamphlet "The Decline and Fall of the Spectacular Commodity-Economy".

As Lukacs correctly showed, revolutionary organisation is this necessary mediation between theory and practice, between man and history, between the mass of workers and the proletariat *constituted as a class* (Lukacs' mistake was to believe that the Bolsheviks fulfilled this role). If they are to be realised in practice "theoretical" tendencies or differences must be translated into organisational problems. It is by its present organisation that a new revolutionary movement will stand or fall. The final criterion of its coherence will be the compatibility of its actual form with its essential project—*the international and absolute power of Workers' Councils* as foreshadowed by the proletarian revolutions of the last hundred years. There can be no compromise with the foundations of existing society—the system of commodity production; ideology in all its guises; the State; and the imposed division of labour from leisure.

The rock on which the old revolutionary movement foundered was the separation of theory and practice. Only at the supreme moments of struggle did the proletariat supersede this division and attain their truth. As a rule the principle seems to have been *hic Rhodus, hic non salta.* Ideology, however "revolutionary", always serves the ruling class; false consciousness is the alarm signal revealing the presence of the enemy fifth column. The lie is the essential product of the world of alienation, and the most effective killer of revolutions: once an organisation which claims the *social truth* adopts the lie as a tactic, its revolutionary career is finished.

All the positive aspects of the Workers' Councils must be already there in an organisation which aims at their realisation. All relics of the Leninist theory of organisation must be fought and destroyed. The spontaneous creation of Soviets by the Russian workers in 1905 was in itself a practical critique of that baneful theory,[1] yet the Bolsheviks continued to claim that working-class spontaneity could not go beyond "trade union consciousness" and would be unable to grasp the "totality". This was no less than a decapitation of the proletariat so that the Party could place itself "at the head" of the Revolution. If once you dispute the proletariat's capacity to emancipate itself, as Lenin did so ruthlessly, then you deny its capacity to organise all aspects of a post-revolutionary society. In such a context, the slogan "All Power to the Soviets" meant nothing more than the subjection of the Soviets to the Party, and the installation of the Party State in place of the temporary "State" of the armed masses.

"All Power to the Soviets" is *still* the slogan, but this time without the Bolshevik afterthoughts. The proletariat can only play the *game* of revolution if the stakes are the whole world, for the only possible form of workers' power—generalized and complete autogestion—can be shared with nobody. Workers' control is the abolition of all authority: it can abide no limitation, geographical or otherwise: any compromise amounts to surrender. "Workers' control must be the means and the end of the struggle: it is at once the goal of that struggle and its adequate form".[2]

A *total* critique of the world is the guarantee of the realism and reality of a revolutionary organisation. To tolerate the existence of an oppresive social system in one place or another, simply because it is packaged and sold as revolutionary, is to condone universal oppression. To accept alienation as inevitable in any one domain of social life is to resign oneself to reification in all its forms. It is not enough to favour Workers' Councils in the abstract; in concrete terms they mean the abolition of commodities and therefore of the proletariat. Despite their superficial disparities, all existing societies are governed by the logic of commodities—and the commodity is the basis of their dreams

---

[1] Compare the theoretical critique of Rosa Luxemburg.

[2] "Les Luttes de Classes en Algérie", in *Internationale Situationniste* 10.

of self-regulation. This famous fetichism[1] is still the *essential* obstacle to a total emancipation, to the free construction of social life. In the world of commodities, external and invisible forces direct men's actions; autonomous action directed towards clearly perceived goals is impossible. The strength of economic laws lies in their ability to take on the appearance of natural ones, but it it also their weakness, for their effectiveness thus depends *only* on "the lack of consciousness of those who help create them".

The market has one central principle—the loss of self in the aimless and unconscious creation of a world beyond the control of its creators. The revolutionary core of autogestion is the attack on this principle. Autogestion *is* conscious direction by all of their whole existence. It is not some vision of a workers' control *of the market*, which is merely to choose one's own alienation, to programme one's own survival (squaring the capitalist circle). The task of the Workers' Councils will not be the autogestion of the world which exists, but its continual qualitative transformation. The commodity and its laws (that vast detour in the history of man's production of himself) will be superseded by a new social form.

With autogestion ends one of the fundamental splits in modern society—between a labour which becomes increasingly reified and a "leisure" consumed in passivity. The death of the commodity naturally means the suppression of *work* and its replacement by a new type of free activity. Without this firm intention, socialist groups like *Socialisme ou Barbarie* or *Pouvoir Ouvrier* fell back on a reformism of labour couched in demands for its "humanization". But it is work itself which must be called in question. Far from being an "Utopia", its suppression is the first condition for a break with the market. The everyday division between "free time" and "working hours", those complementary sectors of alienated life is an *expression* of the internal contradiction between the use-value and exchange-value of the commodity. It has become the strongest point of the commodity ideology, the one contradiction which intensifies with the rise of the consumer. To destroy it, no strategy short of the abolition of work will do. It is only beyond the contradiction of use-value and exchange-value that history begins, that men make their activity an object of their will and their consciousness, and see themselves in the world they have created. The democracy of Workers' Councils is the resolution of all previous contradictions. It makes "everything which exists apart from individuals impossible".

What is the revolutionary project? The conscious domination of history by the men who make it. Modern history, like all past history, is the product of social praxis, the unconscious result of human action. In the epoch of totalitarian control, capitalism has produced its own religion: *the spectacle*. In the spectacle, ideology becomes flesh of our flesh, is realised here on earth. The world itself walks upside down. And like the "critique of religion" in Marx's day, the critique of the spectacle is now the essential precondition of any critique.

The problem of revolution is once again a concrete issue. On one side the grandiose structures of technology and material production; on the other a dissatisfaction which can only grow more profound. The bourgeoisie and its Eastern heirs, the bureaucracy, cannot devise the means to *use* their own over-development, which will be the basis of the *poetry* of the future, simply because they both depend on the *preservation of the old order*. At most they harness over-development to invent new repressions. For they know only one trick, the accumulation of *Capital* and hence of *the proletariat*—a proletarian being a man with no power over the use of his life, and who knows it. The new proletariat inherits the riches of the bourgeois world and this gives it its historical chance. Its task is to transform and destroy these riches, to contitute them as part of a human project: the total appropriation of nature and of human nature by man.

[1] Virginibus puerisque cantamus.

"Yes, Marx's thought really is a critique of everyday life." (*The Return of the Durutti Column*)

A realised human nature can only mean the infinite multiplication of *real desires* and their gratification. These real desires are the underlife of present society, crammed by the spectacle into the darkest corners of the revolutionary unconscious, realised by the spectacle only in the dreamlike delirium of its own publicity. We must destroy the spectacle itself, the whole apparatus of commodity society, if we are to realise human *needs*. We must abolish those pseudo-needs and false desires which the system manufactures daily in order to preserve its power.

The liberation of modern history, and the free use of its hoarded acquisitions, can come only from the forces it represses. In the nineteenth century the proletariat was already the inheritor of philosophy; now it inherits modern art and the first conscious critique of everyday life. With the self-destruction of the working class art and philosophy shall be realised. To transform the world and to change the structure of life are one and the same thing for the proletariat—they are the passwords to its destruction as a class, its dissolution of the present reign of necessity, and its accession to the realm of liberty. As its maximum programme it has the radical critique and free reconstruction of all the values and patterns of behaviour imposed by an alienated reality. The only poetry it can acknowledge is the creativity released in the making of history, the free invention of each moment and each event: Lautréamont's *poésie faite par tous*—the beginning of the revolutionary celebration. For proletarian revolt is a festival or it is nothing; in revolution the road of excess leads once and for all to the palace of wisdom. A palace which knows only one rationality: the *game*. The rules are simple: to live instead of devising a lingering death, and to indulge untrammelled desire.

➤

Postscript: If you make a social revolution, do it for fun

If the above text needed confirmation, it was amply provided by the reactions to its publication. In Strasbourg itself, a very respectable and somewhat olde-worlde city, the traditional reflex of outraged horror was still accessible—witness Judge Llabador's naive admission that our ideas are subversive (see our intro-duction). At this level too, the press seized on the passing encouragements to stealing [1] and hedonism (interpreted, inevitably, in a narrow erotic sense). The union cellars had become the most infamous dive in Strasbourg. The officers had been turned into a pigsty, with students daubing on the walls and relieving them-selves in the corridors. They had come with inflatable mattresses to sleep on the premises "with women and children"! Minors had been perverted . . .

The amoral popular press was of course at wit's end to find adequate labels: the Provos, the Beatniks, and a "weird group of anarchists" were variously reported to have seized power in the city. Under the direction of situationist beatniks, the University restaurant was in the red, and the union's Morsiglia holiday camp had been used free, *gratis* and for nothing by these gentlemen.

Some tried their hand at analysis, but only communicated the stunned incomprehension of a man suddenly caught in quicksands: "The San Francisco and London beatniks, the mods and rockers of the English beaches, the hooligans behind the Iron Curtain, all have been largely superseded by this wave of new-style nihilism. Today it is no longer a matter of outrageous hair and clothes, of dancing hysterically to induce a state of ecstasy, no longer even a matter of entering the artificial paradise of drugs. From now on, the international of young people who are 'against it' is no longer satisfied with provoking society, but intent on destroying it—on destroying the very foundations of a society 'made for the old and rich' and acceding to a state of 'freedom without any kind of restriction whatsoever' ".

It was the Rector of the University who led the chorus of modernist re-pression: "These students have insulted their professors," he declared. "They should be dealt with by psychiatrists. I don't want to take any legal measures against them—they should be in a lunatic asylum. As to their incitement to illegal acts, the Minister of the Interior is looking into that". ("I stand for freedom," he added.) Later, besieged by the press, he reiterated that "We need sociologists and psychologists to explain such phenomena to us". An Italian journalist replied that some of his most brilliant social-science students were in fact responsible for the whole affair. The situationists had an ever better reply to such appeals to the psychiatric cops: through the agency of the student mutual

---

[1] "They believe that all things are common, whence they conclude that theft is lawful for them": the Bishop of Strasbourg, while attacking the Brethren of the Free Spirit in 1317.

LA PRÉSIDENCE PASSE ENCORE, MAIS LA TRÉSORE-
RIE IL N'EN ÉTAIT PAS QUESTION. ILS CONVAINQUIRENT
AISÉMENT UNE PASSANTE, QUE LE HASARD AVAIT MIS
SUR LEUR TROTTOIR, DE PRENDRE LE RÔLE PLUS COM-
PROMETTANT DE TRÉSORIÈRE.

That took care of the presidency, but the treasury was a different kettle of fish.
They easily persuaded a passerby, who came their way by chance, to accept the
more compromising job of treasuress." (The Return of the Durutti Column)

organisation, they officially closed the local student psychiatric clinic. It is to
be hoped that one day such institutions will be physically destroyed rather than
tolerated, but in the meantime this "administrative" decision has such an
exemplary value that it is worth quoting:

> The administrative committee of the Strasbourg section of the Mutuelle
> Nationale des Etudiants de France . . . ,
> considering that the University Psychological Aid Bureaux (BAPU)
> represent the introduction of a para-police control of students, in the form
> of a repressive psychiatry whose clear function everywhere—somewhere
> between outright judicial oppression and the degrading lies of the mass
> spectacle—is to help maintain the apathy of all the exploited victims of
> modern capitalism;
> considering that this type of modernist repression . . . was evoked as soon
> as the Committee of the General Federal Association of the Strasbourg
> Students made known its adhesion to situationist theses by publishing the
> pamphlet "Of Student Poverty . . . ", and that Rector Bayen was quite
> ready to denounce those responsible to the press as "fit cases for the
> psychiatrists";

considering that the existence of a BAPU is a scandal and a menace to all those students of the University who are determined to think for themselves, hereby decides that from the twelfth of January, 1967, the BAPU of Strasbourg shall be closed down.

Another development which must have been predictable to any studious reader of the pamphlet was the attempt to explain away the Strasbourg affair in terms of a "crisis in the universities". *Le Monde*, the most "serious" French paper, and a platform for technocratic liberalism, kept its head while all around were losing theirs. After a long silence to get its breath back, it published an article which shackled situationist activity in Alsace to the "present student malaise" (another symptom: fascist violence in Paris University), for which the only cure is to give "real responsibility" to the students (read: let them direct their own alienation). This type of reasoning refuses *a priori* to see the obvious that so-called student malaise is a symptom of a far more general disease.

Much was made of the unrepresentative character of the union committee, although it had been quite legally elected. It is quite true, however, that our friends got power thanks to the apathy of the vast majority. The action had no mass base whatsoever. What it achieved was to expose the emptiness of student politics and indicate the minimum requirements for any conceivable movement of revolutionary students. At the general assembly of the National Union of French Students in January, the Strasbourg group proposed a detailed motion calling for the dissolution of the organisation, and obtained the implicit support of a large number of honest but confused delegates, disgusted by the corridor politics and phoney revolutionary pretensions of the union. Such disgust, though perhaps a beginning, is not enough: a revolutionary consciousness among students would be the very opposite of student consciousness. Until students realise that their interests coincide with those of *all* who are exploited by modern capitalism, there is *little or nothing to be hoped for from the universities*. Meanwhile, the exemplary gestures of avant-garde minorities are the only form of radical activity available.

This holds good not only in the universities but almost everywhere. In the absence of a widespread revolutionary consciousness, a quasi-terroristic denunciation of the official world is the only possible planned public action on the part of a revolutionary group. The importance of Strasbourg lies in this: it offers one possible model of such action. A situation was created in which society was forced to finance, publicise and broadcast a revolutionary critique of itself, and furthermore to confirm this critique through its reactions to it. It was essentially a lesson in turning the tables on contemporary society. The official world was played with by a group that understood its nature better than the official world itself. The exploiters were elegantly exploited. But despite the virtuosity of the operation, it should be seen as no more than an initial and, in view of what is to come, very modest attempt to create the praxis by which the crisis of this society as a whole can be precipitated; as such, it raises far wider problems of revolutionary organisation and tactics. As the mysterious M.K. remarked to a journalist, Strasbourg itself was no more than "a little experiment".

The concept of "subversion" (*détournement*), originally used by the situationists in a purely cultural context, can well be used to describe the type of activity at present available to us on many fronts. An early definition: "the redeployment of pre-existing artistic elements within a new ensemble . . . Its two basic principles are the loss of importance of each originally independent element (which may even lose its first sense completely), and the organisation of a new significant whole which confers a fresh meaning on each element" (cf. *Internationale Situationniste* 3, pp. 10-11). The historical significance of this technique or game derives from its ability to both *devalue* and *"reinvest"* the heritage of a dead cultural past, so that "subversion negates the value of previous forms of expression . . . but at the same time expresses the search for a broader form, at a higher level—for a *new creative currency*". Subversion counters the manoeuvre of modern society, which seeks to *recuperate* and fossilize the relics of past creativity within its spectacle. It is clear that this struggle on the cultural terrain is no different in structure from the more general revolutionary struggle; subversion can therefore also be conceived as the creation of a new *use value* for political and social *débris*: a student union, for example, recuperated long ago and turned into a paltry agency of repression, can become a beacon of sedition and revolt. Subversion is a form of action transcending the separation between art and politics: it is the art of revolution.

Strasbourg marks the beginning of a new period of situationist activity. The social position of situationist thought has been determined up to now by the following contradiction: the most highly developed critique of modern life has been made in one of the least highly developed modern countries—in a country which has not yet reached the point where the complete disintegration of all values becomes patently obvious and engenders the corresponding forces of radical rejection. In the French context, situationist theory has anticipated the social forces by which it will be realised.

In the more highly developed countries, the opposite has happened: the forces of revolt exist, but without a revolutionary perspective. The Committee of 100 or the Berkeley rebellion of 1964, for example, were spontaneous mass movements which collapsed because they proved incapable of grasping more than the incidental aspects of alienation (the Bomb, Free Speech . . .), because they failed to understand that these were merely specific manifestations of everyone's exclusion from the whole of his experience, on every level of individual and social life. Without a critique of this fundamental alienation, these movements could never articulate the real dissatisfaction which created them—dissatisfaction with the nature of everyday life—while as specialised "causes" they could only become integrated or dissolve. As a shrewd Italian journalist wrote in *L'Europeo*, situationist theory is the "missing link" in the development of the new forces of revolt—the revolutionary perspective of total transformation still absent from the immense discontent of contemporary youth, as from the industrial struggle which continues in all its violence at shop-floor level. The time will come— and our job is to hasten it—when these two currents join forces. Louise Crowley has indicated the reactionary role to which the old workers' movement is now doomed: the maintenance of *work* made potentially unnecessary by the progress of automation.[1] Whatever *Solidarity* may think,[2] outright opposition to forced labour is going to become a rallying-point of revolutionary activity in the most advanced areas of the world.

Already, in the highly industrialised countries, the decomposition of modern society is becoming obvious at a mass level.[3] All previous ideological explanations of the world have collapsed, and left the misery and chaos of everyday life without any coherent dissimulation at all. Politics, morality and culture are all in ruins—and have now reached the point of being marketed as such, as their own parody, the spectacle of decadence being the last desperate attempt to stabilise the decadence of the spectacle. Less and less masks the reduction of the whole of life to the production and consumption of commodities; less and less

---

[1] "Beyond Automation", *Monthly Review*, November, 1964 (reprinted in *Anarchy* 49, March, 1965). Crowley's remarks on the "new lumpenproletariat" are of particular interest.

[2] Cf. their self-criticism, in *Solidarity* vol. 4, number 5, p. 5.

[3] Cf. Raoul Vaneigem's "Banalités de Base" in *Internationale Situationniste* 7 & 8, and translated by us as a pamphlet, "The Totality for Kids".

"*Two thousand years of christianity h a v e fostered the masochism of all these intellectuals. This is our lucky break; and it won't stop here.*" (*The Return of t h e Durutti Column*)

masks the relationship between the isolation, emptiness and anguish of everyday life and this dictatorship of the commodity; less and less masks the increasing waste of the forces cf production, and the richness of lived experience now possible if these forces were only used to fulfil human desires instead of to repress them.

If England is the temporary capital of the spectacular world, it is because no other country could take its demoralization so seriously. The island, having recovered from its fit of satirical giggles, has flipped out. The consumption of hysteria has become a principle of social production, but one where the real banality of the goods keeps breaking the surface, and letting loose a necessary violence—the violence of a man who has been given everything, but finds that every *thing* is phoney. Fashion accelerates because revolution is treading on its tail.

With the end of the first phase of pop, the spectacle is beginning to pitch its convulsive tent in the theatre and the art gallery. Degenerate bourgeois entertainment is dying of self-consciousness and impotent dislike of its audience: rather than mount improvised "political" tear-jerkers, it should learn to destroy itself. Now is the time for a Christopher Fry revival.

Fake culture, fake politics. If we pass over student unionism in Anglo-America, it is out of simple contempt. There is a sharpening of the pseudo-struggle (Reagan versus the Regents, LSE versus Addams), but its only interest is in guessing which side is financed by the CIA. The triumph of Wilsonism is more important, since its harsh mediocrity reveals the logic of modern capitalism: the stronger the Labour Movement, with its bone-hard hierarchies and its school-teacher notions of technology and social justice, the greater the guarantee of total repression. The militant proletariat, whose opposition to the capitalist system is unabated, will remain revolutionary chickenfeed till the myth of the Labour Movement has been finally laid.

With the decline of the spectacular antagonisms (Tory/Labour, East/West, High Culture/Low Culture), the official Left is looking round for new mock battles to fight. It has always had a masochistic urge to embrace the tough-minded alternative. The orthodox "communist" party owed its popularity among the lumpenintelligentsia to an assertion that it was too practical to have time for theory—a claim amply confirmed by its own blend of flaccid intellectual nullity and permanent political impotence. Those who counsel "working within the Labour Movement" play on the same secret craving to rush around with buckets of water trying to light a fire. The latest enthusiasm of the Left is Mao's "cultural revolution", that farce produced by courtesy of the Chinese bureaucracy (complete with blue jokes about red panties). To repeat an old adage, there is no revolution without the arming of the working class. A revolution of unarmed schoolchildren, which even then has to be neutered by the "support" of the army, is a pseudo-revolution serving some obscure need for readjustment within the bureaucracy. As a tactic for bureaucratic reorganisation it is familiar—after the hysterical and ineffective purge of the Right comes the appeal to "discipline", the call "to purify our ranks and eliminate individualism" (*People's Daily*, 21st Feb., 1967), and finally the *essential* purge of the Left. Far from marking an attack on "socialist" bureaucracy, the GPCR marks the bureaucracy's first adjustment to the techniques of neo-capitalist repression, its colonisation of everyday life. It is the beginning of the Great Leap Forward to Kruschov's Russia and Kennedy's America.

The real revolution begins at home: in the desperation of consumer production, in the continuing struggle of the unofficial working class. As yet this unofficial revolt has an official ideology. The notion that modern capitalism is producing new revolutionary forces, new poverties of a new proletariat, is still suppressed. Instead there is an *a priori* fascination with the "conversion" or the "subversion" of the old union movement. The militants are recuperating themselves (and their intellectual "advisers" urge on the process). The *only* real subversion is in a new consciousness and a new alliance—the location of the struggle in the banalities of everyday life, in the supermarket and the beatclub *as well as* on the shopfloor. The enemy is entrism, cultural or political. Art and the Labour Movement are dead! Long live the Situationist International!

Published by Situationist International. All enquiries to :

BCM/Situationist International

London, W.C.1.

printed by Equity Printers Limited
1 Regent Square, London, W.C.1
(Tel.: 01.837.7582)

LA FÊTE PERPÉTUELLE ET SES DÉBORDE-
MENTS DYONISIAQUES LES ACCOMPAGNAIENT
PARTOUT ET RUINÈRENT LE PEU D'ESTIME
QU'AURAIT PU LEUR PORTER ENCORE UN AS-
SEZ PETIT NOMBRE DE GENS...

LA CRISE GÉNÉRALE DES
VIEUX APPAREILS SYNDICAUX,
DES BUREAUCRATIES GAUCHISTES
SE FAISAIT RESSENTIR PAR-
TOUT ET PRINCIPALEMENT CHEZ
LES ÉTUDIANTS, OÙ L'ACTIVIS-
ME N'AVAIT DEPUIS LONG-
TEMPS PLUS D'AUTRE RESSORT
QUE LE DÉVOUEMENT LE PLUS
SORDIDE AUX IDÉOLOGIES DÉFRAÎ-
CHIES ET L'AMBITION LA
MOINS RÉALISTE. LE DERNIER
CARRÉ DE PROFESSIONNELS
QUI ÉLUT NOS HÉROS N'A-
VAIT MÊME PAS L'EXCUSE
D'UNE MYSTIFICATION. ILS
PLACÈRENT LEUR ESPOIR D'UN
RENOUVEAU DANS UN GROUPE
QUI NE CACHAIT PAS SES
INTENTIONS DE SABORDER
AU PLUS VITE ET POUR LE
MIEUX TOUT CE MILITANTIS-
ME ARCHAÏQUE.

AYANT ENTENDU
PARLER DES MŒURS
DE NOS SYMPATHI-
QUES AVENTURI-
ERS, LES HABITUÉS
DU MENSONGE EXIGE-
RENT QU'ILS SE
PLIENT À L'INÉ-
GALITÉ LÉGALE
QUI GARANTISSAIT
DEPUIS SI LONG-
TEMPS LEURS IM-
POSTURES...

3 shillings

50 cents

De la Misère en milieu étudiant
considérée sous ses aspects économique, psychologique,
politique, sexuel et notamment intellectuel
et de quelques moyens pour y remédier

Titre.

Nous pouvons affirmer, sans grand risque de nous tromper,
que l'étudiant en France est, après le flic, l'être le plus
~~universel~~ universellement méprisé. Nous analyserons en détail
les nuances et les subtilités de ce mépris. Nous verrons alors
si les raisons pour lesquelles on le méprise généralement
sont de _fausses_ raisons, qui relèvent de l'idéologie dominante,
tandis que les raisons pour lesquelles il est effectivement
méprisable et méprisé du point de vue de la critique
révolutionnaire sont [refoulées et inavouées,] ~~pour que tous~~
~~tout~~ ~~les tenants de la~~ (aux contestation
justement celles pour lesquelles l'impuissante
intelligentsia de gauche (des Temps modernes à l'Express)
~~en passant par~~ l'Observateur et autres) ~~se pâme~~ devant la
prétendue "montée des étudiants", et les organisations
bureaucratiques (du P.C.F à l'U N E F) ~~qui~~ disputent
~~fabuleusement~~ son appui "moral et matériel. Nous montrons
comment ~~elle par les raisons~~ contribuent au maintien
de la _réalité dominante_, le capitalisme surdéveloppé, et
nous emploierons cette brochure à les dénoncer aux

On the Poverty of Student Life

De la misère en milieu étudiant, considérée sous ses aspects économique, politique, psychologique, sexuel et notamment intellectuel et de quelques moyens pour y remédier: An Early Draft of the First Chapter (1966)

Mustapha Khayati

Mustapha Khayati Papers, GEN MSS 1480, Box 3f, International Situationist, Khayati Papers, Beinecke Rare Book and Manuscript Library, Yale University

En général : vérifiez
bien vos phrases, et
choisissez entre pluriel
et singulier qui se
chevauchent : les étudiants, l'
étudiant ...

Un peu plus de phrases courtes,
coupées par des points.

Un peu moins de grossièretés
faciles : "conneries", etc.

Peut-être faut-il risquer con une seule fois, pour la parade

à une. Le chemin de la désaliénation et celui- (2)
~~même~~ de l'aliénation sont une seule et même chose.

Toutes les ~~études~~ analyses et études faites sur le milieu
étudiant ont ~~négligé~~ jusqu'ici négligé l'essentiel. Elles
~~ne~~ ~~dépassent~~ ~~le~~ ~~pt~~ ~~des~~ ~~spécialités~~ ~~universitaires~~
restent limitées au point de vue du spécialiste (le psychologie,
le sociologie ou l'économiste) et n'apportent qu'un point
~~et~~ ~~détaillent~~
de vue spécial, fondamentalement erroné. Toutes, elles
commettent ce que Fourier appelait déjà, une étourderie
méthodique, ~~~~ puisqu'elle porte régulièrement sur les
questions primordiales, =, en ignorant le point de vue de
vue total de la société moderne, ~~en~~ ~~ne~~ ~~voyant~~ ~~de~~ ~~la~~ ~~recherche~~
~~d'autres~~ ~~détails~~, ils oublient la catégorie fondamentale qui
~~fondamental~~ marchande ~~et~~ spectaculaire. Ainsi
~~la~~ ~~temps~~ ~~le~~ ~~spectacle~~ ~~marchand~~
en viennent-elles à aligner des résultats parcellaires, sans
grand lien entre eux, ~~et~~ ~~s'entassent~~ ~~~~ devant lesquels elles restent désarmées
et qui leur restent incompréhensibles. Nous ~~avons~~ ~~fait~~ à cet égard
par exemple, l'enquête de Bourdieu-Passeron (" ~~les~~ ~~riches~~ un distique
Héritiers"- les étudiants et la culture). les 2 sociologues,
aboutissent à quelques vérités partielles, mais restent tout
à fait incapables de les utiliser, car d'emblée, ils se
sont placés du point de vue réformiste-structuraliste,
qui le point de vue de l'éthique kantienne d'une
démocratisation réelle par une rationalisation réelle.

à une. La création désaliénation n'a ~~sont pas~~ pas d'autre chemin que celui de l'aliénation.

Toutes les analyses et études faites sur le milieu étudiant ont jusqu'ici négligé l'essentiel.

du système de l'enseignement. (enseignement du système)

L'étudiant est fondamentalement et avant tout un rôle provisoire, dans le spectacle du capitalisme moderne, nécessaire à l'accession à un autre rôle permanent, Il y participe comme positif et conservateur, dans le fonctionnement du système.

Une __initiation__ à la machine du journal

✗ Cette initiation retrouve, magiquement, toutes les caractéristiques de l'initiation __mythique__. Elle reste totalement coupée de la réalité historique (individuelle et sociale). L'étudiant est un être partagé entre deux, un statut présent et un statut futur, nettement tranchés et dont la limite est mécaniquement franchie. Dans la fausse conscience qu'ils se font d'eux-mêmes et de leur avenir, les étudiants négligent celui-ci et mettent l'accent sur ce qui les unit, apparemment, dans le premier statut. Dans une sorte de conscience schizophrénique, ils croient s'isoler dans leur "société d'initiation", qui reste sans histoire. Le ressort du renversement de la vérité officielle, c.-à-d. économique, de la société est tellement simple à démasquer : la __réalité__ étudiante est dure à regarder en face. Dans une "société d'abondance",

le statut actuel de l'étudiant est l'extrême pauvreté. ④

Originaires à plus de 80% de couches dont le revenu est supérieur à celui d'un ouvrier, 90% d'entre eux disposent d'un revenu inférieur à celui du plus simple salarié. La misère de l'étudiant reste en deçà de la misère du spectacle, la nouvelle misère du nouveau prolétariat. Son état normal est celui de la minorité prolongée. A une époque où une partie croissante de la jeunesse s'affranchit de plus en plus des préjugés moraux et de l'autorité familiale avant l'âge de 18 ans, les étudiants, dès leur majorité (par le plus simple mécanisme de la dépendance économique) restent tributaires de leur famille jusqu'à l'accession à la profession où ils rentreront dans des familles plus larges de dépendance. Les exigences du capitalisme moderne font que la majeure partie des étudiants seront tout simplement de petits cadres (c'est à dire l'équivalent de ce qu'était au XIXᵉ siècle la fonction d'ouvrier qualifié). Devant le caractère misérable, facilement pressenti, de cet avenir plus ou moins proche, qui paiera la honteuse misère du présent, l'étudiant préfère se tourner vers le présent et le décorer d'un

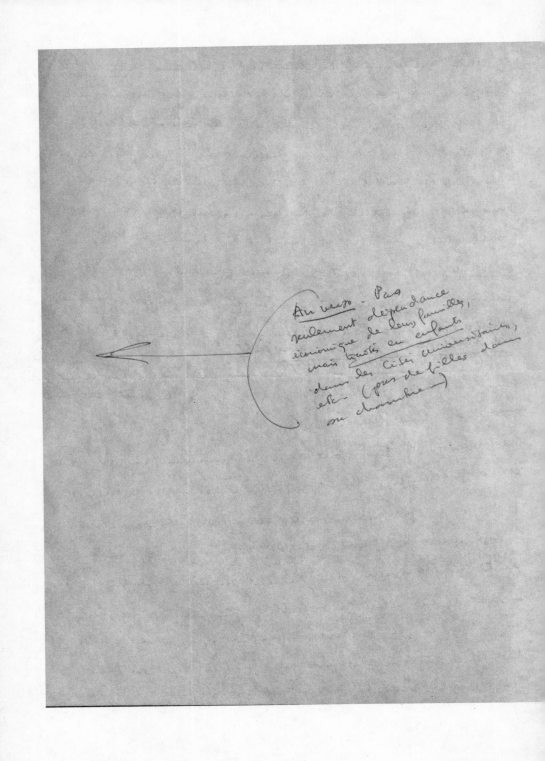

...stige illusoire. La conversation même est trop misérable ⑤
pour qu'on s'y attache; on est sûr que les lendemains ne chanteront pas et baigneront fatalement dans la médiocrité. Alors
rien ne vaut plus le présent, mais irréellement vécu —

Esclave obéissant, l'étudiant se croit d'autant plus libre
que toutes les chaînes de l'autorité le lient. Il se fait de
son existence et de ses conditions de vie les idées les
plus fantastiques et participe aux mythes idéologiques
les plus délirants. Comme sa nouvelle Famille, l'Université
(~~~~~~~~), l'étudiant se voit comme l'Être le plus
                                          social
autonome, alors qu'il relève directement et conjointement
des 2 systèmes les plus puissants de l'autorité sociale :
La Famille et l'État. Il en est leur enfant docile et reconnaissant, le trop le petit ~~~~~ ~~~~~ de l'État — Suivant
                              satisfait
la même logique de l'enfant "~~~~~", l'étudiant
                              "satisfait de l'être"
participe à toutes les valeurs et mystifications du système
et les concentre en lui. — Ce qui était illusions imposées aux
employés, devient idéologie intériorisée ~~~ et véhiculée
par la masse des futurs petits cadres.
   Si la misère sociale a produit les systèmes le plus grandioses
                          ancienne
de l'histoire (les Religions), la misère étudiante n'a trouvé
                                        imaginaire
de réalisation que dans les images les plus éculées de
la société dominante, la répétition burlesque de tous
ses produits aliénés.
   L'étudiant français, en sa qualité d'être idéologique,
arrive trop tard à tout. Toutes les "valeurs" et illusions

qui font la fierté de son monde "fermé" sont déjà condamnés en tant qu' illusions insoutenables, ~~toutes~~ [depuis lgps] ridiculisées par l' histoire.

Être pitoyable, l'étudiant est toujours content d'être étudiant. Trop tard. A ~~une époque~~ où l'enseignement mécanique et spécialisé qu' ~~ils~~ reçoit ~~reçoivent~~ est aussi profondément dégradé (par rapport à l'ancien niveau de la culture générale bourgeoise) que ~~leur~~ [son propre] niveau intellectuel) ~~déjà~~ [au moment où ils accèdent] [du seul fait que la société en domine tout cela,] le système économique, a dû fabriquer massivement des étudiants, incultes et incapables de penser. Que l'Université devienne une organisation (institutionnelle) de l'ignorance, que la "haute culture" elle-même se dissolve au rythme de la production en série des Professeurs, que tous ces professeurs soient des crétins que n'importe quel public lycéen chahuterait; ~~les~~ vétilles que tout cela! Les étudiants continuent à écouter respectueusement ~~leurs~~ [se] maîtres, avec la volonté consciente de perdre tout esprit critique pour pouvoir communier dans l'illusion mystique d'être devenus ~~des~~ "étudiants", ~~des gens~~ [quelqu'un] sérieusement occupés à apprendre ~~à~~ un savoir sérieux. Tla fait rire: tout ce qui se passe aujourd'hui dans les amphithéâtres des écoles et facultés sera condamné dans la future société révolutionnaire comme bruit, socialement nocif.

Prisonnier content de sa prison, l'étudiant ne se rend même pas compte que l'Histoire ~~attend~~ disparaît aussi son dérisoire monde ~~fermé~~ clos. La fameuse "Crise de l'Université", détail d'une crise plus générale du Capitalisme moderne ~~transautratique~~ reste l'objet d'un dialogue de sourds entre différents spécialistes. Elle traduit tout simplement les difficultés d'un ajustement tardif de ce secteur spécial de la production à une transformation de l'ensemble de l'appareil productif. Les résidus de la vieille idéologie de l'université libérale bourgeoise se banalisent au moment où sa base sociale disparaît. L'Université a pu ✗ prendre pour une puissance autonome à ✗ l'époque du Capitalisme de libre échange et de son État libéral qui lui laissait une certaine liberté marginale. Elle défendait en fait étroitement des besoins de ce type de société : donner à la minorité privilégiée qui faisait des études la culture générale adéquate avant qu'elle rejoigne les rangs de la classe dirigeante dont elle était à peine sortie. D'où le ridicule de ces professeurs (nostalgiques), aigris d'avoir perdu leur ancienne fonction de chiens de garde des futurs maîtres pour celle beaucoup moins noble de chiens de bergers conduisant, (suivant les besoins planifiés du système économique) les fournées de "cols blancs" vers leurs usines respectives. Ce sont eux qui opposent leurs archaïsmes à la technocratisation (nécessaire) de l'Université, et continuent imperturbablement à ~~disperser~~ débiter les tribus d'une culture "dite générale, à de

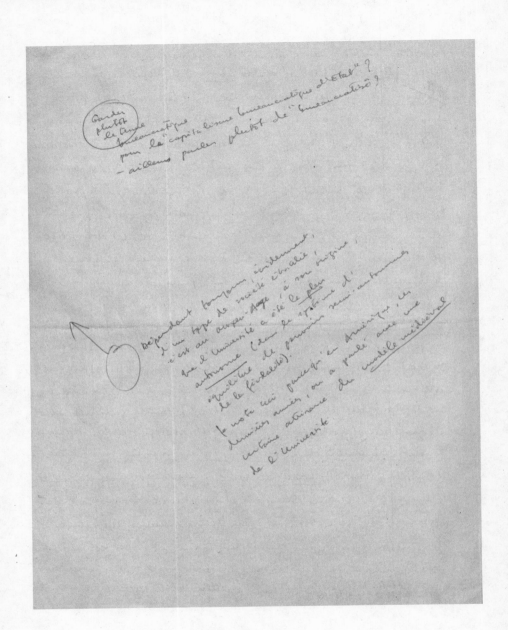

IIᵉ PARTIE

" Il ne suffit pas que la pensée/cherche sa réalisation, il faut que la réalité recherche la pensée.

Depuis quelques années s'esquisse, dans les pays avancés, un renouveau de la contestation dont la jeunesse semble être la porteuse. Mais la société du spectacle impose l'emploi de ses catégories idéologiques ~~propres~~ pour expliquer et s'expliquer le monde et tend ainsi à ramener tout ce qui s'y passe à du déjà connu et les nouveautés réelles à des appendices de son illusoire nouveauté. La révolte de la jeunesse contre les ~~mode~~ de vie qu'on lui impose n'est en réalité que les signes avant-coureurs d'une contestation plus vaste, le prélude à ~~une~~ prochaine époque révolutionnaire ~~qui~~ ~~emportera l'ordre contre lequel la jeunesse s'insurge aujourd'hui.~~

Seulement ~~l~~ l'idéologie dominante ne peut ~~s'arroger~~ cela ~~et~~ selon des mécanismes éprouvés d'inverser la réalité, elle enferme le mouvement historique réel dans cette pseudo-catégorie socio-naturelle qui est le mystère de la jeunesse. Ainsi ramène-t-elle une nouvelle jeunesse de la révolte à l'éternelle révolte de la jeunesse qui renaît à chaque génération pour s'estomper quand le jeune homme est pris par le sérieux de la production / par l'activité en vue des fins concrètes et véritables. »

On the Poverty of Student Life

De la misère en milieu étudiant, considérée sous ses aspects économique, politique, psychologique, sexuel et notamment intellectuel et de quelques moyens pour y remédier (1966)

Members of the Situationist International and Students from Strasbourg

Ce texte peut être librement reproduit même sans indication d'origine.

Ecrire à: LE PAVÉ, B. P. 323 R 8 Strasbourg

Directeur de «21-27 Etudiants de France», J. TERREL

Commission paritaire des papiers de Presse, Paris 40522 - IMPRIMERIE WEIBEL - STRASBOURG

Union Nationale des Etudiants de France
Association Fédérative Générale des Etudiants
de Strasbourg

DE LA MISERE
EN MILIEU
ETUDIANT

considérée
sous ses aspects économique, politique,
psychologique, sexuel et notamment
intellectuel
et de quelques moyens pour y remédier.

1966

Supplément spécial au N° 16 de «21-27 Etudiants de France»

DE LA MISERE EN MILIEU ETUDIANT

*considérée
sous ses aspects économique, politique,
psychologique, sexuel et notamment
intellectuel
et de quelques moyens pour y remédier.*

Rendre la honte
plus honteuse encore en la livrant
à la publicité.

Nous pouvons affirmer sans grand risque de nous tromper que l'étudiant en France est, après le policier et le prêtre, l'être le plus universellement méprisé. Si les raisons pour lesquelles on le méprise sont souvent de fausses raisons qui relèvent de l'idéologie dominante, les raisons pour lesquelles il est effectivement méprisable et méprisé du point de vue de la critique révolutionnaire sont refoulées et inavouées. Les tenants de la fausse contestation savent pourtant les reconnaître et s'y reconnaître. Ils inversent ce vrai mépris en une admiration complaisante. Ainsi l'impuissante intelligentsia de gauche (*des Temps Modernes à l'Express*) se pâme devant la prétendue «montée des étudiants», et les organisations bureaucratiques effectivement déclinantes (du parti dit communiste à l'U.N.E.F.) se disputent jalousement son appui «moral et matériel». Nous montrerons les raisons de cet intérêt pour les étudiants et comment elles participent positivement à la réalité dominante du capitalisme surdéveloppé, et nous emploierons cette brochure à les dénoncer une à une: la désaliénation ne suit pas d'autre chemin que celui de l'aliénation.

Toutes les analyses et études entreprises sur le milieu étudiant ont jusqu'ici négligé l'essentiel. Jamais elles ne dépassent le point de vue des spécialisations universitaires (psychologie, sociologie, économie) et demeurent donc fondamentalement erronées. Toutes, elles commettent ce que Fourier appelait déjà une *étourderie méthodique* «puisqu'elle porte régulièrement sur les questions primordiales», en ignorant le point de vue total de la société moderne. Le fétichisme des

3

faits masque la catégorie essentielle et les détails font oublier la *totalité*. On dit tout de cette société sauf ce qu'elle est effectivement: *marchande et spectaculaire*. Les sociologues Bourderon et Passedieu, dans leur enquête «*Les Héritiers: les étudiants et la culture*», restent désarmés devant les quelques vérités partielles qu'ils ont fini par prouver. Et malgré toute leur volonté bonne ils retombent dans la morale des professeurs, l'inévitable éthique kantienne d'une *démocratisation réelle par une rationalisation réelle du système d'enseignement*, c'est-à-dire de l'enseignement du système. Tandis que leurs disciples, les Kravetz (1) se croient des milliers à se réveiller, compensant leur amertume petite-bureaucrate par le fatras d'une phraséologie révolutionnaire désuète.

La mise en spectacle (2) de la réification sous le capitalisme moderne impose à chacun un rôle dans la passivité généralisée. L'étudiant n'échappe pas à cette loi. Il est un rôle provisoire, qui le prépare au rôle définitif qu'il assumera, en élément positif et conservateur, dans le fonctionnement du système marchand. Rien d'autre qu'une initiation.

Cette initiation retrouve, magiquement, toutes les caractéristiques de l'initiation mythique. Elle reste totalement coupée de la réalité historique, individuelle et sociale. L'étudiant est un être partagé entre un statut présent et un statut futur nettement tranchés et dont la limite va être mécaniquement franchie. Sa conscience schizophrénique lui permet de s'isoler dans une «société d'initiation», méconnait son avenir et s'enchante de l'unité mystique que lui offre un présent à l'abri de l'histoire. Le ressort du renversement de la vérité officielle, c'est-à-dire économique, est tellement simple à démasquer: la réalité étudiante est dure à regarder en face. Dans une «société d'abondance» le statut actuel de l'étudiant est l'extrême pauvreté. Originaires à plus de 80% des couches dont le revenu est supérieur à celui d'un ouvrier, 90% d'entre eux disposent d'un revenu inférieur à celui du plus simple salarié. La misère de l'étudiant reste en deça de la misère de la société du spectacle, de la nouvelle misère du nouveau prolétariat. En un temps où une partie croissante de la jeunesse s'affranchit de plus en plus des préjugés moraux et de l'autorité

---

(1) *Kravetz* (Marc) connut une certaine notoriété dans les milieux dirigeants de l'UNEF; élégant parlementaire, il commit l'erreur de se risquer dans la «recherche théorique»: en 1964, publie dans les *Temps Modernes* une apologie du syndicalisme étudiant qu'il dénonce l'année suivante dans le même périodique.

(2) Il va de soi que nous employons ces concerts de *spectacle*, *rôle*, etc... au sens situationniste.

4

familiale pour entrer au plus tôt dans les relations d'exploitation ouverte, l'étudiant se maintient à tous les niveaux dans une «minorité prolongée», irresponsable et docile. Si sa crise juvénile tardive l'oppose quelque peu à sa famille, il accepte sans mal d'être traité en enfant dans les diverses institutions qui régissent sa vie quotidienne (3).

La colonisation des divers secteurs de la pratique sociale ne fait que trouver dans le monde étudiant son expression la plus criante. Le transfert sur les étudiants de toute la mauvaise conscience sociale masque la misère et la servitude de tous.

Mais les raisons qui fondent notre mépris pour l'étudiant sont d'un tout autre ordre. Elles ne concernent pas seulement sa misère réelle mais sa complaisance envers toutes les misères, sa propension malsaine à consommer béatement de l'aliénation, dans l'espoir, devant le manque d'intérêt général, d'intéresser à son manque particulier. Les exigences du capitalisme moderne font que la majeure partie des étudiants seront tout simplement de *petits cadres* (c'est-à-dire l'équivalent de ce qu'était au XIXe siècle la fonction d'ouvrier qualifié) (4). Devant le caractère misérable, facile à pressentir, de cet avenir plus ou moins proche qui le «dédommagera» de la honteuse misère du présent, l'étudiant préfère se tourner vers son présent et le décorer de prestiges illusoires. La compensation même est trop lamentable pour qu'on s'y attache; les lendemains ne chanteront pas et baigneront fatalement dans la médiocrité. C'est pourquoi il se réfugie dans un présent, irréellement vécu.

Esclave stoïcien, l'étudiant se croit d'autant plus libre que toutes les chaînes de l'autorité le lient. Comme sa nouvelle famille, l'Université, il se prend pour l'être social le plus «autonome» alors qu'il relève *directement et conjointement* des deux systèmes les plus puissants de l'autorité sociale: la famille et l'Etat. Il est leur enfant rangé et reconnaissant. Suivant la même logique de *l'enfant soumis*, il participe à toutes les valeurs et mystifications du système et les concentre en lui. Ce qui était illusions imposées aux employés devient idéologie intériorisée et véhiculée par la masse des futurs petits cadres.

Si la misère sociale ancienne a produit les systèmes de compensation les plus grandioses de l'histoire (les religions),

___

(3) Quand on lui chie pas dans la gueule, on lui pisse au cul.
(4) Mais sans la conscience révolutionnaire; l'ouvrier n'avait pas l'illusion de la promotion.

5

la misère marginale étudiante n'a trouvé de consolation que dans les images les plus éculées de la société dominante, la répétition burlesque de tous ses produits aliénés.

L'étudiant français, en sa qualité d'être idéologique *arrive trop tard à tout*. Toutes les valeurs et illusions qui font la fierté de son monde fermé, sont déjà condamnées en tant qu'illusions insoutenables, depuis longtemps ridiculisées par l'histoire.

Récoltant un peu du prestige en miettes de l'Université, l'étudiant est encore content d'être étudiant. Trop tard. L'enseignement mécanique et spécialisé qu'il reçoit est aussi profondément dégradé (par rapport à l'ancien niveau de la culture générale bourgeoise) (5) que son propre niveau intellectuel au moment où il y accède, du seul fait que la réalité qui domine tout cela, le système économique, réclame une fabrication massive d'étudiants incultes et incapables de penser. Que l'Université soit devenue une organisation — institutionnelle — de l'ignorance, que la «haute culture» elle-même se dissolve au rythme de la production en série des professeurs, que *tous* ces professeurs soient des crétins, dont la plupart provoquerait le chahut de n'importe quel public de lycée — l'étudiant l'ignore et continue d'écouter respectueusement ses maîtres, avec la volonté consciente de perdre tout esprit critique afin de mieux communier dans l'illusion mystique d'être devenu un «étudiant», quelqu'un qui s'occupe sérieusement à apprendre un savoir *sérieux*, dans l'espoir qu'on lui confiera les vérités dernières. C'est une ménopause de l'esprit. Tout ce qui se passe aujourd'hui dans les amphithéâtres des écoles et des facultés sera condamné dans la future société révolutionnaire comme *bruit*, socialement nocif. D'ores et déjà l'étudiant fait rire.

L'étudiant ne se rend même pas compte que l'histoire altère aussi son dérisoire monde «fermé». La fameuse «Crise de l'Université», détail d'une crise plus générale du capitalisme moderne, reste l'objet d'un dialogue de sourds entre différents spécialistes. Elle traduit tout simplement les difficultés d'un ajustement tardif de ce secteur spécial de la production à une transformation d'ensemble de l'appareil productif. Les résidus de la vieille idéologie de l'Université libérale bourgeoise se banalisent au moment où sa base sociale disparaît. L'Université a pu se prendre pour une puissance autonome à l'époque du capitalisme de libre-échange et de

---

(5) Nous ne parlons pas de celle de l'Ecole Normale Supérieure ou des Sorboniqueurs, mais de celle des encyclopédistes ou de Hegel.

6

son Etat libéral qui lui laissait une certaine liberté marginale. Elle dépendait en fait étroitement des besoins de ce type de société: donner à la minorité privilégiée, qui faisait des études, la culture générale adéquate avant qu'elle ne rejoigne les rangs de la classe dirigeante dont elle était à peine sortie. D'où le ridicule de ces professeurs nostalgiques (6), aigris d'avoir perdu leur ancienne fonction de chiens de garde des futurs maîtres pour celle beaucoup moins noble de chiens de berger conduisant, suivant les besoins planifiés du système économique, les fournées de «cols blancs» vers leurs usines et bureaux respectifs. Ce sont eux qui opposent leurs archaïsmes à la technocratisation de l'Université, et continuent imperturbablement à débiter les bribes d'une culture dite générale à de futurs spécialistes qui ne sauront qu'en faire.

Plus sérieux, et donc plus dangereux, sont les modernistes de la gauche et ceux de l'UNEF menés par les «ultras» de la FGEL, qui revendiquent une «réforme de structure de l'Université», une «réinsertion de l'Université dans la vie sociale et économique», c'est-à-dire son adaptation aux besoins du capitalisme moderne. De dispensatrices de la «culture générale» à l'usage des classes dirigeantes, les diverses facultés et écoles, encore parées de prestiges anachroniques, sont transformées en usines d'élevage hâtif de petits cadres et de cadres moyens. Loin de contester ce processus historique qui subordonne directement un des derniers secteurs relativement autonome de la vie sociale aux exigences du système marchand, nos progressistes protestent contre les retards et défaillances que subit sa réalisation. Ils sont les tenants de la future Université cybernétisée qui s'annonce déjà çà et là (7). Le système marchand et ses serviteurs modernes, voilà l'ennemi.

Mais il est normal que tout ce débat passe par dessus la tête de l'étudiant, dans le ciel de ses maîtres et lui échappe totalement: l'ensemble de sa vie, et à fortiori de *la vie*, lui échappe.

De par sa situation économique d'extrême pauvreté, l'étudiant est condamné à un certain mode de *survie* très peu enviable. Mais toujours content de son être, il érige sa triviale misère en «style de vie» original: le misérabilisme et la bohème. Or, la «bohème», déjà loin d'être une solution ori-

---

(6) N'osant pas se réclamer du libéralisme philistin, ils s'inventent des références dans les franchises universitaires du moyen-âge, époque de la «démocratie de la non-liberté».

(7) Cf. Internationale Situationniste, N° 9 (Rédaction B. P. 307.03, Paris). *Correspondance avec un cybernéticien* et le tract situationniste *La tortue dans la vitrine* contre le néo-professeur A. Moles.

7

ginale, n'est jamais authentiquement vécue qu'après une rupture complète et irréversible avec le milieu universitaire. Ses partisans parmi les étudiants (et tous se targuent de l'être un peu), ne font donc que s'accrocher à une version factice et dégradée de ce qui n'est, dans le meilleur des cas, qu'une médiocre solution individuelle. Il mérite jusqu'au mépris des vieilles dames de la campagne. Ces «originaux» continuent, trente ans après W.Reich (8), cet excellent éducateur de la jeunesse, à avoir les comportements érotiques-amoureux les plus traditionnels, reproduisant les rapports généraux de la société de classes dans leurs rapports inter-sexuels. Son aptitude à faire un militant de tout acabit en dit long sur son impuissance. Dans la marge de liberté individuelle permise par le Spectacle totalitaire, et malgré son emploi du temps plus ou moins lâche, l'étudiant ignore encore l'aventure et lui préfère un espace-temps quotidien étriqué, aménagé à son intention par les garde-fous du même spectacle.

Sans y être contraint il sépare de lui-même travail et loisirs, tout en proclamant un hypocrite mépris pour les «bosseurs» et les «bêtes à concours». Il entérine toutes les séparations et va ensuite gémir dans divers «cercles» religieux, sportifs, politiques ou syndicaux sur la non-communication. Il est si bête et si malheureux qu'il va même jusqu'à se confier spontanément et en masse au contrôle parapolicier des psychiatres et psychologues, mis en place à son usage par l'avantgarde de l'oppression moderne et donc applaudi par ses «représentants» qui voient naturellement dans ces Bureaux d'Aide Psychologique Universitaire (BAPU) une conquête indispensable et méritée (9).

Mais la misère réelle de la vie quotidienne étudiante trouve sa compensation immédiate, fantastique, dans son principal opium: la marchandise culturelle. Dans le spectacle culturel, l'étudiant retrouve naturellement sa place de disciple respectueux. Proche du lieu de production sans jamais y accéder — le Sanctuaire lui reste interdit — l'étudiant découvre la «culture moderne» en spectateur admiratif. A une époque où *l'art est mort*, il reste le principal fidèle des théâtres et des ciné-clubs, et le plus avide consommateur de son cadavre congelé et diffusé sous cellophane dans les supermarchés pour

---

(8) Voir *la lutte sexuelle des jeunes* et *la Fonction de l'orgasme*.
(9) Avec le reste de la population la camisole de force est nécessaire pour l'amener à comparaître devant le psychiatre dans sa forteresse asilaire. Avec l'étudiant il suffit de faire savoir que des postes de contrôle avancés ont été ouverts dans le ghetto: il s'y précipite, au point qu'il est nécessaire de distribuer des numéros d'ordre.

8

les ménagères de l'abondance. Il y participe sans réserve, sans arrière-pensée et sans distance. C'est son élément naturel. Si les «maisons de la culture» n'existaient pas, l'étudiant les aurait inventées. Il vérifie parfaitement les analyses les plus banales de la sociologie américaine du marketing: consommation ostentatoire, établissement d'une différenciation publicitaire entre produits identiques dans la nullité (Pérec ou Robbe-Grillet; Godard ou Lelouch).

Et dès que les «dieux», qui produisent ou organisent son spectacle culturel, s'incarnent sur scène, il est leur principal public, leur fidèle rêvé. Ainsi assiste-t-il en masse à leurs démonstrations les plus obscènes; qui d'autre que lui peuplerait les salles quand, par exemple, les curés des différentes églises viennent exposer publiquement leurs dialogues sans rivages (semaines de la pensée dite marxiste, réunions d'intellectuels catholiques) ou quand les débris de la littérature viennent constater leur impuissance (cinq mille étudiants à «Que peut la littérature?»).

Incapable de passions réelles il fait ses délices des polémiques sans passion entre les vedettes de l'Inintelligence, sur de faux problèmes dont la fonction est de masquer les vrais: Althusser - Garaudy - Sartre - Barthes - Picard - Lefebvre - Levi Strauss - Halliday - Chatelet - Antoine. Humanisme - Existentialisme - Structuralisme - Scientisme - Nouveau Criticisme - Dialecto-naturalisme - Cybernétisme - Planétisme - Métaphilosophisme.

Dans son application, il se croit d'avant-garde parce qu'il a vu le dernier Godard, acheté le dernier livre argumentiste (10) participé au dernier happening de Lapassade ce con. Cet ignorant prend pour des nouveautés «révolutionnaires» garanties, par label, les plus pâles ersatz d'anciennes recherches effectivement importantes en leur temps, édulcorées à l'intention du marché. La question est de toujours préserver son standing culturel. L'étudiant est fier d'acheter, comme tout le monde, les rééditions en livre de poche d'une série de textes importants et difficiles que la «culture de masse» répand à une cadence accélérée (11). Seulement il ne sait pas lire. Il se contente de les consommer du regard.

Ses lectures préférées restent la presse spécialisée qui

(10) Sur le gang argumentiste et la disparition de son organe, voir le tract *Aux poubelles de l'Histoire* diffusé par l'Internationale Situationniste en 1963.

(11) A cet effet on ne saurait trop recommander la solution, déjà pratiquée par les plus intelligents, qui consiste à les voler.

9

orchestre la consommation délirante des gadgets culturels; docilement il accepte ses oukases publicitaires et en fait la référence-standard de ses goûts. Il fait encore ses délices de l'*Express* et de l'*Observateur,* ou bien il croit que *le Monde,* dont le style est déjà trop difficile pour lui, est vraiment un journal «objectif» qui reflète l'actualité. Pour approfondir ses connaissances générales, il s'abreuve de *Planète,* la revue magique qui enlève les rides et les points noirs des vieilles idées. C'est avec de tels guides qu'il croit participer au monde moderne et s'initier à la politique.

Car l'étudiant, plus que partout ailleurs, est content d'être *politisé.* Seulement il ignore qu'il y participe à travers le même *spectacle.* Ainsi se réapproprie-t-il tous les restes en lambeaux ridicules d'une gauche qui fut anéantie voilà *plus de quarante ans,* par le réformisme «socialiste» et par la contre-révolution stalinienne. Cela il l'ignore encore, alors que le Pouvoir le sait clairement, et les ouvriers d'une façon confuse. Il participe, avec une fierté débile, aux manifestations les plus dérisoires qui n'attirent que lui. La fausse conscience politique se trouve chez lui à l'état pur et l'étudiant constitue la base idéale pour les manipulations des bureaucrates fantomatiques des organisations mourantes (du Parti dit Communiste à l'UNEF). Celles-ci programment totalitairement ses options politiques; tout écart ou velléité d'«indépendance» rentre docilement, après une parodie de résistance, dans un ordre qui n'a jamais été un instant mis en question (12). Quand il croit aller outre comme ces gens qui se nomment par une véritable maladie de l'inversion publicitaire JCR, alors qu'ils ne sont ni jeunes ni communistes ni révolutionnaires, c'est pour se rallier gaîment au mot d'ordre pontifical: Paix au Viet-Nam.

L'étudiant est fier de s'opposer aux «archaïsmes» d'un De Gaulle, mais ne comprend pas qu'il le fait au nom d'erreurs du passé, de *crimes refroidis* (comme le stalinisme à l'époque de Togliatti - Garaudy - Kroutchev - Mao) et qu'ainsi sa *jeunesse* est encore plus *archaïque* que le pouvoir qui, lui, dispose effectivement de tout ce qu'il faut pour administrer une société moderne.

Mais l'étudiant n'en est pas à un archaïsme près. Il se croit tenu d'avoir des idées générales sur tout, des conceptions

---

(12) Cf.: Les dernières aventures de l'UEC et de leurs homologues chrétiens avec leurs hiérarchies respectives; elles montrent que la seule unité entre tous ces gens réside dans leur soumission inconditionnelle à leurs maîtres.

10

cohérentes du monde qui donnent un sens à son besoin d'agitation et de promiscuité asexuée. C'est pourquoi, joué par les dernières fébrilités des églises, il se rue sur la vieillerie des vieilleries pour adorer la charogne puante de Dieu et s'attacher aux débris décomposés des religions préhistoriques qu'il croit dignes de lui et de son temps. On ose à peine le souligner, le milieu étudiant est avec celui des vieilles femmes de province, le secteur où se maintient la plus forte dose de religion professée et reste encore la meilleure «terre de missions» (alors que dans toutes les autres on a déjà mangé ou chassé les curés) où des prêtres-étudiants continuent à sodomiser, sans se cacher, des milliers d'étudiants dans leurs chiottes spirituelles.

Certes, il existe tout de même, parmi les étudiants, des gens d'un niveau intellectuel suffisant. Ceux-là dominent sans fatigue les misérables contrôles de capacité prévus pour les médiocres, et ils les dominent justement parce qu'ils ont *compris le système*, parce qu'ils le méprisent et se savent ses ennemis. Ils prennent dans le système des études ce qu'il a de meilleur: les bourses. Profitant des failles du contrôle, que sa logique propre oblige actuellement et ici à garder un petit secteur purement intellectuel, la «recherche», ils vont tranquillement porter le trouble au plus haut niveau: leur mépris ouvert à l'égard du système va de pair avec la lucidité qui leur permet justement d'être plus forts que les valets du système, et tout d'abord intellectuellement. Les gens dont nous parlons figurent en fait déjà parmi les théoriciens du mouvement révolutionnaire qui vient et se flattent d'être aussi connus que lui quand on va commencer à en parler. Ils ne cachent à personne que ce qu'ils prennent si aisément au «système des études» est utilisé pour sa destruction. Car l'étudiant ne peut se révolter contre rien sans se révolter contre ses *études*, et la nécessité de cette révolte se fait sentir moins naturellement que chez l'ouvrier, qui se révolte spontanément contre sa condition. Mais l'étudiant est un produit de la société moderne, au même titre que Godard et le Coca-Cola. Son extrême aliénation ne peut être contestée que par la contestation de la société toute entière. En aucune façon cette critique ne peut se faire sur le terrain étudiant: l'étudiant comme tel s'arroge une pseudo-valeur, qui lui interdit de prendre conscience de sa dépossession réelle et, de ce fait, il demeure au comble de la fausse conscience. Mais partout où la société moderne commence à être contestée, il y a révolte de la jeunesse, qui correspond immédiatement à une critique totale du comportement étudiant.

11

Il ne suffit pas que
la pensée recherche sa réalisation,
il faut que la réalité
recherche la pensée.

Après une longue période de sommeil léthargique et de contre-révolution permanente, s'esquisse, depuis quelques années, une nouvelle période de contestation dont la jeunesse semble être la porteuse. Mais la société du spectacle, dans la représentation qu'elle se fait d'elle-même et de ses ennemis, impose ses catégories idéologiques pour la compréhension du monde et de l'histoire. Elle ramène tout ce qui s'y passe à l'ordre naturel des choses et enferme les véritables nouveautés qui annoncent son *dépassement* dans le cadre restreint de son illusoire nouveauté. La révolte de la jeunesse contre le mode de vie qu'on lui impose n'est en réalité que le signe avant-coureur d'une subversion plus vaste qui englobera l'ensemble de ceux qui éprouvent de plus en plus l'impossibilité de vivre, le prélude à la prochaine époque révolutionnaire. Seulement l'idéologie dominante et ses organes quotidiens, selon des mécanismes éprouvés d'inversion de la réalité, ne peut que réduire ce mouvement historique réel à une pseudo-catégorie socio-naturelle: l'Idée de la Jeunesse (dont il serait dans l'essence d'être révoltée). Ainsi ramène-t-on une nouvelle jeunesse de la révolte à l'éternelle révolte de la jeunesse, renaissant à chaque génération pour s'estomper quand «le jeune homme est pris par le sérieux de la production et par l'activité en vue des fins concrètes et véritables». La «révolte des jeunes» a été et est encore l'objet d'une véritable inflation

12

journalistique qui en fait le spectacle d'une «révolte» possible donnée à contempler pour empêcher qu'on la vive, la sphère aberrante — déjà intégrée — nécessaire au fonctionnement du système social; cette révolte contre la société rassure la société parce qu'elle est sensée rester partielle, dans l'apartheid des «problèmes» de la jeunesse — comme il y aurait des problèmes de la femme, ou un problème noir — et ne durer qu'une partie de la vie. En réalité, s'il y a un problème de la «jeunesse» dans la société moderne c'est que la crise profonde de cette société est ressentie avec le plus d'acuité par la jeunesse (1). Produit par excellence de cette société moderne, elle est elle-même moderne, soit pour s'y intégrer sans réserves, soit pour la refuser radicalement. Ce qui doit surprendre, ce n'est pas tant que la jeunesse soit révoltée, mais que les «adultes» soient si résignés. Ceci n'a pas une explication mythologique mais historique: la génération précédente a connu toutes les défaites et consommé tous les mensonges de la période de la désagrégation honteuse du mouvement révolutionnaire.

Considérée en elle-même la «Jeunesse» est un mythe publicitaire déjà profondément lié au mode de production capitaliste, comme expression de son dynamisme. Cette illusoire primauté de la jeunesse est devenue possible avec le redémarrage de l'économie après la deuxième guerre mondiale, par suite de l'entrée en masse sur le marché de toute une catégorie de consommateurs plus malléables, un *rôle* qui assure un brevet d'intégration à la société du spectacle. Mais l'explication dominante du monde se trouve de nouveau en contradiction avec la réalité socio-économique (car en retard sur elle) et c'est justement la jeunesse qui, la première affirme une irrésistible fureur de vivre et s'insurge spontanément contre l'ennui quotidien et le temps mort que le vieux monde continue à secréter à travers ses différentes modernisations. La fraction révoltée de la jeunesse exprime le pur refus sans la conscience d'une perspective de dépassemnt, son refus nihiliste. Cette perspective se cherche et se constitue partout dans le monde. Il lui faut atteindre la cohérence de la critique théorique et l'organisation pratique de cette cohérence.

Au niveau le plus sommaire, les «Blousons noirs», dans tous les pays, expriment avec le plus de violence apparente le refus de s'intégrer. Mais le caractère abstrait de leur refus ne leur laisse aucune chance d'échapper aux contradictions d'un

---

(1) Non seulement le ressent mais veut l'exprimer.

13

système dont ils sont le produit négatif spontané. Les «Blousons noirs» sont produits par tous les côtés de *l'ordre* actuel: l'urbanisme des grands ensembles, la décomposition des valeurs, l'extension des loisirs consommables de plus en plus ennuyeux, le contrôle humaniste-policier de plus en plus étendu à toute la vie quotidienne, la survivance économique de la cellule familiale privée de toute signification. Ils méprisent le travail *mais* ils acceptent les marchandises. Ils voudraient avoir tout ce que la publicité leur montre, tout de suite et sans qu'ils puissent les payer. Cette contradiction fondamentale domine toute leur existence et c'est le cadre qui empoisonne leur tentative d'affirmation dans la recherche d'une véritable liberté dans l'emploi du temps, l'affirmation individuelle et la constitution d'une sorte de communauté. (Seulement, de telles micro-communautés recomposent, en marge de la société développée, un primitivisme où la misère recrée inéluctablement la hiérarchie dans la bande. Cette hiérarchie, qui ne peut s'affirmer que dans la lutte contre d'autres bandes, *isole* chaque bande, et dans chaque bande l'individu.) Pour sortir de cette contradiction, le «Blouson noir» devra finalement travailler pour acheter des marchandises — et là tout un secteur de la production est expressément fabriqué pour sa récupération en tant que consommateur (motos, guitares électriques, vêtements, disques, etc...) — ou bien il doit s'attaquer aux lois de la marchandise, soit de façon primaire en la volant, soit d'une façon consciente en s'élevant à la critique révolutionnaire du monde de la marchandise. La consommation adoucit les mœurs de ces jeunes révoltés, et leur révolte retombe dans le pire conformisme. Le monde des Blousons noirs n'a d'autre issue que la prise de conscience révolutionnaire ou l'obéissance aveugle dans les usines.

Les *Provos* constituent la première forme de dépassement de l'expérience des «Blousons noirs», l'organisation de sa première expression politique. Ils sont nés à la faveur d'une rencontre entre quelques déchets de l'art décomposé en quête de succès et une masse de jeunes révoltés en quête d'affirmation. Leur organisation a permis aux uns et aux autres d'avancer et d'accéder à un nouveau type de contestation. Les «artistes» ont apporté quelques tendances, encore très mystifiées, vers le jeu, doublées d'un fatras idéologique, les jeunes révoltés n'avaient pour eux que la violence de leur révolte. Dès la formation de leur organisation les deux tendances sont restées distinctes; la masse sans théorie s'est trouvée d'emblée sous la tutelle d'une mince couche de diri-

14

geants suspects qui essaient de maintenir leur «pouvoir» par la sécrétion d'une idéologie provotarienne. Au lieu que la violence des «Blousons noirs» passe sur le plan des idées dans une tentative de dépassement de l'art, c'est le réformisme néo-artistique qui l'a emporté. Les *Provos* sont l'expression du dernier réformisme produit par le capitalisme moderne: celui de la vie quotidienne. Alors qu'il ne faut pas moins d'une révolution ininterrompue pour changer la vie, la hiérarchie Provo croit — comme Bernstein croyait transformer le capitalisme en socialisme par les réformes — qu'il suffit d'apporter quelques améliorations pour modifier la vie quotidienne. Les Provos, en optant pour le fragmentaire, finissent par accepter la totalité. Pour se donner une base, leurs dirigeants ont inventé la ridicule idéologie du Provotariat (salade artistico-politique innocemment composée avec des restes moisis d'une fête qu'ils n'ont pas connue) destinée selon eux, à s'opposer à la prétendue passivité et à l'embourgeoisement du Prolétariat, tarte à la crème de tous les crétins du siècle. Parce qu'ils désespèrent de transformer la totalité, ils désespèrent des forces qui, seules, portent l'espoir d'un dépassement possible. Le Prolétariat est le moteur de la société capitaliste et donc son danger mortel: tout est fait pour le réprimer (partis, syndicats bureaucratiques, police, plus souvent que contre les Provos, colonisation de toute sa vie), car il est la seule force réellement menaçante. Les Provos n'ont rien compris de cela; ainsi ils restent incapables de faire la critique du système de production, et donc prisonniers de tout le système. Et quand dans une émeute ouvrière anti-syndicale leur base s'est ralliée à la violence directe, les dirigeants étaient complètement dépassés par le mouvement et, dans leur affolement ils n'ont rien trouvé de mieux que de dénoncer les «excès» et d'en appeler au pacifisme, renonçant lamentablement à leur programme: provoquer les autorités pour en montrer le caractère répressif — et criant qu'ils étaient provoqués par la police —. Et pour comble ils ont appelé, de la radio, les jeunes émeutiers à se laisser éduquer par les «Provos», c'est-à-dire par les dirigeants, qui ont largement montré que leur vague «anarchisme» n'est qu'un mensonge de plus. La base révoltée des Provos ne peut accéder à la critique révolutionnaire qu'en commençant par se révolter contre ses chefs, c'est-à-dire rallier les forces révolutionnaires objectives du Prolétariat et se débarrasser d'un Constant, l'artiste officiel de la Hollande Royale, ou d'un De Vries, parlementaire raté et admirateur de la police anglaise. Là, seulement, les Provos peuvent rejoindre la con-

15

testation moderne authentique qui a déjà une base réelle chez eux. S'ils veulent réellement transformer le monde, ils n'ont que faire de ceux qui veulent se contenter de le peindre en blanc.

En se révoltant contre leurs études, les étudiants américains ont immédiatement mis en question une société qui a besoin de telles études. De même que leur révolte (à Berkeley et ailleurs) contre la hiérarchie universitaire s'est d'emblée affirmée comme *révolte contre tout le système social basé sur la hiérarchie et la dictature de l'économie et de l'Etat*. En refusant d'*intégrer les entreprises* auxquelles les destinaient tout naturellement leurs études spécialisées, ils mettent profondément en question un système de production où toutes les activités et leur produit échappent totalement à leurs auteurs. Ainsi à travers des tâtonnements et une confusion encore très importante, la jeunesse américaine en révolte en vient-elle à chercher, dans la «société d'abondance» une alternative révolutionnaire cohérente. Elle reste largement attachée aux deux aspects relativement accidentels de la crise américaine: les Noirs et le Viet-Nam; et les petites organisations qui constituent «la Nouvelle Gauche» s'en ressentent lourdement. Si dans leur forme une authentique exigence de démocratie se fait sentir, la faiblesse de leur contenu subversif les fait retomber dans des contradictions dangereuses. L'hostilité à la politique traditionnelle des vieilles organisations est facilement récupérée par l'ignorance du monde politique qui se traduit par un grand manque d'informations et des illusions sur ce qui se passe effectivement dans le monde. L'hostilité *abstraite* à leur société les conduit à l'admiration ou à l'appui de ses ennemis les plus apparents: les bureaucraties dites socialistes, la Chine ou Cuba. Ainsi trouve-t-on dans un groupe comme «Resurgence Youth Movement» et en même temps une condamnation à mort de l'Etat et un éloge de la «Révolution Culturelle» menée par la bureaucratie la plus gigantesque des temps modernes: la Chine de Mao. De même que leur organisation semi-libertaire et non directive risque, à tout moment, par le manque manifeste de contenu, de retomber dans l'idéologie de la «dynamique des groupes» ou dans le monde fermé de la Secte. La consommation en masse de la drogue est l'expresson d'une misère réelle et la protestation contre cette misère réelle: elle est la fallacieuse recherche de liberté dans un monde sans liberté, la critique religieuse d'un monde qui a lui-même dépassé la religion. Ce n'est pas par hasard qu'on la trouve surtout dans les milieux beatniks (cette droite des jeunes révoltés) foyers du refus idéolo-

16

gique et l'acceptation des superstitions les plus fantastiques (Zen, spiritisme, mysticisme de la «New Church» et autres pourritures comme le Gandhisme ou l'Humanisme...). A travers leur recherche d'un programme révolutionnaire, les étudiants américains commettent la même erreur que les «Provos» et se proclament «la classe la plus exploitée de la société»; ils doivent dès à présent comprendre qu'ils n'ont pas d'intérêts distincts de tous ceux qui subissent l'oppression généralisée et l'esclavage marchand.

A l'Est, le totalitarisme bureaucratique commence aussi à produire ses forces négatives. La révolte des jeunes y est particulièrement virulente et n'est connue qu'à travers les dénonciations qu'en font les différents organes de l'appareil ou les mesures policières qu'il prend pour les contenir. Nous apprenons ainsi qu'une partie de la jeunesse ne «respecte» plus l'ordre moral et familial (tel qu'il existe sous sa forme bourgeoise la plus détestable), s'adonne à la «débauche», méprise le travail et n'obéit plus à la police du parti. Et en U.R.S.S. on nomme un ministre expressément pour combattre le hooliganisme. Mais parallèlement à cette révolte diffuse une contestation plus élaborée tente de s'affirmer et les groupes ou petites revues clandestines apparaissent et disparaissent selon les fluctuations de la répression policière, et dont le plus important a été la publication par les jeunes Polonais *Kuron* et *Modzelewski* de leur «Lettre ouverte au Parti Ouvrier Polonais», et dans laquelle ils affirment expressément la nécessité de «l'abolition des rapports de production et des relations sociales actuelles» et que pour cela «la révolution est inéluctable». L'intelligentzia des pays de l'Est cherche actuellement à rendre conscientes et à formuler clairement les raisons de cette critique que les ouvriers ont concrétisés à Berlin-Est, à Varsovie et à Budapest, la critique prolétarienne du pouvoir de classe bureaucratique. Cette révolte souffre profondément du désavantage de poser d'emblée les problèmes réels et leur solution. Si dans les autres pays le mouvement est possible, mais le but reste mystifié, dans les bureaucraties de l'Est, la contestation est sans illusion, et ses buts connus. Il s'agit pour elle d'inventer les formes de leur réalisation, de s'ouvrir le chemin qui y mène.

Quant à la révolte des jeunes Anglais elle a trouvé sa première expression organisée dans le mouvement anti-atomique. Cette lutte partielle, ralliée autour du vague programme du *Comité des Cent* — qui a pu rassembler jusqu'à 300.000 manifestants — a accompli son plus beau geste au printemps 1963

17

avec le scandale R.S.G. 6 (2). Elle ne pouvait que retomber, faute de perspectives, récupérée par les débris de la politique traditionnelle et les belles âmes pacifistes. L'archaïsme du contrôle dans la vie quotidienne, caractéristique de l'Angleterre, n'a pu résister à l'assaut du monde moderne, et la décomposition accélérée des valeurs séculaires engendre des tendances profondément révolutionnaires dans la critique de tous les aspects du mode de vie (3). Il faut que les exigences de cette jeunesse rejoignent la résistance d'une classe ouvrière qui compte parmi les plus combatives du monde, celle des shop-stewards et des grèves sauvages et la victoire de leurs luttes ne peut être recherchée que dans des perspectives communes. L'écroulement de la social-démocratie au pouvoir ne fait que donner une chance supplémentaire à leur rencontre. Les explosions qu'occasionnera une telle rencontre seront autrement plus formidables que tout ce qu'on a vu à Amsterdam. L'émeute provotarienne ne sera devant elles qu'un jeu d'enfants. De là seulement peut naître un véritable mouvement révolutionnaire, où les besoins pratiques auront trouvé leur réponse.

Le Japon est le seul parmi les pays industriellement avancés où cette fusion de la jeunesse étudiante et des ouvriers d'avant-garde soit déjà réalisée.

Zengakuren, la fameuse organisation des Etudiants révolutionnaires et la *Ligue des jeunes travailleurs marxistes* sont les deux importantes organisations formées sur l'orientation commune de la *Ligue Communiste Révolutionnaire* (4). Cette formation en est déjà à se poser le problème de l'organisation révolutionnaire. Elle combat simultanément, et sans illusions, le Capitalisme à l'Ouest et la Bureaucratie des pays dits socialistes. Elle groupe déjà quelques milliers d'étudiants et d'ouvriers organisés sur une base démocratique et anti-hiérarchique, sur la participation de tous les membres à toutes les activités de l'organisation. Ainsi les révolutionnaires japonais sont-ils les premiers dans le monde à mener déjà de grandes luttes organisées, se référant à un programme avancé, avec

---

(2) Où les partisans du mouvement anti-atomique ont découvert, rendu public et ensuite envahi des abris anti-atomiques ultra-secrets réservés aux membres du gouvernement.

(3) On pense ici à l'excellente revue «Heatwave» dont l'évolution semble aller vers un radicalisme de plus en plus rigoureux. Adresse: 13, Redcliffe Rd.... London, S W 10, Angleterre.

(4) KAIHOSHA c/o Dairyuso, 3 Nakanockimae, Nakanoku. TOKYO JAPON. ZENGAKUREN Hiroto Building 2-10 Kandajimbocho, Chiyoda-Ku TOKYO JAPON.

18

une large participation des masses. Sans arrêt des milliers d'ouvriers et d'étudiants descendent dans la rue et affrontent violemment la police japonaise. Cependant la L.C.R., bien qu'elle les combatte fermement n'explique pas complètement et concrètement les deux systèmes. Elle cherche encore à définir précisément l'exploitation bureaucratique, de même qu'elle n'est pas encore arrivée à formuler explicitement les caractères du Capitalisme moderne, la critique de la vie quotidienne et la critique du spectacle. La Ligue Communiste Révolutionnaire reste fondamentalement une organisation politique d'avant-garde, héritière de la meilleure organisation prolétarienne classique. Elle est actuellement la plus importante formation révolutionnaire du monde et doit être d'ores et déjà un des pôles de discussion et de rassemblement de la nouvelle critique révolutionnaire prolétarienne dans le monde.

Créer enfin la situation qui rende impossible tout retour en arrière.

«Etre d'avant-garde, c'est marcher au pas de la réalité» (1). La critique radicale du monde moderne doit avoir maintenant pour objet et pour objectif la *totalité*. Elle doit porter indissolublement sur son passé réel, sur ce qu'il *est* effectivement et sur les perspectives de sa transformation. C'est que pour pouvoir dire toute la vérité du monde actuel et a fortiori pour formuler le projet de sa subversion totale, il faut être capable de *révéler* toute son *histoire cachée*, c'est-à-dire regarder d'une façon totalement démystifée et fondamentalement critique l'histoire de tout le mouvement révolutionnaire international inaugurée voilà plus d'un siècle par le prolétariat des pays d'Occident, ses «échecs» et ses «victoires». «Ce mouvement contre l'ensemble de l'organisation du vieux monde est depuis longtemps fini (2)» et a *échoué*. Sa dernière manifestation historique étant la défaite de la révolution prolétarienne en Espagne (à Barcelone en mai 1937). Cependant ses «échecs» officiels, comme ses «victoires» officielles doivent être jugées à la lumière de leurs prolongements, et leurs vérités rétablies. Ainsi nous pouvons affirmer qu'«il y a des défaites qui sont des victoires et des victoires plus honteuses que des défaites» (Karl Liebknecht à la veille de son assassi-

(1) Internationale Situationniste nº 8.
(2) Internationale Situationniste nº 7.

20

nat). La première grande «défaite» du pouvoir prolétarien, la Commune de Paris, est en réalité sa première grande *victoire*, car pour la première fois le Prolétariat primitif a affirmé sa capacité historique de diriger d'une façon *libre* tous les aspects de la vie sociale. De même que sa première grande «victoire», la révolution bolchévik, n'est en définitive que sa défaite la plus lourde de conséquences. Le triomphe de l'ordre bolchévik coïncide avec le mouvement de contre-révolution internationale qui commença avec l'écrasement des Spartakistes par la «Social-démocratie» allemande. Leur triomphe commun était plus profond que leur opposition apparente et cet ordre bolchévik n'était en définitive qu'un déguisement nouveau et une figure particulière de l'ordre ancien. Les résultats de la contre-révolution russe furent, à l'intérieur, l'établissement et le développement d'un nouveau mode d'exploitation, le *capitalisme bureaucratique d'Etat*, et à l'extérieur la multiplication des sections de l'Internationale dite communiste, succursales destinées à le défendre et répandre son modèle. Le capitalisme sous ses différentes variantes bureaucratiques et bourgeoises florissait de nouveau, sur les cadavres des marins de Kronstadt et des paysans d'Ukraine, des ouvriers de Berlin, Kiel, Turin, Shanghaï et plus tard de Barcelone.

La IIIe Internationale, apparemment créée par les Bolcheviks pour lutter contre les débris de la social-démocratie réformiste de la IIe Internationale, et grouper l'avant-garde prolétarienne dans les «partis communistes révolutionnaires» était trop liée à ses créateurs et à leurs intérêts pour pouvoir réaliser, où que ce soit, la *véritable révolution socialiste*. En fait la IIe Internationale était la vérité de la IIIe. Très tôt le modèle russe s'imposa aux organisations ouvrières d'Occident et leurs évolutions furent une seule et même chose. A la dictature totalitaire de la Bureaucratie, nouvelle classe dirigeante, sur le prolétariat russe, correspondait au sein de ces organisations, la domination d'une couche de bureaucrates politiques et syndicaux sur la grande masse des ouvriers dont les intérêts sont devenus franchement contradictoires avec les siens. Le monstre stalinien hantait la conscience ouvrière, tandis que le Capitalisme, en voie de bureaucratisation et de surdéveloppement, résolvait ses crises internes et affirmait tout fièrement sa nouvelle victoire qu'il prétend permanente. Une même forme sociale, apparemment divergente et variée, s'empare du monde, et les principes du *vieux monde* continuent à gouverner notre *monde moderne*. Les morts hantent encore les cerveaux des vivants.

21

Au sein de ce monde, des organisations prétendument révolutionnaires ne font que le combattre apparemment, sur son terrain propre, à travers les plus grandes mystifications. Toutes se réclament d'*idéologies* plus ou moins pétrifiées et ne font en définitive que participer à la consolidation de l'ordre dominant. Les syndicats et les partis politiques forgés par la classe ouvrière pour sa propre émancipation sont devenus de simples régulateurs du système, propriété privée de dirigeants qui travaillent à leur propre émancipation et trouvent un statut dans la classe dirigeante d'une société qu'ils ne pensent jamais mettre en question. Le programme réel de ces syndicats et partis ne fait que reprendre platement la phraséologie «révolutionnaire» et appliquer en fait les mots d'ordre du *réformisme* le plus édulcoré, puisque le capitalisme lui-même se fait officiellement réformiste. Là où ils ont pu prendre le pouvoir — dans des pays plus arriérés que la Russie — ce n'était que pour reproduire le modèle stalinien du totalitarisme contre-révolutionnaire (3). Ailleurs ils sont le complément statique et nécessaire (4) à l'autorégulation du Capitalisme bureaucratisé; la contradiction indispensable du maintien de son humanisme policier. D'autre part ils restent, vis-à-vis des masses ouvrières, les garants indéfectibles et les défenseurs inconditionnels de la contre-révolution bureaucratique, les instruments dociles de sa politique étrangère. Dans un monde fondamentalement mensonger, ils sont les porteurs du mensonge le plus radical, et travaillent à la pérennité de la dictature universelle de l'Economie et de l'Etat. Comme l'affirment les situationistes «un modèle social universellement dominant, qui tend à l'autorégulation totalitaire, n'est qu'apparemment combattu par de fausses contestations posées en permanence sur son propre terrain, illusions qui, au contraire, renforcent ce modèle. Le pseudo-socialisme bureaucratique n'est que le plus grandiose de ces déguisements du vieux monde hiérarchique du travail aliéné» (5). Le syndicalisme étudiant n'est dans tout cela que la caricature d'une caricature, la répétition burlesque et inutile d'un syndicalisme dégénéré.

La dénonciation théorique et pratique du stalinisme sous

(3) Leur réalisation effective c'est tendre à industrialiser le pays par la classique accumulation primitive au dépens de la paysannerie accélérée par la terreur bureaucratique.

(4) Depuis 45 ans, en France, le parti dit Communiste n'a pas fait un pas vers la prise du pouvoir; il est de même dans tous les pays avancés où n'est pas venue l'Armée dite rouge.

(5) Lutte de classe en Algérie. Internationale Situationniste N° 10.

22

toutes ses formes doit être la banalité de base de toutes les futures organisations révolutionnaires. Il est clair qu'en France, par exemple, où le retard économique recule encore la conscience de la crise, le mouvement révolutionnaire ne pourra renaître que sur les ruines du stalinisme anéanti. La destruction du stalinisme doit devenir le *delenda Carthago* de la *dernière* révolution de la préhistoire.

Celle-ci doit elle-même rompre, *définitivement,* avec sa propre préhistoire, et tirer toute sa poésie de l'avenir. Les «Bolcheviks ressuscités» qui jouent la farce du «militantisme» dans les différents groupuscules gauchistes sont des relents du passé et en aucune manière n'annoncent l'avenir. Epaves du grand naufrage de la «révolution trahie», ils se présentent comme les fidèles tenants de l'orthodoxie bolchévik: la défense de l'U.R.S.S. est leur indépassable fidélité et leur scandaleuse démission.

Ils ne peuvent plus entretenir d'illusions que dans les fameux pays sous-développés (6) où ils entérinent eux-mêmes le sous-développement théorique. De *Partisans* (organe du stalino-trotskisme réconciliés) à toutes les tendances et demi-tendances qui se disputent «Trotsky» à l'intérieur et à l'extérieur de la *IVe Internationale,* règne une même *idéologie* révolutionnariste et une même incapacité pratique et théorique de comprendre les problèmes du monde moderne. Quarante années d'histoire contre-révolutionnaire les séparent de la Révolution. Ils ont tort parce qu'ils ne sont plus en 1920, et en 1920 ils avaient déjà tort. La dissolution du groupe «ultra-gauchiste» *Socialisme ou Barbarie* après sa division en deux fractions «moderniste cardaniste» et «vieux marxiste» de *Pouvoir Ouvrier,* prouve, s'il en était besoin, qu'il ne peut y avoir de révolution hors du moderne, ni de pensée moderne hors de la critique révolutionnaire à réinventer (7). Elle est significative en ce sens que toute séparation entre ces deux aspects retombe inévitablement soit dans le musée de la Préhistoire révolutionnaire achevée, soit dans la modernité du pouvoir, c'est-à-dire dans la contre-révolution dominante: *Voix ouvrière* ou *Arguments.*

Quant aux divers groupuscules «anarchistes», ensemble prisonniers de cette appellation, ils ne possèdent rien d'autre que cette idéologie réduite à une simple étiquette. L'incroyable

---

(6) Sur le rôle en Algérie cf. La lutte de classes en Algérie, Internationale Situationniste n° 10.
(7) Internationale Situationniste n° 9.

23

«Monde Libertaire» évidemment rédigé par des *étudiants*, atteint le degré le plus fantastique de la confusion et de la bêtise. Ces gens-là *tolèrent effectivement tout*, puisqu'ils se tolèrent les uns les autres.

La société dominante qui se flatte de sa modernisation permanente doit maintenant trouver à qui parler, c'est-à-dire à la négation modernisée qu'elle produit elle-même (8): «Laissons maintenant aux morts le soin d'enterrer leurs morts et de les pleurer.» Les démystifications pratiques du mouvement historique débarrassent la conscience révolutionnaire des fantômes qui la hantaient; la révolution de la vie quotidienne se trouve face à face avec les tâches immenses qu'elle doit accomplir. La révolution, comme la vie qu'elle annonce, est à réinventer. Si le projet révolutionnaire reste fondamentalement le même: l'abolition de la société de classes, c'est que nulle part les conditions dans lesquelles il se forme n'ont été radicalement transformées. Il s'agit de le reprendre avec un radicalisme et une cohérence accrus par l'expérience de la faillite de ses anciens porteurs, afin d'éviter que sa réalisation fragmentaire n'entraîne une nouvelle division de la société.

La lutte entre le pouvoir et le nouveau prolétariat ne pouvant se faire que sur la *totalité*, le futur mouvement révolutionnaire doit abolir, en son sein, tout ce qui tend à reproduire les produits aliénés du *système marchand* (9); il doit en être en même temps la critique vivante et la négation qui porte en elle tous les éléments du *dépassement* possible. Comme l'a bien vu Lukacs (mais pour l'appliquer à un objet qui n'en était pas digne: le parti bolchevik), l'organisation révolutionnaire est cette médiation nécessaire entre la théorie et la pratique, entre l'homme et l'histoire, entre la masse des travailleurs et le prolétariat *constitué en classe*. Les tendances et divergences «théoriques» doivent immédiatement se transformer en question d'organisation si elles veulent montrer la voie de leur réalisation. La question de l'organisation sera le jugement dernier du nouveau mouvement révolutionnaire, le tribunal devant lequel sera jugée la cohérence de son projet *essentiel: la réalisation internationale du pouvoir absolu des Conseils Ouvriers*, tel qu'il a été esquissé par l'expérience des révolutions prolétariennes de ce siècle. Une telle organisation doit mettre en avant la critique radicale de tout ce qui fonde la société qu'elle combat, à savoir: la production marchande,

---

(8) Adresse aux révolutionnaires... Internationale Situationniste Nº 10.
(9) Défini par la prédominance du travail-marchandise.

24

l'idéologie sous tous ses déguisements, l'Etat et les scissions qu'il impose.

La scission entre théorie et pratique a été le roc contre lequel a buté le vieux mouvement révolutionnaire. Seuls les plus hauts moments des luttes prolétariennes ont dépassé cette scission pour retrouver leur *vérité*. Aucune organisation n'a encore *sauté* ce Rhodus. L'*idéologie*, si «révolutionnaire» qu'elle puisse être est toujours au service' des maîtres, le *signal d'alarme* qui désigne l'ennemi déguisé. C'est pourquoi la critique de l'idéologie doit être, en dernière analyse, le problème central de l'organisation révolutionnaire. Seul le monde aliéné produit le mensonge, et celui-ci ne saurait réapparaître à l'intérieur de ce qui prétend porter la *vérité sociale*, sans que cette organisation ne se transforme elle-même en un mensonge de plus dans un monde fondamentalement mensonger.

L'organisation révolutionnaire qui projette de réaliser le pouvoir absolu des Conseils Ouvriers doit être le milieu où s'esquissent tous les aspects positifs de ce pouvoir. Aussi doit-elle mener une lutte à mort contre la théorie léniniste de l'organisation. La révolution de 1905 et l'organisation spontanée des travailleurs russes en Soviets était déjà une critique en actes (10) de cette théorie néfaste. Mais le mouvement bolchevik persistait à croire que la spontanéité ouvrière ne pouvait dépasser la conscience «trade-unioniste», et était incapable de saisir «la totalité». Ce qui revenait à décapiter le prolétariat pour permettre au parti de prendre la «tête» de la Révolution. On ne peut contester, aussi impitoyablement que l'a fait Lénine, la capacité historique du prolétariat de s'émanciper par lui-même, sans contester sa capacité de gérer totalement la société future. Dans une telle perspective le slogan «tout le pouvoir aux Soviets» ne signifiait rien d'autre que la conquête des Soviets par le Parti, l'instauration de l'Etat du parti à la place de «l'Etat» dépérissant du prolétariat en armes.

C'est pourtant ce slogan qu'il faut reprendre radicalement et en le débarrassant des arrière-pensées bolchéviks. Le prolétariat ne peut s'adonner au *jeu* de la révolution que pour gagner *tout* un monde, autrement il n'est rien. La forme unique de son pouvoir, *l'autogestion généralisée*, ne peut être partagée avec aucune autre force. Parce qu'il est la dissolution effective de tous les pouvoirs, il ne saurait tolérer aucune limitation (géographique ou autre); les compromis qu'il

---

(10) Après la critique théorique menée par Rosa Luxembourg.

25

accepte se transforment immédiatement en compromissions, en démission. «L'autogestion doit être à la fois le moyen et la fin de la lutte actuelle. Elle est non seulement l'enjeu de la lutte, mais sa forme adéquate. Elle est pour elle-même la matière qu'elle travaille et sa propre présupposition (11)».

La critique unitaire du monde est la garantie de la cohérence et de la vérité de l'organisation révolutionnaire. Tolérer l'existence des systèmes d'oppression (parce qu'ils portent la défroque «révolutionnaire» par exemple) dans un point du monde, c'est reconnaître la légitimité de l'oppression. De même, si elle tolère l'aliénation, dans un domaine de la vie sociale, elle reconnaît la fatalité de toutes les réifications. Il ne suffit pas d'être pour le pouvoir abstrait des Conseils Ouvriers, mais il faut en montrer la signification concrète: la suppression de la production marchande et donc du prolétariat. La *logique de la marchandise* est la rationalité première et ultime des société actuelles, elle est la base de l'autorégulation totalitaire de ces sociétés comparables à des puzzles dont les pièces, si dissemblables en apparence, sont en fait équivalentes. La réification marchande est l'obstacle *essentiel* à une émancipation totale, à la construction libre de la vie. Dans le monde de la production marchande la praxis ne se poursuit pas en fonction d'une fin déterminée de façon autonome, mais sous les directives de puissances extérieures. Et si les lois économiques semblent devenir des lois naturelles d'une espèce particulière, c'est que leur puissance repose *uniquement* sur «l'absence de conscience de ceux qui y ont part».

Le principe de la production marchande c'est la perte de soi dans la création chaotique et inconsciente d'un monde qui échappe totalement à ses créateurs. Le noyau radicalement révolutionnaire de l'autogestion généralisée c'est au contraire la direction consciente par tous de l'ensemble de la vie. L'autogestion de l'aliénation marchande ne ferait de tous les hommes que les programmateurs de leur propre survie: c'est la quadrature du cercle. La tâche des Conseils Ouvriers ne sera donc pas l'autogestion du monde existant, mais sa transformation qualitative ininterrompue: le dépassement concret de la marchandise (en tant que gigantesque détour de la production de l'homme par lui-même).

Ce dépassement implique naturellement la suppression du *travail* et son remplacement par un nouveau type d'acti-

(11) La lutte des classes en Algérie (Internationale Situationniste n° 10).

26

vité libre, donc l'abolition d'une des scissions fondamentales de la société moderne, entre un travail de plus en plus réifié et des loisirs consommés passivement. Des groupuscules aujourd'hui en liquéfaction comme S ou B ou P.O. (12), pourtant ralliés sur le mot d'ordre moderne du Pouvoir Ouvrier, continuent à suivre, sur ce point central, le vieux mouvement ouvrier sur la voie du réformisme du travail et de son «humanisation». C'est au travail lui-même qu'il faut aujourd'hui s'en prendre. Loin d'être une «utopie», sa suppression est la condition première du dépassement effectif de la société marchande, de l'abolition — dans la vie quotidienne de chacun — de la séparation entre le «temps libre» et le «temps de travail», secteurs complémentaires d'une vie aliénée, où se projette indéfiniment la contradiction interne de la marchandise entre valeur d'usage et valeur d'échange. Et c'est seulement au-delà de cette opposition que les hommes pourront faire de leur activité vitale un objet de leur volonté et de leur conscience, et se contempler eux-mêmes dans un monde qu'ils ont eux-mêmes créé. La démocratie des Conseils Ouvriers est l'énigme résolue de toutes les scissions actuelles. Elle rend «impossible tout ce qui existe en dehors des individus».

La domination consciente de l'histoire par les hommes qui la font, voilà tout le projet révolutionnaire. L'histoire moderne, comme toute l'histoire passée, est le produit de la praxis sociale, le résultat — inconscient — de toutes les activités humaines. A l'époque de sa domination totalitaire, le capitalisme a produit sa nouvelle religion: le *spectacle*. Le *spectacle* est la réalisation terrestre de l'*idéologie*. Jamais le monde n'a si bien marché sur la tête. «Et comme la „critique de la religion" la critique du spectacle est aujourd'hui la condition première de toute critique» (13).

C'est que le problème de la *révolution* est historiquement posé à l'humanité. L'accumulation de plus en plus grandiose des moyens matériels et techniques n'a d'égale que l'insatisfaction de plus en plus profonde de tous. La bourgeoisie et son héritière à l'Est, la bureaucratie, ne peuvent avoir le mode d'emploi de ce surdéveloppement qui sera la base de la *poésie* de l'avenir, justement parce qu'elles travaillent, toutes les deux, au *maintien d'un ordre ancien*. Elles ont tout

---

(12) Socialisme ou Barbarie, Pouvoir Ouvrier, etc... Un groupe comme ICO au contraire, en s'interdisant toute organisation et une théorie cohérente est condamné à l'inexistence.
(13) Internationale Situationniste n° 9.

27

au plus le secret de son usage policier. Elles ne font qu'accumuler le *Capital* et donc le *prolétariat;* est *prolétaire* celui qui n'a aucun pouvoir sur l'emploi de sa vie et qui le sait. La chance historique du nouveau prolétariat est d'être le seul héritier conséquent de la richesse sans valeur du *monde bourgeois* à transformer et à *dépasser* dans le sens de l'homme total, l'appropriation totale de la nature et de sa propre nature. Cette réalisation de la *nature* de l'homme ne peut avoir de sens que par la satisfaction sans bornes et la multiplication infinie des *désirs réels* que le *spectacle* refoule dans les zones lointaines de l'inconscient révolutionnaire, et qu'il n'est capable de réaliser que fantastiquement dans le délire onirique de sa publicité. C'est que la réalisation effective des désirs réels, c'est-à-dire l'abolition de tous les pseudo-besoins et désirs qu'il crée quotidiennement pour perpétuer son pouvoir, ne peut se faire sans la suppression du spectacle marchand et son dépassement positif.

L'histoire moderne ne peut être libérée, et ses acquisitions innombrables librement utilisées que par les forces qu'elle refoule: les travailleurs sans pouvoir sur les conditions, le sens et le produit de leurs activités. Comme le prolétariat était déjà au XIXᵉ siècle l'héritier de la philosophie, il est en plus devenu l'héritier de l'art moderne et de la première critique consciente de la vie quotidienne. Il ne peut se supprimer sans réaliser, en même temps, l'art et la philosophie. Transformer le monde et changer la vie sont pour lui une seule et même chose, les mots d'ordre inséparables qui accompagneront sa suppression en tant que classe, la dissolution de la société présente en tant que règne de la nécessité, et l'accession enfin possible au règne de la liberté. La critique radicale et la reconstruction libre de toutes les conduites et valeurs imposées par la réalité aliénée sont son programme maximum, et la créativité libérée dans la construction de tous les moments et événements de la vie est la seule *poésie* qu'il pourra reconnaître, la poésie faite par tous, le commencement de la fête révolutionnaire. Les révolutions prolétariennes seront des *fêtes* ou ne seront pas, car la vie qu'elles annoncent sera elle-même créée sous le signe de la fête. Le *jeu* est la rationalité ultime de cette fête, vivre sans temps mort et jouir sans entraves sont les seules règles qu'il pourra reconnaître.

28

III
Cataloging *On the Poverty of Student Life*

On the Poverty of Student Life

An Illustrated Bibliography

About this Bibliography

We have been able to locate about a hundred editions of *On the Poverty of Student Life* in twenty or so languages. We have attempted to follow an order where the languages are roughly grouped by language family, starting with French, then English, then Romance languages, then other European languages, then non-European languages. Excluded from the bibliography are the following editions:

- Editions that are part of a compendium or anthology, *unless*:
  - This is the first time the text is published in a particular language.
  - The compendium/anthologies were printed before 1975.
- Editions that have only been released digitally.
  - This includes editions in Macedonian, Romanian, Polish, and more.
- Editions that we have not been able to physically trace.
  - This includes editions in Spanish, Indonesian, and more.

We invite our readers to alert us to editions that are not featured here. These could then be included in a revised edition of this book. Please contact us via Mehdi El Hajoui, elhajoui@gmail.com.

De la misère en milieu étudiant

Une bibliographie illustrée

A propos de cette bibliographie

Nous avons pu retrouver la trace d'une centaine d'éditions de *La misère en milieu étudiant*, publiées dans une vingtaine de langues. Nous avons tenté un regroupement des éditions par groupe de langue, en commençant par le français, suivi de l'anglais, des langues romanes, des autres langues européennes, et enfin des langues non-européennes. En outre, nous avons exclu de notre bibliographie les éditions suivantes :

- Editions présentes dans une anthologie ou autre recueil de
  textes, sauf dans les cas suivants :
  - Lorsqu'il s'agit de la première traduction du texte dans une
    langue donnée.
  - Lorsque les anthologies ou recueils de textes datent d'avant 1975.
- Editions publiées uniquement de manière électronique.
  - Par exemple, des éditions en roumain, macédonien, ou en polonais.
- Editions dont nous n'avons pas pu confirmer l'existence physique.
  - Par exemple, certaines éditions en Espagnol et en Indonésien.

Nous invitons nos lecteurs à prendre en contact avec nous s'ils retrouvent des éditions qui nous auraient échappées. Il sera possible de les inclure dans une édition revue et corrigée de cet ouvrage. Notre courriel, via Mehdi El Hajoui, est le suivant: elhajoui@gmail.com.

French

(France, Belgium, Switzerland)

1. *De la Misère en Milieu Étudiant, Considérée sous ses Aspects Économique, Politique, Psychologique, Sexuel et Notamment Intellectuel et de Quelques Moyens pour y Remédier.* Strasbourg: AFGES, November 1966[1].

28 pages. Dark green wrappers. Spelling mistake in the title ("Psyschologique" instead of "Psychologique.") At the bottom of the front wrapper, the pamphlet ironically describes itself as a "special insert for Issue 16 of 21–27 *Étudiants de France*, the periodical of the National French Student Association (UNEF)."

This first edition, printed in 10,000 copies, appeared in two versions: a standard edition, featuring light blue wrappers (9,000 copies); and a limited edition featuring green wrappers (1,000 copies). The color coincidentally matches that of the first German edition of *The Communist Manifesto*.[2] The rear wrapper features the now famous anti-copyright statement: "This text can be freely reproduced even without indication of origin." Jean-Jacques Raspaud and Jean-Pierre Voyer reference this edition in *Situationist International: Chronology, Bibliography, Protagonists (with an Index of Insulted Names)*, listing Mustapha Khayati as the author.

* * *

Français

(France, Belgique, Suisse)

1. *De la misère en milieu étudiant, considérée sous ses aspects économique, politique, psychologique, sexuel et notamment intellectuel et de quelques moyens pour y remédier.* Strasbourg : AFGES, Novembre 1966. 28 p. Couverture vert foncé.

Faute d'orthographe au titre (« psyschologique » pour « psychologique »). L'ouvrage est ironiquement référencé comme « supplément spécial au numéro 16 de « 21-27 Étudiants de France », organe de l'UNEF. Edition originale tirée à 10.000 exemplaires : une version ordinaire, sous couverture bleu ciel (9.000 exemplaires), et une version « de luxe », sous une couverture verte (1.000 exemplaires) dont la couleur est – pure coïncidence – semblable à celle de l'édition originale du *Manifeste du part communiste*. C'est cette dernière que nous présentons ici. Au dos, on trouve la célèbre mention « ce texte peut être librement reproduit même sans indication d'origine ». Edition référencée par Jean-Jacques Raspaud et Jean-Pierre Voyer dans leur ouvrage *L'Internationale Situationniste : chronologie, bibliographie, protagonistes (avec un index des noms insultés)* qui attribue la paternité du texte à Mustapha Khayati.

Union Nationale des Etudiants de France
Association Fédérative Générale des Etudiants
de Strasbourg

DE LA MISERE
EN MILIEU
ETUDIANT

*considérée
sous ses aspects économique, politique,
psychologique, sexuel et notamment
intellectuel
et de quelques moyens pour y remédier.*

1966

Supplément spécial au N° 16 de «21-27 Etudiants de France»

2. *De la Misère en Milieu Étudiant, Considérée sous ses Aspects Économique, Politique, Psychologique, Sexuel et Notamment Intellectuel et de Quelques Moyens pour y Remédier.* Strasbourg: AFGES, November 1966.

28 pages. Light blue wrappers. Identical to the previous entry. This standard edition was printed in a run of 9,000 copies.

* * *

2. *De la misère en milieu étudiant, considérée sous ses aspects économique, politique, psychologique, sexuel et notamment intellectuel et de quelques moyens pour y remédier.* Strasbourg : AFGES, novembre 1966. 28 p. Couverture bleu ciel.

Le même que le précèdent. Il s'agit ici de l'édition « ordinaire » publiée à 9.000 exemplaires.

Union Nationale des Étudiants de France
Association Fédérative Générale des Étudiants
de Strasbourg

DE LA MISERE
EN MILIEU
ETUDIANT

considérée
*sous ses aspects économique, politique,
psychologique, sexuel et notamment
intellectuel
et de quelques moyens pour y remédier.*

1966

Supplément spécial au N° 16 de «21-27 Etudiants de France»

3. *De la Misère en Milieu Étudiant, Considérée sous ses Aspects Économique, Politique, Psychologique, Sexuel et Notamment Intellectuel et de Quelques Moyens pour y Remédier*, n.p., c. 1966–1967.

28 pages. Light grey wrappers. Unauthorized reprint of the 1966 edition (identical text and layout), except for the correction of the spelling mistake ("psyschologique") and the removal of all authorship information from the front wrapper.

* * *

3. *De la misère en milieu étudiant, considérée sous ses aspects économique, politique, psychologique, sexuel et notamment intellectuel et de quelques moyens pour y remédier.* s.l.: s.d., 1966–67. 28 p. Couverture gris clair.

Contrefaçon de l'édition de 1966 (texte et mise en page identique), sauf pour l'absence de faute à « psychologique » et la suppression des informations concernant les auteurs du texte.

DE LA MISERE EN MILIEU ETUDIANT

considérée
sous ses aspects économique, politique,
psychologique, sexuel et notamment
intellectuel
et de quelques moyens pour y remédier

4. *De la Misère en Milieu Étudiant, Considérée sous ses Aspects Économique, Politique, Psychologique, Sexuel et Notamment Intellectuel et de Quelques Moyens pour y Remédier.* Paris: Internationale Situationniste, 1967.

32 pages. Light grey wrappers. Second edition, without the "psyschologique" spelling mistake. Issued as a supplement to the periodical *Internationale Situationniste*, P.O. Box 307-03, Paris. The text and layout are identical to the 1966 edition, with one important change: for the first time, authorship is attributed to "members of the Situationist International and students of Strasbourg" on the front wrapper. In our interview, Khayati describes how the SI made the decision to reprint the text in Paris rather than Strasbourg. This time, they ran 20,000 copies, which were sold primarily at a bookstall in Saint-Michel (with a few copies for a bookstall in Saint-Germain).

* * *

4. *De la misère en milieu étudiant, considérée sous ses aspects économique, politique, psychologique, sexuel et notamment intellectuel et de quelques moyens pour y remédier.* Paris : Internationale Situationniste, 1967. 32 p. Couverture gris clair.

Deuxième édition, 20e mille, sans la faute à « psyschologique ». Supplément à la revue *Internationale Situationniste*, Boite Postale 307-03, Paris. Texte et mise en page identiques à l'édition de 1966, sauf pour l'ajout pour la première fois de la mention « par des membres de l'Internationale Situationniste et des étudiants de Strasbourg » sur la couverture. Dans notre entretien, Mustapha Khayati explique le choix de rééditer le texte à Paris (plutôt qu'à Strasbourg). Les 20,000 exemplaires sont principalement distribués au kiosque Saint-Michel (avec quelques exemplaires pour le kiosque Saint-Germain).

DE LA MISERE
EN MILIEU
ETUDIANT

considérée
sous ses aspects économique, politique,
psychologique, sexuel et notamment
intellectuel
et de quelques moyens pour y remédier

par
des membres de l'Internationale Situationniste
et des étudiants de Strasbourg

— 1967 —

deuxième édition - 20e mille

5. *De la Misère en Milieu Étudiant, Considérée sous ses Aspects Économique, Politique, Psychologique, Sexuel et Notamment Intellectuel et de Quelques Moyens pour y Remédier,* n.p., 1967.

32 pages. Salmon wrappers. Unauthorized reprint of the 1967 edition (identical text and layout). Price (2,50 F) stamped on the rear wrapper.

* * *

5. *De la misère en milieu étudiant, considérée sous ses aspects économique, politique, psychologique, sexuel et notamment intellectuel et de quelques moyens pour y remédier.* s.l.: s.d., 1967. 32 p. Couverture saumon.

Contrefaçon de l'édition de 1967 (texte et mise en page identique). Prix (2,50 F) indiqué en quatrième de couverture.

6. *De la Misère en Milieu Étudiant, Considérée sous ses Aspects Économique, Politique, Psychologique, Sexuel et Notamment Intellectuel et de Quelques Moyens pour y Remédier,* n.p., 1967.

28 pages. Green wrappers. Unauthorized reprint of the 1966 edition (with identical text and layout, except for the addition of "by members of the Situationist International and students of Strasbourg" on the front wrapper.

***

6. *De la misère en milieu étudiant, considérée sous ses aspects économique, politique, psychologique, sexuel et notamment intellectuel et de quelques moyens pour y remédier.* s.l.: s.e., 1967. 28 p. Couverture verte.

Contrefaçon de l'édition de 1966, (texte et mise en page identique, hormis l'ajout de « par des membres de l'Internationale Situationniste et des étudiants de Strasbourg » au bas de la couverture.

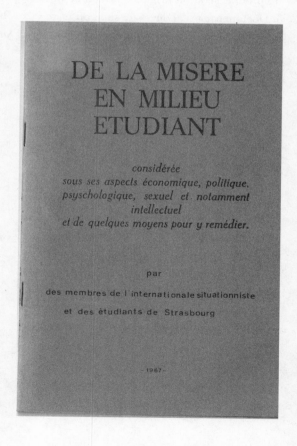

7. "De la Misère en Milieu Étudiant, Considérée sous ses Aspects Économique, Politique, Psychologique, Sexuel et Notamment Intellectuel et de Quelques Moyens pour y Remédier." René Vienet, *Enragés and Situationists in the Occupation Movement*. Paris : Gallimard (1968) : 219–243.

Illustrated white cover. Reproduction of the original edition, in a condensed layout. This reproduction can be found in the "Documents" section of the book, followed by the text "Our Goals and Our Methods in the Strasbourg Scandal" (originally published in *Internationale Situationniste* 11, October 1967).

* * *

7. « De la misère en milieu étudiant, considérée sous ses aspects économique, politique, psychologique, sexuel et notamment intellectuel et de quelques moyens pour y remédier ». Vienet, René. *Enragés et situationnistes dans le mouvement des occupations*. Paris: Gallimard, 1968. p. 219-243. Couverture blanche illustrée.

Reproduit l'édition originale, avec une mise en page condensée, dans la partie « Documents » de l'ouvrage, suivi du texte « Nos buts et nos méthodes dans le scandale de Strasbourg » (paru dans *Internationale Situationniste* 11, octobre 1967).

8. *De la Misère en Milieu Étudiant*. Brussels: J-C Klur, c. 1968–1969.

27 pages. Front wrapper illustrated by a black-and-white photomontage. Unauthorized Belgian reprint, most likely published at the end of the 1960s. The layout is identical to the version published in *Enragés and Situationists in the Occupation Movement*. This edition is illustrated with a centerfold of a détourned comics series by Blake and Mortimer, "The Point of No Return": "An increasing number of decent travelers had become scoundrels . . . who reject the conditions of modern existence . . ."

8. *De la misère en milieu étudiant.* Bruxelles: J-C Klur, ca. 1968 ou 69. 27 p. Couverture illustrée d'un photomontage en noir et blanc.

Contrefaçon belge, vraisemblablement publiée à la fin des années 60. Mise en page identique à celle du texte paru dans *Enragés et situationnistes dans le mouvement des occupations.* Cette édition est illustrée, en page centrale, d'une bande dessinée détournée de Blake et Mortimer intitulée « Point de non-retour » : « Un nombre croissant d'honnêtes passagers se muaient en canailles [...] qui niaient les conditions modernes d'existence... »

9. *De la Misère en Milieu Étudiant, Considérée sous ses Aspects Économique, Politique, Sexuel et Notamment Intellectuel et de Quelques Moyens pour y Remédier*, n.p., 1969.

18 pages. No wrappers (stapled sheets). Large-format pirate edition, followed by a "Supplement to 'On the Poverty of Student Life' As it Relates to the Occupation Movement of May–June '68," an excerpt from *Enragés and Situationists in the Occupation Movement* by René Viénet (Paris: Gallimard, 1968). Note the absence of the "psychologique" in the title. According to Louis-Jean Marty, "This activist edition (from 1969) is surprising and uncommon. A few dozen copies must have been printed . . . I was 16 and an active member of the School Action Committee)."[3]

* * *

9. *De la misère en milieu étudiant, considérée sous ses aspects économique, politique, sexuel et notamment intellectuel et de quelques moyens pour y remédier.* s.l.: s.e., 1969. [18 p.]. Sans couverture (feuillets agrafées).

Edition pirate grand format, enrichie d'un « Additif à 'la Misère', relatif au mouvement des occupations de Mai-Juin 68 », extrait de *Enragés et Situationnistes dans le Mouvement des Occupations de René Viénet* (Paris : Gallimard, 1968). Noter l'absence de « psychologique » au titre. Selon Louis-Jean Marty, « cette édition militante (de 1969) est étonnante et rare elle a dû être tirée à quelques dizaines d'exemplaires seulement (à la ronéo). J'avais 16 ans en 1968 et je militais au CAL ».

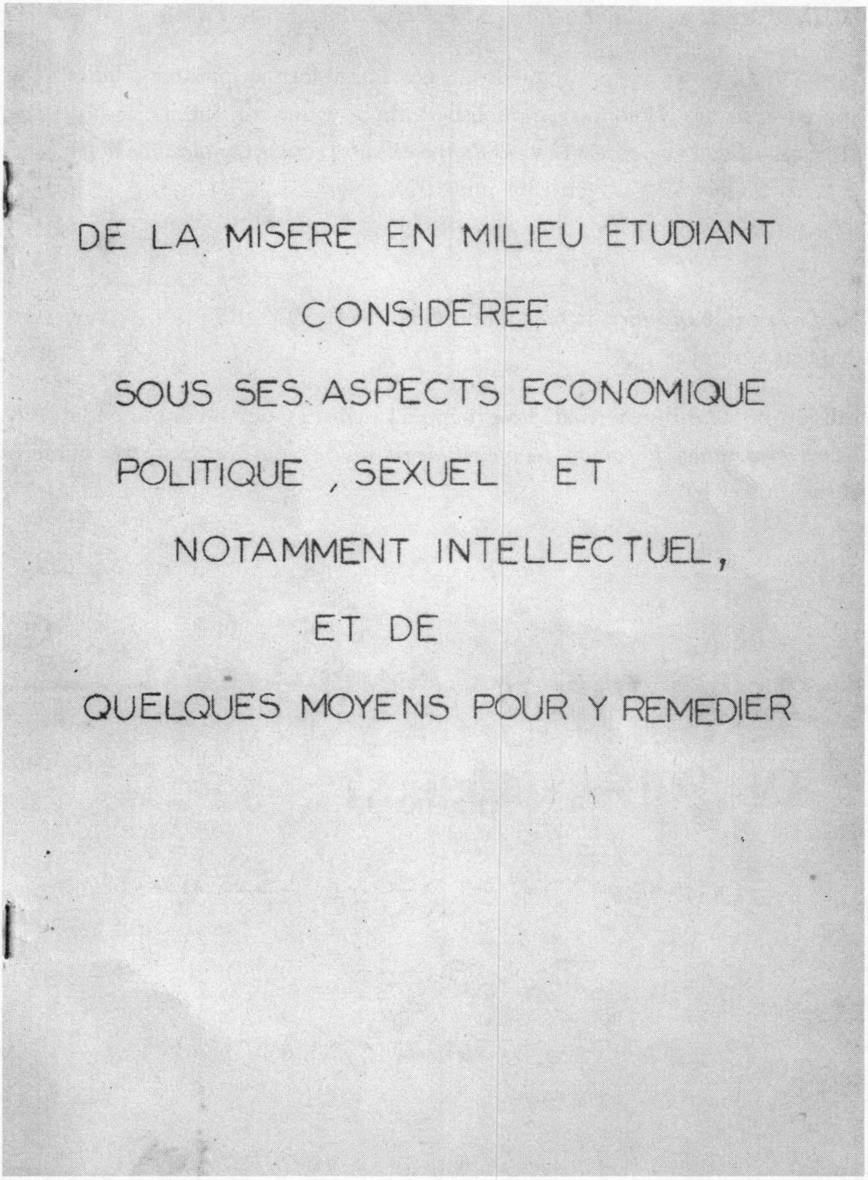

DE LA MISERE EN MILIEU ETUDIANT

CONSIDEREE

SOUS SES ASPECTS ECONOMIQUE

POLITIQUE , SEXUEL   ET

NOTAMMENT INTELLECTUEL,

ET DE

QUELQUES MOYENS POUR Y REMEDIER

10. *De la Misère en Milieu Étudiant.* Nice: Colonne L, 1970.

17 pages. No wrappers (stapled sheets). Large-format pirated edition. The anarchist group Colonne L published three issues of the periodical *Pour l'Organisation du Pouvoir des Conseils de Travailleurs* [*For the Organization of the Power of Workers' Councils*] between 1969 and 1971.

* * *

10. *De la misère en milieu étudiant.* Nice: Colonne L, 1970 . 17 p.. Sans couverture (feuillets agrafés).

Edition pirate grand format. Le groupe anarchiste Colonne L publie la revue *Pour l'organisation du pouvoir des conseils de travailleurs*, qui a connu trois numéros entre 1969 et 1971.

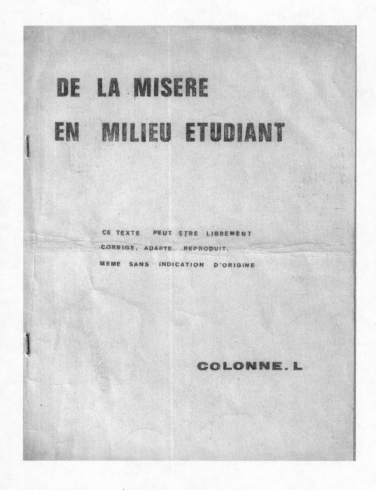

11. *De la Misère en Milieu Étudiant, Considérée sous ses Aspects Économique, Politique, Psychologique, Sexuel et Notamment Intellectuel et de Quelques Moyens pour y Remédier.* Grenoble: Coordination Anarchiste de Grenoble, 1974.

27 pages. Yellow wrappers. Unauthorized reprint (including pagination) of the version published in the "Documents" section of *Enragés and Situationists in the Occupation Movement.*

* * *

11. *De la misère en milieu étudiant, considérée sous ses aspects économique, politique, psychologique, sexuel et notamment intellectuel et de quelques moyens pour y remédier.* Grenoble: Coordination Anarchiste de Grenoble, 1974. 27 p. Couverture jaune.

Réimpression sauvage à l'identique (y compris la pagination) de la version publiée dans la partie « documents » de *Enragés et situationnistes dans le mouvement des occupations.*

DE LA MISERE
EN MILIEU
ETUDIANT

*considérée
sous ses aspects économique, politique,
psychologique, sexuel et notamment
intellectuel
et de quelques moyens pour y remédier*

par
des membres de l'Internationale Situationniste
et des étudiants de Strasbourg

— 1967 —

deuxième édition - 20ᵉ mille

12. *De la Misère en Milieu Étudiant, Considérée sous ses Aspects Économique, Politique, Psychologique, Sexuel et Notamment Intellectuel et de Quelques Moyens pour y Remédier*, n.p., c. 1974–1975.

28 pages. Pink-orange wrappers. Pirate edition with no listed place or date of publication, but most likely published in the mid-1970s. The text and layout are identical to those of the 1966 edition.

* * *

12. *De la misère en milieu étudiant, considérée sous ses aspects économique, politique, psychologique, sexuel et notamment intellectuel et de quelques moyens pour y remédier.* s.l.: s.e., 1974-75. 28 p. Couverture rose-orange.

Edition pirate, sans indication de lieu ou date, mais vraisemblablement publiée au milieu des années 70. Le texte et la mise en page de cette contrefaçon reprennent celles de l'édition de 1966.

DE LA MISERE EN MILIEU ETUDIANT

considérée
sous ses aspects économique, politique,
psychologique, sexuel et notamment
intellectuel
et de quelques moyens pour y remédier

13. *De la Misère en Milieu Étudiant*. Geneva: Zoé, January 1976.

64 pages. Red cover. First Swiss edition, first printing. The text and layout are identical to those of the 1966 edition, but the work is augmented by numerous illustrations that include posters with slogans from May 1968, détourned comics (including "The Return of the Durutti Column"), posters, etc.

* * *

13. *De la misère en milieu étudiant*. Genève: Zoé, janvier 1976. 64 p. Couverture rouge.

Première édition suisse, premier tirage. Le texte et la mise en page reprennent celles de l'édition de 1966, mais l'ouvrage est enrichi de nombreuses illustrations : slogans de Mai 1968, bandes dessinées détournées (dont « Le retour de la colonne Durutti »), affiches, etc.

14. *De la Misère en Milieu Étudiant.* Geneva: Zoé, March 1976.

64 pages. Red cover. Second printing, identical to the first printing.

* * *

14. *De la misère en milieu étudiant.* Genève: Zoé, mars 1976. 64 p. Couverture rouge.

Le même que le précédent, second tirage.

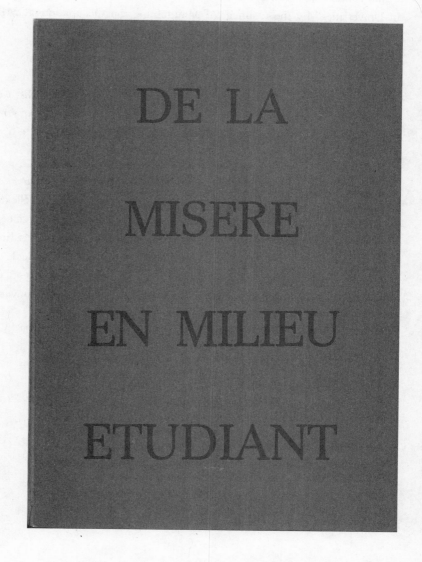

15. *De la Misère en Milieu Étudiant, Considérée sous ses Aspects Économique, Politique, Psychologique, Sexuel et Notamment Intellectuel et de Quelques Moyens pour y Remédier – 1966–1976.* Toulouse: Centre de Recherches Sociales, March 1976.

33 pages. Light blue wrappers. The text and layout are identical to the version published in *Enragés and Situationists in the Occupation Movement*, but the front wrapper is inspired by the 1966 edition (with the "psyschologique" spelling mistake.) This edition is augmented by a short preface providing a retrospective consideration of the historical context of the text ten years after its release: "1968 marked the end of an era, [but] the revolutionary movement erased by a half-century of counterrevolution reemerges everywhere." The poster "End of Universities" by the Council for Maintaining the Occupations (CMDO) is reproduced on the rear wrapper.

* * *

15. *De la misère en milieu étudiant, considérée sous ses aspects économique, politique, psychologique, sexuel et notamment intellectuel et de quelques moyens pour y remédier – 1966-1976.* Toulouse: Centre de Recherches Sociales, mars 1976. 33 p. Couverture bleu ciel.

Texte et mise en page identiques à ceux du texte paru dans *Enragés et situationnistes dans le mouvement des occupations*, mais sous une couverture proche de celle de 1966 (avec la faute à « psyschologique »). Edition enrichie d'une courte préface visant à contextualiser le texte 10 ans après sa parution : « 1968 a marqué la fin d'une époque, le mouvement révolutionnaire écrasé par plus d'un demi-siècle de contre-révolution renaît partout… ». L'affiche « Fin de l'Université » du Conseil pour le maintien des occupations (CMDO) est reproduite en quatrième de couverture.

DE LA MISERE
EN MILIEU
ETUDIANT

considérée
sous ses aspects économique, politique,
psychologique, sexuel et notamment
intellectuel
et de quelques moyens pour y remédier.

- 1966 -   - 1976 -

16. *De la Misère en Milieu Étudiant, Considérée sous ses Aspects Économique, Politique, Psychologique, Sexuel et Notamment Intellectuel et de Quelques Moyens pour y Remédier.* Paris: Champ Libre, October 1976.

59 pages. Gray wrappers. In the appendix, there is a short article from *Le Monde* from April 25–26, 1968, referencing the high school and student strikes of April 1976.

The commercial reprint of the text by Champ Libre led to a conflict between Mustapha Khayati and Gérard Lebovici, who owned the Paris-based publishing house. After hearing about Champ Libre's decision to reprint *On the Poverty of Student Life*, Khayati wrote to Lebovici, "This text isn't intended for the commercial form that you wish to give it. . . . It is necessary to let this text continue to circulate in its many pirate editions" (letter from October 12, 1976). In a response dated October 24, 1976, Lebovici disputed Khayati's sole authorship of the text—and thus Khayati's right to decide on its reprinting. As a rejoinder, Khayati responded with the leaflet, *On the Reprinting of "On The Poverty of Student Life. . . ,"* which was followed by a forged signature from Lebovici. In this sardonic text, Khayati declared to Lebovici that "selling radicalism won't hurt an organization, far from it. It can—with some risks, it's true—lead to success." Khayati then tried to include the leaflet as a sidebar in the Champ Libre edition of *On the Poverty of Student Life* before it was distributed to bookstores. Lebovici was made aware of the scheme and stopped it at the last minute. The letters exchanged by the two men are published in *Champ Libre: Correspondance Vol. 1.*[4]

16. *De la misère en milieu étudiant, considérée sous ses aspects économique, politique, psychologique, sexuel et notamment intellectuel et de quelques moyens pour y remédier.* Paris: Champ Libre, 21 octobre 1976. 59 p. Couverture grise.

En annexe, un court article du *Monde* du 25-26 avril 1976 référençant les grèves lycéennes et étudiantes d'avril 1976.

La réédition commerciale du texte par Champ Libre donne lieu à un conflit entre Mustapha Khayati et Gérard Lebovici. Apprenant la réédition de *La misère en milieu étudiant* aux éditions Champ Libre, Khayati écrit à Lebovici que « ce texte n'est point fait pour la forme commerciale officielle…il faut le laisser continuer son chemin à travers les nombreuses éditions sauvages » (lettre du 12 octobre 1976). Dans une réponse datée du 24 octobre 1976, Lebovici conteste à Khayati la seule paternité du texte – et donc son droit à statuer sur sa réédition. En guise de réponse, Khayati rédige le tract *A propos de la réédition de « La misère en milieu étudiant... »* et lui appose la (fausse) signature de l'éditeur. Dans ce texte burlesque, Khayati fait déclarer à Lebovici que « la marchandise radicale, loin de saboter les affaires, peut – avec quelques risques, il est vrai – travailler à leur salut ». Khayati tente ensuite d'insérer le tract comme encart dans l'édition Champ Libre de *La misère* avant sa livraison en librairie. Averti, Lebovici fait échouer le projet. Les missives échangées par les deux hommes firent l'objet d'une publication dans *Editions Champ Libre, Correspondance vol. 1.*

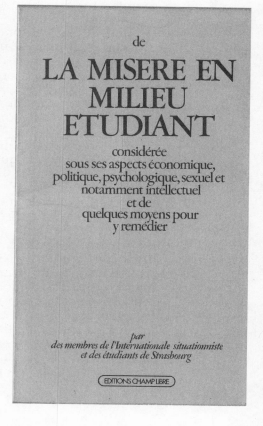

de
LA MISERE EN MILIEU ETUDIANT

considérée
sous ses aspects économique,
politique, psychologique, sexuel et
notamment intellectuel
et de
quelques moyens pour
y remédier

*par
des membres de l'Internationale situationniste
et des étudiants de Strasbourg*

EDITIONS CHAMP LIBRE

« LA MISERE EN MI[

Voici d'étranges rumeurs qui sont capables d'intoxiquer les gens : puisqu'on se moque de moi, on se peut bien moquer d'un autre. Oui ! Sans demander l'autorisation à personne, j'ai pris, seul, l'initiative de rééditer la brochure intitulée : « De la misère en milieu étudiant »..., publiée, voici dix ans, par les situationnnistes.

D'aucuns se demandent naïvement : « Pourquoi reprendre commercialement un texte qui a eu le rare mérite de se diffuser par lui-même, dans divers pays et dans diverses langues, qui a trouvé tant de lecteurs sans la moindre publicité, qui a occasionné quelques dégâts dans l'Université, et qui n'a financièrement jamais rien rapporté à personne, jusqu'à ce jour ? » Je réponds : « Justement ! pourquoi pas ? »

Ce texte, anonyme et libre de tout copyright, me semble être à la disposition de n'importe qui. Quel mal y a-t-il à ce que je sois ce n'importe qui ?

De fait, depuis l'effondrement de l'Empire romain d'Occident, il ne s'est pas trouvé un seul éditeur qui ait rendu, en si peu de temps, autant de services à la cause révolutionnaire, que moi. Des misérables qui n'ont réussi ni dans le monde des affaires ni dans les affaires de la révolution, me reprochent aujourd'hui — à moi qui n'ai jamais connu de frontières entre la bonne cause et la bonne soupe — de m'enrichir aux dépens de cette cause. Feint-on d'ignorer que j'ai souvent risqué mon argent pour diffuser les idées dangereuses ? Pourquoi les idées dangereuses ne courraient-elles pas parfois le risque de me rapporter un peu d'argent ? Les imposteurs ne devaient-ils pas s'ensevelir dans les ténèbres le jour que j'ai produit « La Société du Spectacle » et que j'ai gagné le privilège de rééditer l'Internationale Situationniste ?

La médisance est venue me chercher jusque dans mon métier d'homme du spectacle. J'ai honte pour tous les gens de ma profession qui n'ont pas encore compris que, depuis Mai 68, les temps ont changé et que la marchandise radicale, loin de saboter les affaires, peut — avec quelques risques, il est vrai — travailler à leur salut.

Un de mes amis, dont j'estime beaucoup le juge-

réédition de
[LIEU ETUDIANT»...

ment, parce que c'est J.-P. Belmondo, et Louis de Funès, dont je prenais ordinairement conseil, m'avaient déjà prévenu contre les risques et les tracas de l'édition, et m'avaient conseillé de demeurer tranquillement aux Champs-Elysées. Seulement, voilà ! quoique je sois un homme d'affaires, je ne laisse pas d'être révolutionnaire par une manière qui est, à la vérité, difficile à expliquer, mais qui ne laisse pas d'être véritable, quoique je n'aie jamais réussi à la faire entendre à ceux avec qui j'en ai conféré.

Des esprits mal tournés et qui empoisonnent tout ont trouvé encore dans ma générosité de quoi porter atteinte à ma réputation. Ils disent que mes prétentions d'éditeur révolutionnaire sont fort éloignées de ma réalité d'imprésario, et que je n'ai été engagé dans l'édition que pour les mêmes motifs qui ont fait de moi « Monsieur 10 % du cinéma ». Je leur dis : « L'histoire jugera si mes intérêts peuvent, un jour, faire partie des affaires de la Révolution. »

Je me suis trouvé, certes, dans la funeste nécessité de gagner sans trève de l'argent ; mais que l'on sache que c'est dans l'unique but d'être de quelque utilité à une révolution qui, me libérant de cette odieuse obligation, me rendra à moi-même et aux miens.

Je sais que l'on dit à chaque quart d'heure, dans le public des envieux, que je ne comprends pas les livres que je publie, que je ne suis pour rien dans ce que fait Champ Libre et que, de surplus, je paie très mal mes employés. Mais, même les journalistes qui nous boycottent n'osent nier notre indiscutable contribution à la science de la publicité et à la précision des méthodes de récupération. On peut surprendre les esprits pour deux jours, mais il est difficile de les aveugler pour longtemps : ne croyez point aux médisances qu'on fait de moi ; j'irai si droit dans mon chemin, que si les bons révolutionnaires ne m'aiment de droit, au moins ils m'aimeront de bricole.

G. LEBOVICI
EDITEUR, PRODUCTEUR ET IMPRESARIO

17. "De la Misère en Milieu Étudiant, Considérée sous ses Aspects Économique, Politique, Psychologique, Sexuel et Notamment Intellectuel et de Quelques Moyens pour y Remédier." *Tripot 25 / Hors II*. 5–6. Lys: Editions d'Utovie (1978): 4–13.

Blue cover. Reproduces substantial excerpts of the pamphlet. The remainder of the periodical features slogans and leaflets from May '68, along with some contemporary analyses (for example, "Is Ten Years Too Long? That Depends on What We Do with Them").

* * *

17. « De la misère en milieu étudiant, considérée sous ses aspects économique, politique, psychologique, sexuel et notamment intellectuel et de quelques moyens pour y remédier ». *Tripot 25 / Hors II 5-6*. Lys: Editions d'Utovie, 1978. p. 4-13. Couverture bleue.

Reprend de larges extraits du texte (p. 4-13). Le reste de l'ouvrage reproduit des slogans et tracts de Mai 68, ainsi que quelques analyses contemporaines (par exemple, « Dix ans, c'est trop ? Ça dépend ce qu'on en fait »).

TRIPOT

HORS II 5·6

25

dix ans c'est nor !

MAI 68 MAI 78

18. De la Misère en Milieu Étudiant, Considérée sous ses Aspects Économique, Politique, Psychologique, Sexuel et Notamment Intellectuel et de Quelques Moyens pour y Remédier. Aix-en-Provence: Sulliver, November 30, 1995.

47 pages. Olive-green cover. The edition includes the text, "Our Goals and Methods in the Strasbourg Scandal," which appeared in *Internationale Situationniste* 11 (October 1967), as well as a short preface stating, "With or without students, the dominant system will continue to be against everyone. They can choose to continue to act as accomplices in their own misfortune; they just should know that there are no benefits to doing so."

* * *

18. *De la misère en milieu étudiant, considérée sous ses aspects économique, politique, psychologique, sexuel et notamment intellectuel et de quelques moyens pour y remédier.* Aix-en-Provence : Sulliver, 30 novembre 1995. 47 p. Couverture vert olive.

Edition enrichie du texte « Nos buts et nos méthodes dans le scandale de Strasbourg » (paru dans *Internationale Situationniste* 11, octobre 1967) et d'un bref avant-propos (« Avec ou sans les étudiants, le système dominant continuera à se faire contre tous. Ils peuvent choisir d'être les complices de leur malheur ; ils doivent seulement savoir qu'ils n'auront aucune récompense »).

DE LA MISERE
EN MILIEU
ETUDIANT

considérée
sous ses aspects économique, politique,
psychologique, sexuel et notamment
intellectuel
et de quelques moyens pour y remédier

Suivi de

NOS BUTS ET NOS METHODES
DANS LE SCANDALE DE STRASBOURG

(extrait de la revue *Internationale Situationniste* n° 11)

19. *De la Misère en Milieu Étudiant*. Paris: Mille et une nuits, October 1996.

56 pages. Illustrated cover. Brief two-page afterword that contextualizes the text and offers some reading recommendations, including *The Society of the Spectacle* by Guy Debord and *The Revolution of Everyday Life* by Raoul Vaneigem.

* * *

19. *De la misère en milieu étudiant*. Paris : Mille et une nuits, octobre 1996. 56 p. Couverture illustrée.

Brève notice de deux pages (en guise de postface) qui contextualise le texte et offre quelques recommandations de lecture, dont *La Société du spectacle* de Guy Debord et le *Traité de savoir-vivre à l'usage des jeunes générations* de Raoul Vaneigem.

20. *De la Misère en Milieu Étudiant, Considérée sous ses Aspects Économique, Politique, Psychologique, Sexuel et Notamment Intellectuel et de Quelques Moyens pour y Remédier.* Grenoble: Zanzara Athée, 2000.

35 pages. White wrappers. Pirate reprint of the text by Zanzara Athée, a collective which formed in 1997 and describes itself as "an independent distributor of subversive readings and publisher of similarly subversive brochures."[5] The rear wrapper features an excerpt from the summary order issued on December 13, 1966 by the Strasbourg District Court, with Judge Llabador presiding.

* * *

20. *De la misère en milieu étudiant, considérée sous ses aspects économique, politique, psychologique, sexuel et notamment intellectuel et de quelques moyens pour y remédier.* Grenoble : Zanzara Athée, 2000. 35 p. Couverture blanche.

Réédition pirate du texte par Zanzara Athée, un collectif crée en 1997 et qui se définit comme « à la fois diffuseur autonome de lectures subversives et éditeur de brochures (tout aussi subversives) ». La quatrième de couverture reproduit un extrait de l'ordonnance de référé rendue le 13 décembre 1966 par le Tribunal de Grande Instance de Strasbourg, présidé par le Juge Llabador.

DE LA MISÈRE EN MILIEU ÉTUDIANT

considérée sous ses aspects économique, politique, psychologique, sexuel et notamment intellectuel et de quelques moyens pour y remédier

par des membres de l'Internationale situationniste et des étudiants de Strasbourg (1966)

21. *De la Misère en Milieu Étudiant, Considérée sous ses Aspects Économique, Politique, Psychologique, Sexuel et Notamment Intellectuel et de Quelques Moyens pour y Remédier.* Cabris: Sulliver, January 2005.

60 pages. Blue wrappers. The edition includes the text, "Our Goals and Our Methods in the Strasbourg Scandal," which first appeared in *Internationale Situationniste* 11, October 1967, as well as a brief preface (identical to that of the 1995 edition).

***

21. *De la misère en milieu étudiant, considérée sous ses aspects économique, politique, psychologique, sexuel et notamment intellectuel et de quelques moyens pour y remédier.* Cabris : Sulliver, janvier 2005. 60 p. Couverture bleue.

Edition enrichie du texte « Nos buts et nos méthodes dans le scandale de Strasbourg » (paru dans *Internationale Situationniste* 11, octobre 1967) et d'un bref avant-propos identique à celui de l'édition de 1995.

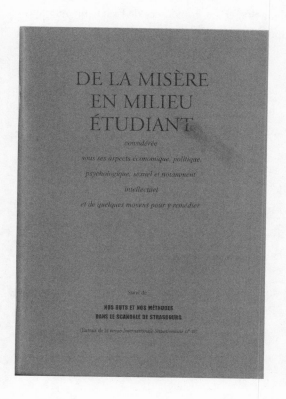

22. *De la Misère en Milieu Étudiant, Considérée sous ses Aspects Économique, Politique, Psychologique, Sexuel et Notamment Intellectuel et de Quelques Moyens pour y Remédier.* Strasbourg: Fédération Hiéro Strasbourg, 2016.

32 pages. Illustrated wrappers. Reprint of the 1966 original edition, on the fiftieth anniversary of the pamphlet. This commemorative edition was released as part of "Situationist Trajectory", a cultural program that took place in Strasbourg from November 21–29, 2016. Events included a screening of Guy Debord's films at Cinéma Star as well as a lecture by Eric Brun, who authored the first comprehensive sociological study of the Situationist International. [6]

***

22. *De la misère en milieu étudiant, considérée sous ses aspects économique, politique, psychologique, sexuel et notamment intellectuel et de quelques moyens pour y remédier.* Strasbourg : Fédération Hiéro Strasbourg, 2016. 32 p. Couverture illustrée.

Réédition de l'édition originale de 1966, à l'occasion du cinquantième anniversaire de la brochure. Celle-ci a lieu dans le cadre de « Trajectoire situationniste », une programmation culturelle qui se déroule à Strasbourg entre le 21 et le 29 novembre 2016. Parmi les nombreux évènements, on remarquera entre autres une projection des films de Guy Debord au Cinéma Star et une conférence de Eric Brun, auteur de la première étude sociologique approfondie du mouvement situationniste.

23. *De la Misère en Milieu Étudiant, Considérée sous ses Aspects Économique, Politique, Psychologique, Sexuel et Notamment Intellectuel et de Quelques Moyens pour y Remédier.* Maisons-Laffitte: Ampélos, 2018.

85 pages and front matter (i–xviii). The cover is illustrated by a détourned comic. Jean Baubérot, a friend of Daniel Joubert, authored the preface, which is followed by "Editor's Notes: On the Poverty," which argues for a joint authorship by Guy Debord, Daniel Joubert, and Mustapha Khayati. This edition is augmented by the text "Our Goals and Methods in the Strasbourg Scandal," which first appeared in *Internationale Situationniste* 11, October 1967, along with a poster reproduction of the famous comic strip by André Bertrand, "The Return of the Durutti Column," which announces the release of "the most scandalous pamphlet of the century."

* * *

23. *De la misère en milieu étudiant, considérée sous ses aspects économique, politique, psychologique, sexuel et notamment intellectuel et de quelques moyens pour y remédier.* Maisons-Laffitte : Ampélos, 2018. xviii + 85 p. Couverture illustrée d'une bande dessinée détournée.

Jean Baubérot, ami de Daniel Joubert, rédige la préface. Elle est suivie de « Notes de l'éditeur sur : *De la misère* », ou est avancée l'idée que Guy Debord, Daniel Joubert et Mustapha Khayati partageraient la paternité du texte. Cette édition est également enrichie du texte « Nos buts et nos méthodes dans le scandale de Strasbourg » (paru dans *Internationale Situationniste* 11, octobre 1967) ainsi que d'une reproduction du célèbre tract-affiche d'André Bertrand, « Le retour de la colonne Durutti » qui annonce la parution prochaine de « la brochure la plus scandaleuse du siècle ».

24. *De la Misère en Milieu Étudiant.* Paris: Coralie de Castro, 2019.

36 pages. Illustrated white wrappers. This edition reproduces the pamphlet with a revised layout in form of a user manual. A small figure—a didactic caricature with an animatedly mischievous personality—guides the reader and is overlaid upon images from May 1968. The figure demonstrates ways to apply lessons from the manifesto to everyday life. Fifty copies were produced.

* * *

24. *De la misère en milieu étudiant.* Paris : Coralie de Castro, 2019. 36 p. Couverture blanche illustrée.

Edition qui reproduit le pamphlet avec une remise en page sous forme de notice d'utilisation. Un petit personnage guide le lecteur ; un trouble-fête qui s'incruste dans les illustrations de Mai 68 et qui présente dans des schémas des moyens d'appliquer le manifeste dans la vraie vie. Edition indépendante tirée à 50 exemplaires.

English

(United Kingdom, United States, Australia)

25. "Finally to Create the Situation Which Renders Return Backwards Impossible." *The Seattle Group Bulletin* 38 (1967): 1–3.[7]

First translation of excerpts (specifically, pages 24–28) from the pamphlet, only a few months after its publication in Strasbourg. Translation and notes by Jim Evrard. Evrard was a contributor to the magazine *Rebel Worker*. In 1967, he voraciously opposed the Situationists in "On the Situationists' 'Intellectual Terrorism.'"

* * *

Anglais

(Royaume-Uni, Etats-Unis, Australie)

25. « Finally to create the situation which renders return backwards impossible ». *The Seattle Group Bulletin* 38. Seattle : The Seattle Group, 1967. p. 1-3.

Première traduction d'extraits (plus précisément des pages 24 à 28) de la brochure, quelques mois seulement après sa parution à Strasbourg. Traduction et notes de Jim Evrard. Evrard fut membre du collectif qui publia la revue *Rebel Worker*. Il est l'auteur d'un libelle contre les situationnistes : « Sur le 'terrorisme intellectuel' des situationnistes ».

Submitted for your consideration without endorsement other than the
author's except as it represents a contribution pertinent to the
problems of our times.

The only concurrence we solicit is that which the Devil asked of
Wicked John: "Here -- take a chunk of fire and go start your own hell".

We do ask you, in turn, to submit your ideas to us on the same basis.
the experience of non-involvement....
scious will of men, and this presupposes insight. JE]

...The dominant society, which flatters itself on its permanent modernisation,
ought now to find someone with whom to speak, namely with the modernized negation
which it itself produces: "Let us now leave to the dead the charge of burying their
dead and weeping for them". The practical demystifications of the historical movement
are unburdening revolutionary consciousness of the phantoms which haunt it; the revolution of everyday life finds itself faced by immense tasks to accomplish. The revolution, like the life it announces, must be reinvented. If the revolutionary task
remains fundamentally the same: abolition of class society, we must remember that no
part of the conditions in which it forms itself has not been radically transformed.
The task is to take work up anew with a radicalism and a coherence accrued through
experience with the bankruptcy of its earlier carriers, in order to avoid that its
fragmentary realization entail a new division of society.

The struggle between these in power and the new proletariat can be fought only in
its totality; the future revolutionary movement will have to abolish in its breast
everything which tends to reproduce the alienated products of the commodity system"
(* defined by the prevalence of work as commodity [needless to say, they are not using
this term in the banal sense in which Cardan understands it] . It will at the same
time have to be its living critique and the negation which carries in itself all the
elements of possibly transcending [this is the Hegel concept aufheben] it. As Lukacs
saw correctly (altho he applied it to an object unworthy of it: the Bolshevik party),
the revolutionary organization [they are using the term too in a sense more profound
than that vapid sense in which you are used to hearing it] is that necessary mediation
[= Hegel's Vermittlung] between theory and practice, between man and history, between
the mass of workers and the proletariat constituted as a class. "Theoretical" tendencies and divergences must immediately transform themselves into questions of organization if they want to point out the way to their realization. The question of organization will be the last judgement of the new revolutionary movement, the tribunal
before which will be judged the coherence of its essential task, international realization of the absolute power of Workers' Councils such as has been sketched out by the
experiences of the proletarian revolutions of this century. [They mean 1905 and '17 in
Russia, 1919 in Germany, 1956 in Hungary.] Such an organization must give priority to
radical criticism of all foundations of the society which it combats, namely: commodity production, ideology in all its disguises, the state and the dichotomes it imposes.

The dichotome between theory and practice has been the rock on which the old
revolutionary movement rested. Only the high points of proletarian struggle have
transcended that dichotome to rediscover their own truth [another Hegel term; see
Herbert Marcuse, Reason and Revolution, index]. No organization has yet jumped this
Rhodus. Ideology [this word is used throughout in the Marxist sense] "revolutionary"
as it may be, is always in the service of rulers, the alarm signal which designates
the disguised enemy. That is why criticism of ideology must be, in the last analysis,
the central problem of the revolutionary organization. Only an alienated world produces illusion, and illusion can not reappear in the interior of those who pretend to
carry social truth, except in that the organization itself transform itself into just
another illusion in a fundamentally illusory world. [There you have one of the central ideas in the situationist concept of the "spectacle".]

The revolutionary organization which proposes to realize the absolute power of
Workers' Councils must be the milieu where all the positive aspects of that power are
sketched. It will also have to conduct a struggle to the death against the Leninist
theory of organization. The revolution of 1905 and the spontaneous organization of
Russian workers in Soviets was already a criticism in action of that nefarious theory.
But the Bolshevik movement persisted in believing that workers' spontaneity was incapable of seizing "the totality". The outcome was the beheading of the proletariat
to allow the Party to take the "head" of the Revolution. You cannot contest, as
ruthlessly as Lenin did, the historical capability of the proletariat to emancipate
itself unaided, without contesting its capability of ruling the future society. In
such a context the slogan, "All power to the Soviets" means nothing else but the conquest of the Soviets by the Party, the installation of the party State instead of
the perishing "State" of the armed proletariat.

26. *Ten Days That Shook the University: The Situationists at Strasbourg*. London: BCM/ Situationist International, April 1967.[8]

30 pages. White wrappers illustrated with images from "The Return of the Durutti Column." This first English translation, which deviates from the French original, was envisioned as a militant text and hence was significantly adapted for an English-language audience. The title was borrowed from John Reed's famous eyewitness account of the 1917 Russian Revolution, *Ten Days That Shook the World*.[9]

This edition is the work of T.J. Clark and Donald Nicholson-Smith in Paris, with contributions from Situationists Christopher Gray and Charles Radcliffe in London. The English translation of the original text is augmented by a short preface, as well as by partial reproductions of "The Return of the Durutti Column." It also includes a six-page postscript entitled "If You Make a Social Revolution, Do It for Fun!"—a détournement of D.H. Lawrence's poem "A Sane Revolution." In this now acclaimed text, Clark and Nicholson-Smith describe reactions to the incendiary brochure in Strasbourg and beyond, emphasizing its relevance to a British context. The postscript would later be reproduced in nearly all subsequent English-language reprints of the pamphlet. The price, 3 shillings/50 cents, is listed on the rear wrapper.

* * *

26. *Ten days that shook the university : the situationists at Strasbourg*. Londres : BCM / Situationist International, avril 1967. 30 p. Couverture blanche illustrée d'un extrait du tract-affiche « Le retour de la colonne Durutti ».

Edition originale anglaise – en fait, une version adaptée au contexte anglo-saxon et envisagée comme un texte de combat – réalisée par T.J. Clark et Donald Nicholson-Smith à Paris, avec l'aide notamment des situationnistes Christopher Gray et Charles Radcliffe à Londres. Le titre est une allusion à l'ouvrage de John Reed, *Dix jours qui ébranlèrent le monde*, un témoignage de la révolution russe de 1917. Le texte est enrichi d'une courte préface, de reproductions de vignettes du tract-affiche « Le retour de la colonne Durutti » et surtout du texte devenu célèbre « Si vous faite une révolution sociale, faites-la pour le plaisir ! », un détournement du poème de D.H. Lawrence « Une revolution saine ». En six pages, Clark et Nicholson-Smith décrivent les réactions à la brochure incendiaire, à Strasbourg et ailleurs, et mettent en avant sa pertinence dans le contexte britannique. Cette postface sera reproduite dans la quasi-totalité des rééditions en langue anglaise du pamphlet. Prix (3 shillings / 50 cents) indiqué en bas de page sur la quatrième de couverture.

27. *On the Poverty of Student Life. A Consideration of its Economic, Political, Sexual, Psychological and Notably Intellectual Aspects and of a Few Ways to Cure It.* Trans. Robert Chasse. New York, n.p., April 1967.[10]

36 pages. White wrappers. The work of Tony Verlaan, this first American edition was initially conceived as a supplement to the *Situationist International Bulletin* (but the periodical itself would not be published until 1969). The pamphlet includes a short list of other Situationist texts available in English and is stamped "Situationist International, P.O. Box 491, Cooper Station, N.Y., N.Y., 10003." The English translation is by Robert Chasse, who became a member of the Situationist International in November 1968. The rear wrapper lists addresses of the Situationist International in Paris (Boite Postale 307-03), London (Attn: Heatwave), and New York (Cooper Station PO BOX).

* * *

27. *On the poverty of student life. A consideration of its economic, political, sexual, psychological and notably intellectual aspects and of a few ways to cure it.* New York : Situationist International, avril 1967. 36 p. Couverture blanche.

Réalisée par Tony Verlaan, l'édition originale américaine est initialement envisagée comme supplément à *Situationist International Bulletin* (qui ne paraîtra néanmoins qu'en 1969). Brève liste d'autres textes situationnistes disponibles en langue anglaise, et tampon (vraisemblablement apposé postérieurement) « Situationist International, P.O. Box 491, Cooper Station, NY, NY 10003 ». Traduction en anglais (États-Unis) de Robert Chasse, qui rejoint l'Internationale Situationniste en novembre 1968. En quatrième de couverture, on retrouve les adresses de l'Internationale Situationniste à Paris (Boite Postale 307-03), Londres (aux soins de Heatwave) et New York (Cooper Station PO BOX).

ON THE POVERTY
OF
STUDENT LIFE

A CONSIDERATION OF ITS ECONOMIC, POLITICAL, SEXUAL, PSYCHOLOGICAL and notably INTELLECTUAL ASPECTS AND OF A FEW WAYS TO CURE IT

–April, 1967–

First American edition, New York.

by
some members of the Situationiste International
and some students from Strasbourg and New York.

28. *Ten Days That Shook the University*. Paris, London, and New York: BCM/Situationist International, 1967.[11]

25 pages. Beige wrappers illustrated with a simplification of a piece of the Bayeux Tapestry depicting Normans feasting with Odo, Bishop of Bayeux, saying grace.[12] This image also appeared as a détourned comic in "The Return of the Durutti Column." This edition reprints the translation by Donald Nicholson-Smith and T.J. Clark, as well as the short preface and postscript from the 1967 edition (but excluding the illustrations). The rear wrapper lists addresses of the Situationist International in Paris, London, and New York.

* * *

28. *Ten days that shook the university*. Paris, Londres et New York : BCM/Situationist International, 1967. 25 p. Couverture beige illustrée d'une image provenant de la tapisserie de Bayeux ; on y voit des Normands célébrant un banquet en compagnie d'Odo, évêque de Bayeux. Cette illustration est également reprise sous forme de vignette de bande dessinée détournée dans « Le retour de la colonne Durutti ».

Reprend l'adaptation en langue anglaise de Donald Nicholson-Smith et T.J. Clark, ainsi que la courte préface et la postface présentes dans l'édition de 1967 (mais pas les illustrations). En quatrième de couverture, on retrouve les adresses de l'Internationale Situationniste à Paris, Londres et New York.

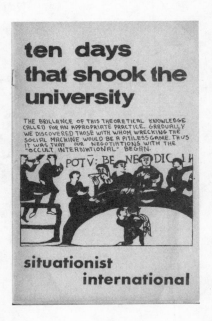

29. *Ten Days That Shook the University*. Paris, London, and New York: BCM/ Situationist International, 1967.[13]

25 pages. Blue wrappers illustrated with a simplification of a piece of the Bayeux Tapestry depicting Normans feasting with Odo, Bishop of Bayeux, saying grace.[14] This image also appeared as a détourned comic in "The Return of the Durutti Column." Identical to the previous edition except for the addition of an English translation of "The Return of the Durutti Column," printed as a centerfold insert.

* * *

29. *Ten days that shook the university*. Paris, Londres et New York : BCM / Situationist International, 1967. 25 p. Couverture bleue illustrée d'une image provenant de la tapisserie de Bayeux. Cette illustration est également reprise sous forme de vignette de bande dessinée détournée dans « Le retour de la colonne Durutti ». Identique au précédent, mais enrichi d'une traduction en anglais de « Le retour de la colonne Durutti », agrafé à la page centrale.

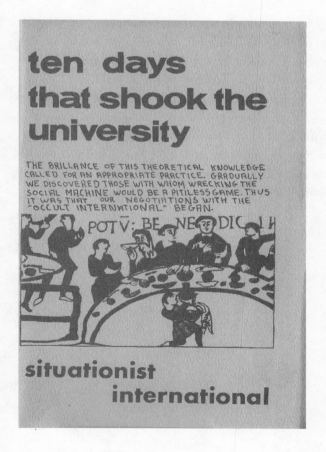

30. *On the Poverty of Student Life*. New York: Situationist International, 1968.[15]

24 pages. White wrappers illustrated with a détourned comic strip. This American edition reuses the Donald Nicholson-Smith and T.J. Clark translation, as well as the short preface and postscript to the first English edition. The illustrations in the text are taken from "In Our Spectacular Society Where All You Can See is Things and Their Price," a famous poster dated December 1967 announcing the publication of *Internationale Situationniste* 11. A partial reproduction of the English translation of "The Return of the Durutti Column" appears on the front and rear endpapers. The rear wrapper features an excerpt from the "Address to New York City Public School Students," a détourned comic by Bruce Elwell and Robert Chasse, as well as the address of the Situationist International in New York.

* * *

30. *On the poverty of student life*. New York : Situationist International, ca.1968. 24 p. Couverture blanche illustrée d'une bande dessinée détournée.

Edition américaine. Reprend la traduction de Donald Nicholson-Smith et T.J. Clark, ainsi que la courte préface et la postface de l'édition originale anglaise. Les illustrations dans le texte sont issues de « Dans le décor spectaculaire où le regard ne rencontre que les choses et leur prix », célèbre affiche de décembre 1967 qui annonce la parution du onzième numéro de la revue *Internationale Situationniste*. Une reproduction partielle de la traduction anglaise du tract-affiche « Le retour de la colonne Durutti » apparait pour sa part en deuxième et troisième de couverture. La quatrième de couverture comprend un extrait de « Adresse aux élèves des écoles publiques de New-York », bande dessinée détournée par Bruce Elwell et Robert Chasse, ainsi que l'adresse de l'Internationale Situationniste à New York.

ON THE POVERTY OF STUDENT LIFE

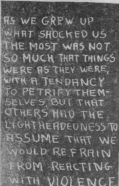

AS WE GREW UP WHAT SHOCKED US THE MOST WAS NOT SO MUCH THAT THINGS WERE AS THEY WERE, WITH A TENDANCY TO PETRIFY THEM-SELVES, BUT THAT OTHERS HAD THE LIGHTHEADEDNESS TO ASSUME THAT WE WOULD REFRAIN FROM REACTING WITH VIOLENCE

PRICK YOUR LIFE!

COMMODITY

SPECTACLE OF OPPOSITION

situationist international

31. "Ten Days That Shook the University," *Berkeley Barb* 5, no. 124 (December 1967): 1, 8–9.

"Ten Days That Shook the University," *Berkeley Barb* 6, no. 125 (January 1968): 2, 14.

"Ten Days That Shook the University," *Berkeley Barb* 6, no. 126 (January 1968): 8–9.[16]

Publication spread across three issues of the countercultural periodical *Berkeley Barb*. The illustrations are taken from the English translation of "The Return of the Durutti Column," as they were already featured in *Ten Days That Shook the University* (1967). One of the détourned comics reproduces Eugène Delacroix's painting *The Death of Sardanapalus*. Here, Sardanapalus is made to say, "Yes, the thought of Marx is really a critique of everyday life." The original painting reproduces Lord Byron's *Sardanapalus*[17] which envisioned the fall of ancient Assyria. He orders all the women in his harem as well as his possessions to be burned with him. In *The Absolute Bourgeois*, former Situationist International member T.J. Clark analyzes the original *The Death of Sardanapalus*, where he discusses the painting in relation to class conflict following the Paris Commune and the 1848 uprisings. He juxtaposes it to Delacroix's *Liberty Leading the People*, which shows a liberated revolutionary woman, whereas *Sardanapalus* pictures "the Assyrian's obedient entourage."[18]

* * *

31. « Ten days that shook the university ». *Berkeley Barb*, Vol. 5, Issue 124. Berkeley : Berkeley Barb, décembre 1967. p. 1, 8-9.

« Ten days that shook the university ». *Berkeley Barb*, Vol. 6, No.1, Issue 125. Berkeley : Berkeley Barb, janvier 1968. p. 2, 14.

« Ten days that shook the university ». *Berkeley Barb*, Vol. 6, No. 2, Issue 126. Berkeley : Berkeley Barb, janvier 1968. p. 8-9.

Publication en feuilleton (échelonné sur trois numéros) du texte par la revue de contre-culture *Berkeley Barb*. Illustrations tirées de la traduction en anglais de « Le retour de la colonne Durutti », que l'on trouve dans l'édition originale anglaise de *La misère en milieu étudiant*. Une des vignettes de bande dessinée détourne le tableau *La mort de Sardanapale* de Eugène Delacroix. Sardanapale s'exclame : « Oui, la pensée de Marx est d'abord une critique de la vie quotidienne ». La toile originale était basée sur le *Sardanapale* de Lord Byron, où est dépeinte la chute de l'ancien royaume assyrien. Dans *Le bourgeois absolu*, T.J. Clark – un ancien membre de l'Internationale Situationniste – présente une analyse du *Sardanapale*, replaçant le tableau dans le contexte du conflit des classes au lendemain de la Commune et des manifestations de 1848. Il contraste *La mort de Sardanapale*, qui dépeint « l'entourage obéissant de l'Assyrien », à une autre toile de Delacroix, *La Liberté guidant le peuple*, portrait d'une une femme libérée et révolutionnaire.

ten days
that shook t

The poverty of student activism is the main thrust of argument in a pamphlet by Situationist International, a Marxists-anarchist group born in France. This BARB series is a reprint of that pamphlet.

A small group os students at Strasbourg University in 1966 got elected to power in the students union. Instead of devoting themselves to sandbox reform, they proclaimed their intention to dissolve the student union, and they used its funds to publish Situationist-inspired propaganda.

Synopsis of Part One

The revolt of youth, the pamphlet asserts, is the seed of a total overthrow of the dead life produced by modern capitalism. But the revolt of youth is, itself, subverted by its over-exposure by social scientists and the mass media. It becomes a categorized social aberration within the system, rather than a revolution against the system.

Youthful delinquency is a violent expression of the rejection of the sterile choices offered by society. The delinquent's revolt, however, gives no way of excaping the system. He either yields to the lure of commodity consuption and gets a job, or attacks the commodity system itself. The attack on the laws of the market can take the form of stealing, or of a revolutionary critique of commodity society.

The Provos, a combination of artists and hippies ("beatniks" in the 1966 European terminology of the pamphlet), revolt against the commodity system by means of neo-artistic reformism of everyday life. They choose a limited, fragmentary attack, and in the end remain the servants of the system of production. "If they want to change the world, they must get rid of those who are content to paint it white," say the Situationists.

UC Berkeley students from the start, Part One of this series points out, "have

he university

organisation.

They are the first to carry the struggle on to the streets, holding fast to a real revolutionary programme, and with a mass participation. Thousands of workers and students have waged a violent struggle with the Japanese police. In many ways the C.R.L. lacks a complete and concrete theory of the two systems it fights with such ferocity. It has not yet defined the precise nature of bureaucratic exploitation, and it has hardly formulated the character of modern capitalism, the critique of everyday life and the critique of the spectacle. The Communist Revolutionary League is still fundamentally an avant-garde *political* organisation, the heir of the best features of the classic proletarian movement. But it is at present the most important group in the world—and should henceforth be one of the poles of discussion and a rallying point for the new proletarian critique.

To make shame more shameful by giving it publicity

We might very well say, and no-one would disagree with us, that the student is the most universally despised creature in France, apart from the priest and the policeman. Naturally he is usually attacked from the wrong point of view, with specious reasons derived from the ruling ideology. He may be worth the contempt of a true revolutionary, yet a revolutionary critique of the student situation is currently taboo on the official Left. The licensed and impotent opponents of capitalism repress the obvious—that what is wrong with the students is also what is wrong with them. They convert their unconscious contempt into a blind enthusiasm. The radical intelligentsia (from *Les Temps Modernes* to *L'Express*) prostrates itself before the so-called "rise of the student" and the declining bureaucracies of the Left (from the "Communist" party to the Stalinist National Union of Students) bids noisily for his moral and material support.

There are reasons for this sudden enthusiasm, but they are all *provided* by the present form of capitalism, in its overdeveloped state. We shall use this pamphlet for denunciation. We shall expose these reasons one by one, on the principle that the end of alienation is only reached by the straight and narrow path of alienation itself.

Up to now, studies of student life have ignored the essential issue. The surveys and analyses have all been psychological or sociological or economic: in other words, academic exercises, content with the false categories of one specialization or another. None of them can achieve what is most needed—a view of modern society as a whole. Fourier denounced their error long ago as the attempt to apply scientific laws to the basic assumptions of the science ("*porter régulièrement sur les questions primordiales*"). Everything is said about our society except what it *is*, and the nature of its two basic principles—the commodity and the spectacle. The fetishism of facts masks the essential category, and the details consign the totality to oblivion.

Modern capitalism and its spectacle allot everyone a specific role in a general passivity. The student is no exception to the rule. He has a provisional part to play, a rehearsal for his final role as an element in market society as conservative as the rest. Being a student is a form of initiation. An initiation which echoes

32. "Ten Days That Shook the University." *Helix* 3, no. 4 (March 1968): 11–14.

Excerpts from *On the Poverty of Student Life* appear in this issue of *Helix*, a biweekly Seattle-based countercultural periodical. Also includes the postscript to the first English edition ("If You Make a Social Revolution, Do It for Fun!") and an English translation of "In Our Spectacular Society Where All You Can See is Things and Their Price," a 1967 poster announcing the publication of the eleventh issue of *Internationale Situationniste*. Illustrations in the text are taken from "The Return of the Durutti Column."

* * *

32. « Ten days that shook the university ». *Helix*, Vol. 3, No. 4. Seattle: Helix, March 1968. p. 11-14.

Publication d'extraits du pamphlet par *Helix*, bimensuel de contre-culture de Seattle. On retrouve également la postface à l'édition originale anglaise (« Si vous faites une révolution sociale, faites-la pour le plaisir ! ») et une traduction de « Dans le décor spectaculaire où le regard ne rencontre que les choses et leur prix », affiche de 1967 qui annonce la parution du onzième numéro de la revue *Internationale Situationniste*. Les illustrations dans le texte sont tirées de « Le retour de la colonne Durutti ».

situationnist international

In November 1966, Strasbourg University was the scene of a preliminary skirmish between modern capitalism and the new revolutionary forces which it is beginning to engender.

For the first time, a few students abandoned pseudo-revolt and found their way to a coherent radical activity of a kind which has everywhere been repressed by reformism. This small group got itself elected, amidst the apathy of Strasbourg's 18,000 students, to the committee of the left-wing students' union. Once in this position of power, they began to put union funds to good use. They founded a Society for the Rehabilitation of Karl Marx and Ravachol. They plastered the walls of the city with a Marxist comic-strip, "The Return of the Durutti Column". They proclaimed their intention to dissolve the union once and for all. Worst of all, they enlisted the aid of the notorious Situationist International, and ran off ten thousand copies of a lengthy pamphlet which poured shit on student life and loves (and a few other things).

THE RETURN OF THE DURUTTI COLUMN

OF STUDENT POVERTY

When this was handed out at the official ceremony marking the beginning of the academic year, only de Gaulle was unaffected. The press—local, national and international—had a field-day. It took three weeks for the local Party of Order—from right-wing students to the official left, via Alsatian mill-owners—to eject these fanatics. The union was closed by a court order on the 14th of December. The judge's summing-up was disarmingly lucid:

> *The accused have never denied the charge of misusing the funds of the students' union. Indeed, they openly admit to having made the union pay some £500 for the printing and distribution of 10,000 pamphlets, not to mention the cost of other literature inspired by "Internationale Situationniste". These publications express ideas and aspirations which, to put it mildly, have nothing to do with the aims of a student union. One has only to read what the accused have written, for it to be obvious that these five students, scarcely more than adolescents, lacking all experience of real life, their minds confused by ill-digested philosophical, social, political and economic theories, and perplexed by the drab monotony of their everyday life, make the empty, arrogant and pathetic claim to pass definitive judgements, sinking to outright abuse, on their fellow-students, their teachers, God, religion, the clergy, the governments and political systems of the whole world. Rejecting all morality and restraint, these cynics do not hesitate to commend theft, the destruction of scholarship, the abolition of work, total subversion and a world-wide proletarian revolution with "unlicensed pleasure" as its only goal.*
>
> *In view of their basically anarchist character, these theories and propaganda are eminently noxious. Their wide diffusion in both student circles and among the general public, by the local, national and foreign press, are a threat to the morality, the studies, the reputation and thus the very future of the students of the University of Strasbourg.*

The phenomena of revolt, preceding the Strasbourg explosion have been adequately delt with in the pamphlet of which portions are reprinted ,pages 12,13. No use repeating. However we will have a good look at significant developments ever since.

(See next page.)

Keiner Partei dürfen wir vertrauen!

Berlin, January. Here, to understand the sudden upheaval of the summer and fall, we have appreciate two representative lines. The Horror kommunes and S.D.S , to be compared with respectively Abbie Hoffmans NY Provos (see page 12) and American S.D.S.

The horror kommune, although raising havoc, has rather blurred the issues, in an ideology of confusion, following the confusion of ideoligies. Intending to horrify the square world, they hardly succeeded in being funny with their costumery and sub-sexual revolution that had to be performed while all the rest was still in place. They got lost in the web of legalistic explanations: why one of their members could not have thrown a stone during the anti-shah demonstration where he should have thrown it in the first place. Likewise their anarchistic outlooks were obscured by a loud acclamation of the cultural revolution and super bureaucratic chairman Maos redbook.

S.D.S. however, rising from a youth subsidiary of the Socialist party, turned finally against their fathers, their academical factories and their obsolete professors. It formulated a confused but in its partiality, an often true analysis: The task of the student since he is more informed and cannot make the revolution by himself (after all), is to raise and organize the conciousness of all who are repressed thus creating the revolutionary class. Knowing also, however that to be positivist now would only lead to further manipulation. Opposing all political parties (but not the party system with its' inevitable manipulation), they espouse vaguely, ideas of workers' councils, soviets and do realize the necessity of a workers'alliance on common terms. (compare Japans' Zengakeren) They know the last admissable profession is to be a revolutionary.

Due, however, to their socialistic descendance, they still reason within 19th century terms of state control; The "revolutionary"party. They acclaim, foolishly like Godard the state-engendered cultural revolution and take Lubars on Jugoslavias' illusory self-management for revolutionary. They practice a schizophrenic conciousness, living in two worlds, on one hand: the state, culture, leadership (Dutchke, the German Mario de Savio) and the family on the other: revolution, the refusal of the old order. They still have to learn that the basis of the old world is separation and partial truth.

Thousands in Poland Fight Police

Warsaw March. The events of this month prove our former analysis (see"10 days"pamphlet.) The state capitalistic bureaucracy, denounced in 1965 by two brillant students, Kuron and Modzelewski (son of party bureaucrats!) in their "Open Letter to the Workers Party," and did not fail to imprison them again, as soon as opposition broke into the streets. As our two comrades affirmed, it was necessary to abolish the present system of production and social relations and hereto "revolution is unavoidable." This consciousness now has reached the breaking point. Students supported in fact by adult workers include solidarity messages from the rolling-stock factory in Wroclaw, do not claim a return to the old order, but on the contrary, a relization of a revolutionary society composed of free individuals. They finally took to the streets. Invariably, however, the totalitarian state bureaucracies, U.S.S.R. China (see our pamphlet-"Shattering Point of Ideology in China") and now, Poland have to take recourse to the most savage repression. Youth in revolt are termed and treated as hooligans, i.e., ministeries do exist to fight this delinquancy that consists in wanting true freedom instead of the bourgeois morality of the fucking family, of work and the party.

The proprietors of the state Gomulka and his bunch, take recourse to some idiological tinkering. Thus the Zionist plot is discovered. The nightmare of evident religous counter-revolution is brought in, to purge in affect any opposition from the left. Although Polands "Leaders"keep in the same hand the possibilities to economical and ideological control unlike in China where a division led to the shattering conflicts between the ideological masters of Pekin and the tenants of the economical gravity center inShanghai, it has never undergone the same total (and totalitarian) eradication of all traces of religious and racial minorities. As a consequence an exaggeration of a Zionist threat would backfire immediately. (See N.Y. Times, March 26th). Neither does Poland have Chinese walls behind which schoolchildren can be massively drilled into a redbook waving appearance of revolution and progroms so-called counter-revolutionary minorities can be waged. Nor can it boast an independance from its Russian benefactors On the contrary, changes in the distribution process, due to a relativestate of abundance, imposed a loosening of the economical ham-strings and a widening of contacts with the West. Thus the currents might be irreversible since the problem in the East is not so much to define the aims of revolution, but to learn how to fight for them. In the West struggle may be easy, but the goals are left obscure or ideological in the Eastern bureaucracies there are no illusions about what is being fought for, hence the bitterness of the struggle In the East the main task is The proletarian critique of the dictatorship of the proletariat next to devising the forms revolution must take in the immediate future.

TORINO, March. Three months of sustained agitation at this university succeeded in spreading a new spirit of revolt over 25 cities in Italy, climaxing in the Roman Head-mashing story. What started as a partial protest against the usual manipulation of student life, (dislocation of dormitories, obsolescence of facilities and programs, sexual repression) grew into the comprehensive awareness of the oppressive nature of actual society as a whole. The agents of this transition, as in Strasbourg, have been associates of the situationist international. As a matter of fact, they are applying the same methods and even the Italian version of the pamphlet. Thus our friends (with their friends: 30) in an effort to materialise their demands, managed to knock down the door of the deans office, and told him what he was, a schmuck. The tone of the revolt was set. An agitation committee arose. Study groups tried to grasp a coherent picture of their problems, in terms of quality of life, cultural exploitation, university equals factory, etc. To transform their analysis in action, self-managing reunions were set up to break with the already growing dirigism of the committee.

S.I.conspirator (85 lbs.) dismissed as assistant in Political Sciences, charged with lifting a door (200 lbs.) out of its hinges.

30 studenti occupano l'Università
Un appello del Senato Accademico

NOV. 27th. The built strength broke free. The doors of the University broke down. The university fell in student hands and was to stay there till Dec. 27th. Allentrances were chained except one, passes issued only to those who practiced agreement. The study groups were continued in so-called anti-lectures in which participated students, assistants and even some late-coming leftists professors. Reunions continued to decide upon all matters relevant to the occupation. Information-commandos were sent to factories, communities and faculties: even to the ousted careerists, who had taken refuge in an old unheated administration building, and whose lectures were constantly disrupted. By Dec. 25th the insurgents counted 700. Dec. 27th. Finally, the police charged. The administration counted their peanuts and thought the Xmas vacation with its' low-tide, would be ideal to do away with the nuisance, gently, without noise. But, although heads were smashed and the university vacated, the rebels quickly overcame this one day of defeat and charged the university the next day, bringing disruption and despair to the authorities. The university was forcibly closed. The same pattern was repeated, as soon as the semester started. In spite of permanent police-presence terror, the blackmailing of students and assistants, the communist rent-a-cops and an elaborate cooption effort, which promised that complaints would be heard and charges dropped if the student would stick to the rules of the administrations game, the horrible extremists refused to the shipload of insults, anything but the implementation of their minium demands: self management by the student committees. Jan. 23., the University of Turine, after two more days of turmoil, closed down indefinitely.

Chiuse a tempo indeterminato
le facoltà di Palazzo Campana

During that week, the same kind of action spread to 25 other cities and finally caused the infamous skull cracking in Rome (200)wounded)

THE STRUGGLE IS POSSIBLE!!

Seattle, March. Worldwide struggle is going on.....yeah! However the coherence of these aims has still to be assured. Americas problem is not that no fight can be put up but how and for what. The recent Howard University occupation (cf. p. 5) shows that Italian tactics can be applied, as well for Black Power's neo0capitalistic illusions and courses in Black histor (as if it would be less mystifying than university taught white history) as for student participation. Likewise, Tuskegees black college is boycotted but so are the high-schools in L.A. and the N.Y. bronx. It shows that although grievances are the same and mainly found in the oppression of everyday life which is the real source of revolutionary potential, solutions are still sought according to the rules of the old world they should reject They are still bl... before being exploited, brown before being kicked around, students before being subdued. The point is to realize that the conditions are the same for everyone. All our lives are daily dissipated in nonsensical jobs in order to get our throats stuffed with needless goodies and cultural gadgets (from Godart to modern art) in a growingly urbanistic as well as politically totalitarian environment. While our insight is intentionally fucked up by the obsolescence of the family and religious schmucks, from the pope to Leary This old world stands increasingly on its head It is now that we must refuse absolutely this old world and concentrate on the real world, in order to produce again great men of great character, to produce a new life and great actions.

ITS YOUR TURN TO PLAY

Long live the situationist international.

Situationist International P.O. Box 491 N.Y.,N.Y. 10003

11

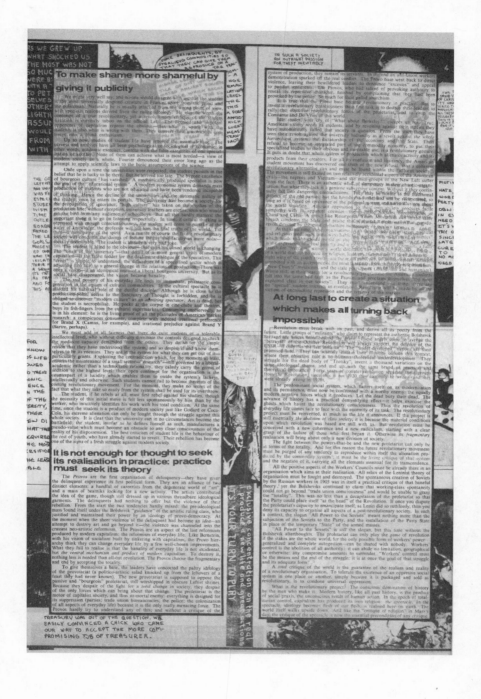

33. "How to Smash a System," *Circuit* 6 (June 1968): 32–45.[19]

Illustrated wrappers. Excerpts from *On the Poverty of Student Life* appear in this issue of *Circuit*, a British countercultural periodical. It is preceded by a brief introduction, which quickly summarizes the events that took place at Strasbourg and goes on to enthusiastically endorse the text: "The Situationist position and by derivation this pamphlet (though more purely polemical) are the result of one of the most developed and coherent radical critiques of contemporary capitalist society in the West. Their position cannot be ignored by anyone concerned with the possibility of radical political action or thoughts in the context of a developed industrial system."

* * *

33. « How to smash a system ». *Circuit* 6. Londres : Circuit, juin 1968. p. 32-45. Couverture illustrée.

Des extraits de *La misère en milieu étudiant* sont reproduits dans ce numéro de la revue de contre-culture britannique *Circuit*. Le texte est précédé d'une courte préface qui résume brièvement le scandale de Strasbourg avant de soutenir avec enthousiasme le pamphlet situationniste : « La pensée situationniste (et par conséquent ce pamphlet, malgré son caractère ouvertement polémique) découle d'une critique radicale, parmi les plus développées et les plus cohérentes, de la société capitaliste contemporaine en occident. Quiconque s'intéresse à la possibilité d'une action ou d'une pensée politique radicale, et ce dans le contexte d'un système industriel développé, ne peut ignorer cette pensée ».

HOW TO SMASH
A SYSTEM

The manifesto partially reprinted below was the immediate out-
come of one of the most coherent outbursts of radical activity by
European students in the last few years. When in November 1966
a small group of students at Strasbourg abandoned pseudo revolt
(three day 'free universities', and suchlike), got itself elected to
the committee of the left-wing students union, plastered the walls
of the city with a marxist comic strip 'The Return of the Durutti
Column', the result was Ten Days That Shook the University.
The most subtle reaction—that of 'Le Monde'—was to shackle
situationist activity in Alsace to the 'present student malaise', for
which the only cure is to give 'real responsibility' to the students,
thus confirming the Situationist arguments: the a priori refusal
to see the obvious, that the so-called student malaise is a symptom
of a far more general disease. Le Monde's solution becomes 'let
them direct their own alienation'.
The Situationist position and by derivation this pamphlet (though
more purely polemical) are the result of one of the most developed
and coherent radical critiques of contemporary capitalist society, in
the West. Their position cannot be ignored by any concerned with
the possibility of radical political action or thought in the context
of a developed industrial system (i.e. thought and action which is
derived from and is concerned with the problem of radical change
within such a system, as opposed to mere flag waving over the
bodies of those fighting on the system periphery). A more general
text has also appeared in English under the title The Totality For

32

Kids (*Banalitsés de Base, Internationale Situationniste, 7/8), and*
last year two of the movement's initiators published books: Guy
Debord—La Société Du Spectacle (Buchet/Chastel); Raoul
Vaneigem—Traité de Savoir-vivre à l'usage des jeunes générations,
about which we hope to have more in the next Circuit.

The student in France is usually attacked from the wrong point of
view, with specious reasons derived from the ruling ideology. The
radical intelligentsia (from *Les Temps Modernes* to *L'Express*)
prostrates itself before the so-called 'rise of the student', the
declining bureaucracies of the Left bid noisily for his moral and
material support; neither realise that what is wrong with the
students is also wrong with them. There are reasons for this sudden
enthusiasm, but they are all *provided* by the present form of
capitalism in its present over-developed state. We shall use this
pamphlet for denunciation. We shall expose these reasons one by
one, on the principle that the end of alienation is only reached by
the straight and narrow path of alienation. Up to now, studies of
student life have ignored the essential issue. The surveys and
analysis have all been psychological or sociological or economic:
in other words, academic exercises, content with the false categories
of one specialization or another. None of them can achieve what is
most needed—a view of modern society as a whole. Fourier
denounced their error long ago as the attempt to apply scientific
laws to the basic assumptions of the science ('*porter régulièrement*

33

34. "Of Student Poverty," *Black & Red* 3 (November 1968): 49–57.

"It is Not Enough for Thought to Seek its Realization in Practice: Practice Must Seek its Theory," *Black & Red* 4 (December 1968): 47–53.

"To Create at Long Last a Situation which Goes Beyond the Point of No Return," *Black & Red* 5 (January 1969): 50–57.

"If You Make a Social Revolution, Do It for Fun!" *Black & Red* 6 (March 1969): 79–84.

Red wrappers. Serial reprint of Donald Nicholson-Smith and T.J. Clark's translation by the anarchist periodical *Black & Red*, edited by Fredy Perlman. The first three issues reproduce the complete text of *On the Poverty of Student Life*, while the fourth issue reprints the postscript from the original English edition.

* * *

34. « Of student poverty ». *Black & Red* 3. Kalamazoo : Black & Red, novembre 1968. p. 49-57. Couverture rouge.

« It is not enough for thought to seek its realization in practice: Practice must seek its theory ». *Black & Red* 4. Kalamazoo : Black & Red, décembre 1968. p. 47-53. Couverture rouge.

« To create at long last a situation which goes beyond the point of no return ». *Black & Red* 5. Kalamazoo : Black & Red, janvier 1969. p. 50-57. Couverture rouge.

« If you make a social revolution, do it for fun! ». *Black and Red* 6. Kalamazoo : Black & Red, mars 1969. p. 79-84. Couverture rouge.

Publication en feuilleton de la traduction anglaise de Donald Nicholson-Smith et T.J. Clark par la revue anarchiste *Black & Red*, éditée par Fredy Perlman. Les trois premiers numéros reproduisent le texte intégral de *La misère en milieu étudiant*, tandis que le quatrième numéro reprend la postface de l'édition originale anglaise.

BLACK & RED

NUMBER 3   NOVEMBER, 1968

35 Cents

Number 4   Christmas   1968

Black & Red

BLACK AND RED NO. 5. JAN 69

B & R 6

BLACK & RED

6

35. *Once upon a Time the Universities Were Respected*. New York: The Eye-Makers, 1969.

48 pages. Illustrated mustard wrapper. A short preface, referred to as "Prehistory" asks, "'Who are the Situationists? Your guess is as good as ours. We only know they produced this pamphlet with a group of French students at Strasbourg U. . . . Strasbourg was a prelude to the May revolt in France and the Situationist pamphlet is its *Allegro Resoluto*" (1). The spacious layout is reminiscent of books of poetry, but the editors are clear that this is a revolutionary text: "Don't mistake this for poetry. It's only the end of the typographic error. Relax. Stop marching. Break the routine. You may even regain consciousness" (1). The postscript from the original English edition ("If You Make a Social Revolution, Do It for Fun!") is also reproduced. This unofficial reprint is mentioned in *Situationist International: Review of the American Section of the SI* (New York: Situationist International, 1969), where it was positively received despite some liberties in the translation: "Recently, the 'Eye-Makers' (in New York) have issued an attractive edition of the text under the title, *Once upon a Time the Universities Were Respected*; in their introduction, they capture the spirit many have missed. . . . [However,] in the text, they have substituted the word 'co-opt' for the word 'recuperate'; and on the last page—in what is perhaps a proofreader's error—they have used the word 'centrism' in the phrase which in the original reads: 'the enemy is entrism, cultural or political'" (34).

* * *

35. *Once upon a time the universities were respected*. New York : The Eye-Makers, 1969. 48 p. Couverture moutarde illustrée.

Courte préface : « 'Qui sont les situationnistes ?' Votre supposition est aussi bonne que la nôtre. Nous savons seulement qu'ils ont produit ce pamphlet avec un groupe d'étudiants de l'Université de Strasbourg [...] Strasbourg était le prélude à Mai 68, et ce pamphlet situationniste son *Allegro Resoluto* » (p. 1). La mise en page aérée n'est pas sans rappeler un recueil de poésie, mais les éditeurs précisent bien qu'il s'agit là d'un texte révolutionnaire : « Ne prenez pas ceci pour de la poésie – il s'agit seulement d'une erreur typographique. Détendez-vous. Arrêtez de défiler. Brisez la routine. Vous reprendrez même peut-être conscience » (p. 1). Comme souvent, on retrouve également la postface de l'édition anglaise (« Si vous faites une révolution sociale, faites-la pour le plaisir ! »). Cette réédition sauvage est mentionnée dans *Situationist International : Review of the American section of the SI* (New York : Situationist International, 1969), où elle reçoit l'aval de l'IS et ce malgré quelques libertés dans la traduction : « Récemment, les 'Eye-Makers' (à New York) ont publié une séduisante édition du texte sous le titre *Il fut un temps où les universités étaient respectées.* Leur préface reflète l'esprit du texte, qui a échappé à beaucoup […] Dans le texte, ils ont substitué le mot « coopter » au mot « récupérer » ; et à la dernière page – dans ce qui est peut-être une erreur du correcteur – ils ont utilisé le mot 'centrisme' dans la phrase qui, dans l'original, se lit comme suit : 'l'ennemi est l'entrisme, culturel ou politique' » (p. 34).

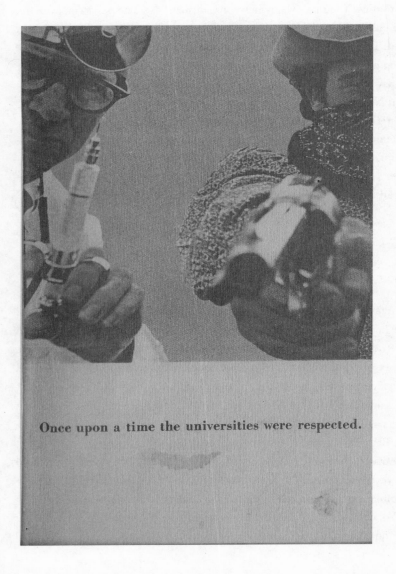

Once upon a time the universities were respected.

36. *On the Poverty of Student Life.* Berkeley: Council for the Eruption of the Marvelous, May 1970.

26 pages and front matter. Beige wrappers. A preface (i–vi) connects the events of October 1966 in Strasbourg and the student movement of May 1968. The text is followed by a two-page note praising revolution and workers' councils and connecting revolutionary theory to New Age ideas. The coda may have been written by Wendy Mann. When this edition was presented to René Viénet in Paris, the coda had been removed. The Council for the Eruption of the Marvelous (CEM), an American pro-Situationist group active in the 1970s, rewrote Chapter 2 almost in its entirety, omitting references to Zengakuren and the Provos, and replacing them with critiques of the contemporary California milieu. These include attacks against astrology, Zen, mysticism, anarchism, Vietnam protesters, and white anti-imperialists. The changes were driven by a desire to create a militant text which would be provocative in its American context. 2,000 copies of this brochure were printed.

* * *

36. *On the poverty of student life.* Berkeley : Council for the Eruption of the Marvelous, mai 1970. vi + 26 p. Couverture beige.

Une préface (p. i-vi) fait le lien entre les évènements de Strasbourg en octobre 1966 et le mouvement étudiant de Mai 1968. Le texte est suivi d'une coda de deux pages qui fait l'apologie de la révolution et des conseils ouvriers et qui tisse un lien entre la théorie révolutionnaire et les idées « New Age ». Celle-ci serait l'œuvre de Wendy Mann. Lorsque le texte sera présenté à René Viénet à Paris, cette dernière aura été retiré. Le Council for the Eruption of the Marvelous (CEM), groupe pro-situationniste américain actif en 1970, réécrit le deuxième chapitre dans sa quasi-totalité, remplaçant les références aux Zengakuren et aux Provos par des critiques du contexte californien de l'époque. On note par exemple des attaques contre l'astrologie, le Zen, le mysticisme, l'anarchisme, le mouvement contre la guerre au Vietnam, et l'anti-impérialisme blanc. Il s'agissait avant tout de publier un texte de combat susceptible de choquer le public américain. La brochure fut tirée à 2.000 exemplaires.

37. "Ten Days That Shook the University," *Neon Lights* 1 (c. 1972): 1–18.

An unauthorized reprint of the entire text of *On the Poverty of Student Life* appears in the ephemeral countercultural periodical *Neon Lights* in its first and only issue. *Neon Lights* was printed in Manchester by the Grassroots Bookshop. Also included are the preface and postscript to the original English edition, as well as détourned comics. Special Collections at University College London list 1972 as the publication date.

* * *

37. « Ten days that shook the university ». *Neon Lights* no. 1. Manchester : Grassroots Bookshop, 1972. p. 1-18.

Reproduction intégrale de *La misère en milieu étudiant* par l'éphémère magazine de contre-culture *Neon Lights* dans son premier (et unique) numéro. Bien complet de la préface et la postface de l'édition originale anglaise. On retrouve également quelques ajouts de bandes dessinées détournées. La bibliothèque de l'Université College London indique 1972 comme date de parution.

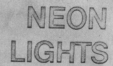

NEON LIGHTS

CONTENTS include

NEON LIGHTS NUMBER ONE

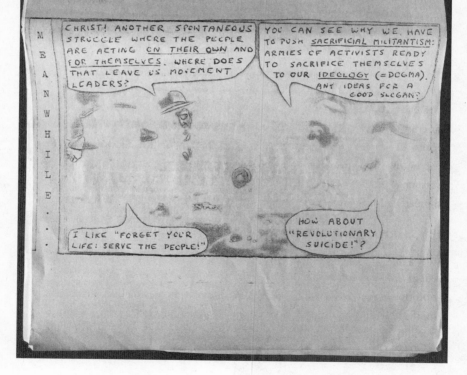

38. *On the Poverty of Student Life*. Berkeley: Contradiction/Bureau of Public Secrets, May 1972.

20 pages. Olive-green wrappers. Reprint of the text by the American pro-Situationist group Contradiction, which was briefly active in the early 1970s. Ken Knabb, Isaac Cronin, and Dan Hammer were among the group's members. It includes the preface and text from the first English edition (1967) with some corrections to Nicholson-Smith and Clark's translation, but it omits the first English postscript. The layout is simple with no illustrations.

* * *

38. *On the poverty of student life*. Berkeley : Contradiction / Bureau of Public Secrets, mai 1972. 20 p. Couverture vert olive.

Réédition du texte par le groupe pro-situationniste américain Contradiction, qui connut une brève existence au début des années 1970. Celui-ci compta parmi ses membres Ken Knabb, Isaac Cronin et Dan Hammer. Le texte reprend la courte préface ainsi que la traduction (avec quelques petites corrections au texte) de l'édition originale anglaise, mais omet de reproduire la postface. Aucune illustration ne vient enrichir une mise en page plutôt austère.

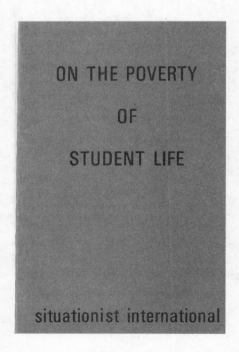

39. *On the Poverty of Student Life.* Berkeley: Point-Blank!, 1972.

31 pages. White wrappers illustrated with a photograph of students in a lecture hall. Reprint of the text by the American pro-Situationist group Point-Blank!, which was active in the early to mid-1970s. Members included David Jacobs, Gina Rosenberg, Chris Shutes, and Christopher Winks. The brochure is a facsimile of the original English translation from 1967—including its pagination—with two brief additions: a short introduction where the group expresses its allegiance to the Situationists: ("Although we are not members of the Situationist International . . . we are Situationists. The theoretical critique of modern capitalism developed by the SI forms a point of departure for ourselves and for anyone who considers himself a revolutionary. Point-Blank!") and a postface regarding Nixon's visit to China is illustrated by détourned comics.

* * *

39. *On the poverty of student life.* Berkeley : Point-Blank !, 1972. 31 p. Couverture blanche illustrée d'une photographie d'étudiants dans un amphithéâtre.

Réédition du texte par le groupe pro-situationniste américain Point-Blank ! (A Bout Portant !) Actif au début et au milieu des années 1970, celui-ci compta parmi ses membres David Jacobs, Gina Rosenberg, Chris Shutes ou encore Christopher Winks. La brochure reproduit à l'identique l'édition originale anglaise de 1967 (pagination comprise) avec deux brefs ajouts : une courte introduction où le groupe déclare son allégeance à la pensée situationniste (« Bien que nous ne soyons pas membres de l'Internationale Situationniste [...] nous somme situationnistes. La critique théorique du capitalisme moderne développée par l'IS constitue un point de départ pour nous et pour quiconque se considère comme un révolutionnaire. Point-Blank ! ») et une postface concernant la visite de Nixon en Chine, illustrée de comics détournés.

FREE

on the poverty of student life

situationist international

fire
point-blank
on
our enemies!

In the wake of Nixon's visit to China, no one can maintain any illusions as to what constitutes a genuine revolutionary opposition to capitalism. As the bureaucrats of the New Left fade into oblivion, capitalism begins to unify itself on a global scale. But those who proclaim that the proletariat has either disappeared or sold out to the system are being decisively answered by a new radical current. This global movement has manifested itself most clearly in the May-June events of 1968 in France, where the workers occupied their factories, and in the Poland insurrection of 1970. Here in the United States, young workers, through acts of sabotage and wildcat strikes, have spontaneously revolted against capitalism and its unions. These autonomous actions, which demonstrate a practical critique of alienation and all commodity production, have yet to find an adequate theoretical and practical expression.

comrades, it's your turn to play!

40. *On the Poverty of Student Life.* Detroit: Black & Red, 1973.

24 pages. Illustrated yellow wrappers featuring a collage of various editions of the text. Reprint by the anarchist American editor Black & Red, which also produced the first American edition of *The Society of the Spectaclee*.[20] Black & Red had already featured *On the Poverty of Student Life* as a serial in their eponymous periodical in 1968–1969. The front endpaper contains a very brief preface, while the rear wrapper proposes an English language translation of an excerpt from the summary order issued on December 13, 1966, by the Strasbourg District Court. According to *Having Little, Being Much: A Chronicle of Fredy Perlman's Fifty Years* by Lorraine Perlman, translation was sometimes a collective effort between group members, and other times, Fredy Perlman would take the lead.[21]

* * *

40. *On the poverty of student life.* Detroit : Black & Red, 1973. 24 p. Couverture jaune illustrée d'un collage reprenant plusieurs autres éditions du texte.

Réédition par l'éditeur anarchiste américain Black & Red, à qui l'on doit également l'édition originale américaine de *La Société du spectacle*. Black & Red avait déjà fait paraitre *De la misère en milieu étudiant* en feuilleton dans sa revue éponyme en 1968-69. La deuxième de couverture contient une très brève préface, tandis que la quatrième de couverture propose une traduction en langue anglaise d'un extrait de l'ordonnance de référé rendue le 13 décembre 1966 par le Tribunal de Grande Instance de Strasbourg. Dans sa biographie *Having Little, Being Much: A Chronicle of Fredy Perlman's Fifty Years (Posséder peu, être beaucoup : chronique de cinquante ans de vie de Fredy Perlman)*, Lorraine Perlman explique que les traductions étaient parfois un travail collectif et, dans d'autres cas, principalement l'œuvre de Fredy Perlman.

MISÄREN
I STUDENTENS MILJÖ

on the poverty
of student life

ON THE POVERTY
OF
STUDENT LIFE

A CONSIDERATION OF ITS
ECONOMIC, POLITICAL, SEXUAL,
PSYCHOLOGICAL and notably
INTELLECTUAL ASPECTS
AND OF A FEW WAYS TO
CURE IT

De la miseria en el medio estudiante

DE LA MISERE
EN MILIEU
ETUDIANT

considérée
sous ses aspects économique, politique,
psychologique, sexuel et notamment
intellectuel
et de quelques moyens pour y remédier

ten days
that shook the
university

THE BRILLANCE OF THIS THEORETICAL KNOWLEDGE
CALLED FOR AN APPROPRIATE PRACTICE. GRADUALLY
WE DISCOVERED THOSE WITH WHOM WRECKING THE
SOCIAL MACHINE WOULD BE A PITILESS GAME. THUS
IT WAS THAT OUR NEGOTIATIONS WITH THE
"OCCULT INTERNATIONAL" BEGAN.

situationist
international

The accused have never denied the charge of misusing the funds of the student union. Indeed, they openly admit to having made the union pay some $1500 for the printing and distribution of 10,000 pamphlets, not to mention the cost of other literature inspired by "Internationale Situationniste". These publications express ideas and aspirations which, to put it mildly, have nothing to do with the aims of a student union. One has only to read what the accused have written, for it is obvious that these five students, scarcely more than adolescents, lacking all experience of real life, their minds confused by ill-digested philosophical, social, political and economic theories, and perplexed by the drab monotony of their everyday life, make the empty, arrogant, and pathetic claim to pass definitive judgements, sinking to outright abuse, on their fellow-students, their teachers, God, religion, the clergy, the governments and political systems of the whole world. Rejecting all morality and restraint, these cynics do not hesitate to commend theft, the destruction of scholarship, the abolition of work, total subversion, and a world-wide proletarian revolution with "unlicensed pleasure" as its only goal.

In view of their basically anarchist character, these theories and propaganda are eminently noxious. Their wide diffusion in both student circles and among the general public, by the local, national and foreign press, are a threat to the morality, the studies, the reputation and thus the very future of the students of the University of Strasbourg.

—*Summation of the judge, Strasbourg, 1966.*

41. "Of Student Poverty," *Red and Black – An Anarchist Journal* 6 (1975): 38–43.

Red wrappers feature an illustration by Anglo-Irish anarchist, artist, and writer Arthur Moyse (1914–2003). This is most likely the first (albeit partial) reprint of *On the Poverty of Student Life* in Australia, published in the journal *Red and Black* (not to be confused with *Black & Red*, published in the United States by Fredy Perlman.) The editor, Jelesko Grancharoff (1925–2016), was a famous anarchist. Only the first chapter of *On the Poverty of Student Life* is included.

* * *

41. « Of student poverty ». *Red and Black – An Anarchist Journal* no. 6. Sydney : J. Grancharoff, 1975. p. 38-43. Couverture rouge illustrée d'un dessin de l'anarchiste, écrivain et artiste Anglo-Irlandais Arthur Moyse (1914-2003).

Il s'agit vraisemblablement de la première réédition (partielle) de *La misère en milieu étudiant* en Australie, parue dans la revue *Red and Black* (à ne pas confondre avec *Black & Red*, publié aux États-Unis par Fredy Perlman). Son éditeur, Jelesko Grancharoff (1925-2016) fut un anarchiste notoire. Seul le premier chapitre est reproduit.

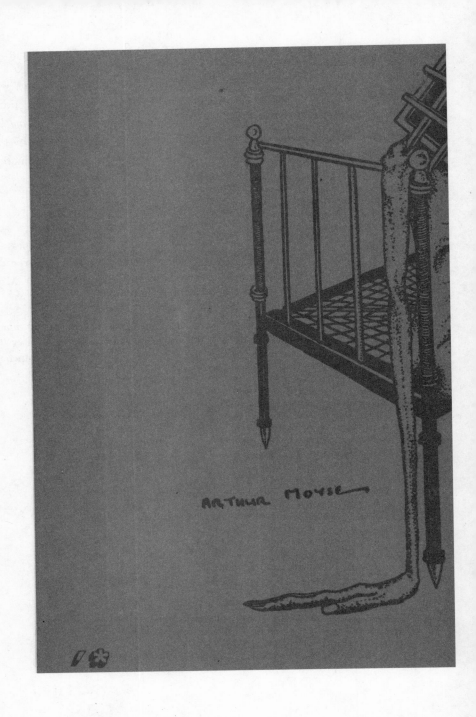

RED
AND
BLACK

N⁰.6

an anarchist journal

50¢

RED & BLACK

AN ANARCHIST JOURNAL

No. 6   **AUTUMN, 1975**

CONTENTS

42. *Of Student Poverty.* London: Spontaneous Combustion, 1977.

18 pages. White wrappers illustrated with a drawing of a police officer in riot gear. This unauthorized reprint was produced by the pro-Situationist group Spontaneous Combustion, with Nick Brandt as the founding member. The text features the short preface as well as the translation (with a few minor corrections) of the first English edition but does not include the first English postscript. The rear wrapper features a derisive photomontage wherein Harry Houdini prepares a slipknot at the gallows as he claims that the text "is not objective . . . ten years out of date . . . inapplicable to British students . . . completely negative . . . no practical suggestions . . . price 25 p."

* * *

42. *Of student poverty.* Londres : Spontaneous Combustion, 1977. 18 p. Couverture blanche illustrée d'un dessin représentant un policier anti-émeute.

Réédition du texte par le groupe pro-situationniste Spontaneous Combustion dont Nick Brandt est le principal membre. Le texte reprend la courte préface ainsi que la traduction (avec quelques corrections mineures au texte) de l'édition originale anglaise, mais ne reproduit pas la postface. La quatrième de couverture consiste en un photomontage railleur où Harry Houdini prépare un nœud coulant pour la potence tout en s'exclamant que le texte n'est : « Pas objectif…Démodé dix ans après…Sans intérêt pour les étudiants britanniques…Totalement négatif… Aucun conseil pratique…Prix : 25p. ».

OF STUDENT POVERTY

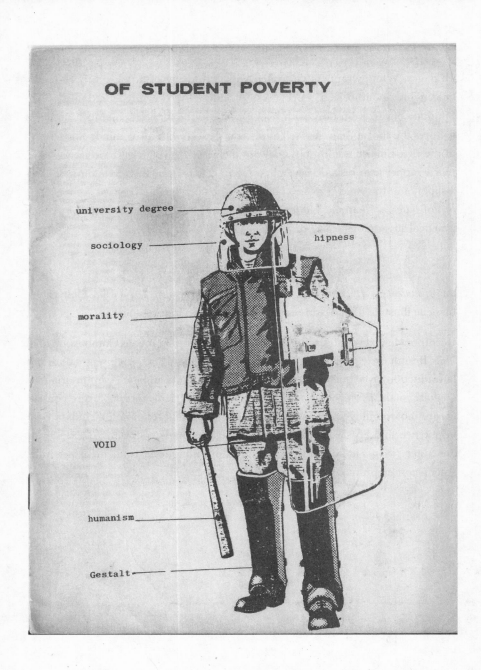

university degree

sociology

hipness

morality

VOID

humanism

Gestalt

* conspicuous consumers <u>always</u> pay.

43. *On the Poverty of Student Life*. Brisbane: Brickburner Press, 1981.

25 pages. Blue wrappers illustrated with an image of diplomas from the University of Queensland (for the Graduate Diploma in Legal Practice) being photocopied. This is perhaps the first full Australian reprint of the text. The postface by Christopher Gray is titled after a quote by Louis Antoine de Saint-Just: "Those who Make Half a Revolution only Dig their Own Graves: The Situationists Since 1969." This postface is excerpted from his book, *Leaving the 20th Century: The Incomplete Work of the Situationist International*.[22] The author, who was also a member of the Situationist International, hypothesizes reasons for the failure of the Situationist movement.

* * *

43. *On the poverty of student life*. Brisbane : Brickburner Press, 1981. 25 p. Couverture bleue illustrée d'une photographie d'un inconnu passant des diplômes de l'Université du Queensland (maitrise en droit appliqué) à la photocopieuse.

Il s'agit vraisemblablement de la première réédition australienne du texte dans son intégralité. Postface de Christopher Gray (« 'Ceux qui font les révolutions à moitié n'ont fait que se creuser un tombeau' : les Situationnistes depuis 1969 ») extraite de son ouvrage *Leaving the 20th Century : The Incomplete Work of the Situationist International (Sortir du XXe siècle : l'œuvre inachevée de l'Internationale Situationniste)*. L'auteur, qui fut aussi membre de l'Internationale Situationniste, revient sur les raisons de l'échec du mouvement.

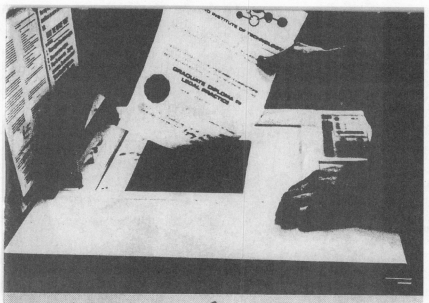

on the poverty
of student life

SITUATIONIST INTERNATIONAL

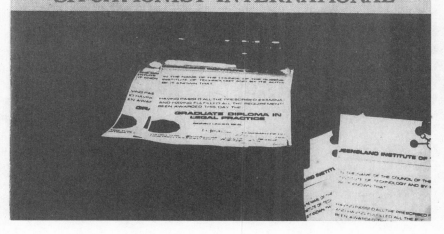

44. *On the Poverty of Student Life.* Detroit: Black & Red, 1983.

24 pages. Red wrappers illustrated with a collage of various editions of the text. This second printing from Black & Red is identical to the 1973 printing apart from the color of the wrappers.

* * *

44. *On the poverty of student life.* Detroit : Black & Red, 1983. 24 p. Couverture rouge illustrée d'un collage reprenant plusieurs autres éditions du texte.

Second tirage chez Black & Red, identique à celui de 1973 à l'exception de la couleur de la couverture.

The accused have never denied the charge of misusing the funds of the student union. Indeed, they openly admit to having made the union pay some $1500 for the printing and distribution of 10,000 pamphlets, not to mention the cost of other literature inspired by "Internationale Situationniste". These publications express ideas and aspirations which, to put it mildly, have nothing to do with the aims of a student union. One has only to read what the accused have written, for it is obvious that these five students, scarcely more than adolescents, lacking all experience of real life, their minds confused by ill-digested philosophical, social, political and economic theories, and perplexed by the drab monotony of their everyday life, make the empty, arrogant, and pathetic claim to pass definitive judgements, sinking to outright abuse, on their fellow-students, their teachers, God, religion, the clergy, the governments and political systems of the whole world. Rejecting all morality and restraint, these cynics do not hesitate to commend theft, the destruction of scholarship, the abolition of work, total subversion, and a world-wide proletarian revolution with "unlicensed pleasure" as its only goal.

In view of their basically anarchist character, these theories and propaganda are eminently noxious. Their wide diffusion in both student circles and among the general public, by the local, national and foreign press, are a threat to the morality, the studies, the reputation and thus the very future of the students of the University of Strasbourg.

—*Summation of the judge, Strasbourg, 1966.*

45. *On the Poverty of Student Life, Considered in Its Economic, Political, Psychological, Sexual, and Particularly Intellectual Aspects, and a Modest Proposal for Its Remedy.* London: Dark Star/Rebel Press, 1985.

32 pages. Dark blue wrappers. Reprint of the English edition with the postscript, "If You Make a Social Revolution, Do It for Fun!" Minimalist edition without any illustrations. Price (75 p.) listed on the rear wrapper. The "modest proposal" in the subtitle is a reference to Jonathan Swift's *A Modest Proposal for Preventing the Children of Poor People from Being a Burthen to Their Parents or Country, and for Making Them Beneficial to the Publick* (1729).[23]

* * *

45. *On the poverty of student life, considered in its economic, political, psychological, sexual, and particularly intellectual aspects, and a modest proposal for its remedy.* Londres : Dark Star / Rebel Press, 1985. 32 p. Couverture bleu foncé.

Réédition de l'édition anglaise et de la postface « Si vous faites une révolution sociale, faites-la pour le plaisir ! ». Edition sobre dénuée de toute illustration. Prix (75 p.) indiqué en quatrième de couverture. La « modeste proposition » dans le sous-titre est une référence au pamphlet de Jonathan Swift, *Modeste proposition pour empêcher les enfants des pauvres d'être à la charge de leurs parents ou de leur pays et pour les rendre utiles au public* de 1729.

on the poverty of student life

considered in its economic, political, psychological, sexual, and particularly intellectual aspects, and a modest proposal for its remedy

by members of the internationale situationniste and students of strasbourg

46. *On the Poverty of Student Life*. Trans. Lorraine Perlman. Detroit: Black & Red, 2000.

31 pages. Maroon illustrated wrappers. The cover design by Ralph Franklin pictures "A Sculpture Garden," originally published by Hieronymus Cock. It is most likely based on a drawing by Marten van Heemskerck. New translation: "The version published here was done by Lorraine Perlman. It mimics the Champ Libre edition published in Paris in 1976" (2). This is the second edition (after two printings of the first edition, in 1973 and 1983) from Black & Red. It refrains from including either a preface or an afterword.

* * *

46. *On the poverty of student life*. Detroit : Black & Red, 2000. 31 p. Œuvre de Ralph Franklin, la couverture marron reproduit une gravure imprimée par Hieronymus Cock. Celle-ci est très probablement inspirée d'un dessin de Marten van Heemskerck.

Nouvelle traduction de Lorrain Perlman, établie d'après la version française parue chez Champ Libre en 1976 (p. 2). Il s'agit de la seconde édition chez Black & Red (la première édition date de 1973, avec une réimpression en 1983). Absence de préface ou de postface.

47. *On the Poverty of Student Life.* Santa Cruz: Black Powder Press, c. 2000s.

31 pages. Illustrated grey wrappers. Pirate of an identical Black & Red edition (2000) by Black Powder Press, an anarchist printing and distribution collective.

* * *

47. *On the poverty of student life.* Santa Cruz, Californie : Black Powder Press, années 2000. 31 p. Couverture grise illustrée.

Réimpression pirate à l'identique de l'édition Black & Red de 2000 par un éditeur et diffuseur de brochures anarchistes.

48. *On the Poverty of Student Life, Considered in Its Economic, Political, Psychological, Sexual, and Particularly Intellectual Aspects, and a Modest Proposal for Its Remedy.* London: Active Distribution, May 2008.

24 pages. Illustrated grey-blue wrappers with a drawing inspired from a May '68 poster that stated, "Return to Normal." Reprint of the Dark Star edition from 1985. It includes posters from May '68 in the text. Active Distribution is a British collective that distributes anarchist and related texts.

* * *

48. *On the poverty of student life, considered in its economic, political, psychological, sexual, and particularly intellectual aspects, and a modest proposal for its remedy.* Londres : Active Distribution, mai 2008. 24 p.

Couverture bleu-grise illustrée d'un dessin reprenant une affiche de Mai 68 intitulée « Retour à la normale ». Réimpression de l'édition Dark Star de 1985, avec ajout d'affiches de Mai 68 dans le texte. Active Distribution est un collectif britannique qui distribue de nombreux textes à tendance libertaire.

49. *Of Student Poverty, Considered in Its Economic, Political, Psychological, Sexual, and Particularly Intellectual Aspects, and a Modest Proposal for Its Remedy.* Paris: Bibliothèque Fantastique, December 2009.

26 pages. White wrappers. Pirate of the first English edition, including the postscript, "If You Want to Make a Social Revolution, Do It for Fun!" but without the short preface. Run by Antoine Lefebvre between 2009 and 2013, Bibliothèque Fantastique was both a publishing house and artistic project inspired by Michel Foucault.

* * *

49. *Of student poverty, considered in its economic, political, psychological, sexual, and particularly intellectual aspects, and a modest proposal for its remedy.* Paris : Bibliothèque Fantastique, décembre 2009. 26 p. Couverture blanche.

Réimpression pirate de l'édition originale anglaise, bien complète de la postface « Si vous faites une révolution sociale, faites-la pour le plaisir ! » mais sans la courte préface. Animée par Antoine Lefebvre entre 2009 et 2013, la Bibliothèque Fantastique fut à la fois une structure d'édition et un projet artistique inspiré par Michel Foucault.

OF STUDENT POVERTY

Considered in its economic, political, psychological, sexual and, particularly intellectual aspects, and a modest proposal for its remedy

50. *On the Poverty of Student Life* . . . Brooklyn: Bright Spot, June 2018.

30 pages. Illustrated yellow wrappers. Reprint of the American translation by Ken Knabb (published online and in his *Situationist International Anthology*[24]), with one key adjustment: all masculine pronouns are changed to gender-neutral pronouns (i.e., from "he" to "they.") Some May '68 posters are translated into English and included in the text. One hundred issues were printed to celebrate the fiftieth anniversary of May '68. A public reading of the English translation took place in Brooklyn on May 12, 2018.

* * *

50. *On the poverty of student life...* Brooklyn : Bright Spot, juin 2018. 30 p. Couverture jaune illustrée.

Reprend la traduction américaine par Ken Knabb (publiée sur internet et dans *Situationist International Anthology*), mais en changeant les pronoms masculins en pronoms neutres. Des affiches de Mai 68 sont traduites en anglais et reproduites dans le texte. Imprimé à 100 exemplaires à l'occasion du cinquantième anniversaire de Mai 68. Le texte fit l'objet d'une lecture le 12 mai, 2018 à Brooklyn.

In an era when art is dead, the student remains the most loyal patron of the theaters and film clubs and the most avid consumer of the packaged fragments of its preserved corpse displayed in the cultural supermarkets.

51. *On the Poverty of Student Life*. Olympia: Last Word Press, 2021.

30 pages. Illustrated black-and-white wrappers featuring a photograph of sheep. This reprint of Ken Knabb's translation was produced by Last Word Press, founded in 2007 as the publishing arm of Last Word Books, an independent bookshop in Olympia, WA.

* * *

51. *On the poverty of student life*. Olympia : Last Word Press, 2021. 30 p. Couverture en noir et blanc illustrée d'une photographie de moutons.

Réédition de la traduction de Ken Knabb par Last Word Press, une maison d'édition fondée en 2007. Celle-ci dépend de Last Word Books, une librairie indépendante basée à Olympia, dans l'état de Washington.

Spanish

(Spain, Chile, Argentina)

52. *Sobre la Miseria en el Medio Estudiantil.* Barcelona: Mayo 37, 1974–1975.

31 pages. Beige wrappers. First known Castilian edition. However, there is evidence the text circulated undercover in Spain as early as 1968.[25] The translation of *On the Poverty of Student Life* is preceded by a preface on the history, ideas, and dissolution of the Situationist movement. The translation is anonymous.

* * *

Espagnol

(Espagne, Chili, Argentine)

52. *Sobre la miseria en el medio estudiantil.* Barcelone : Mayo 37, 1974-75. 31 p. Couverture beige.

Première édition en castillan de *La misère en milieu étudiant* dont on ait retrouvé la trace. Il semble néanmoins que le texte ait circulé « sous le manteau » en Espagne dès 1968. Le texte est précédé d'une préface qui présente le mouvement situationniste : son histoire, ses idées, sa disparition. Le traducteur demeure anonyme.

sobre la miseria en el medio estu diantil

53. *Sobre la Miseria en el Medio Estudiantil: Opúsculo Situacionista*. Barcelona: Anagrama, 1977.

80 pages. Brown cover. In a short introductory note, the editor presents this text as the first "authorized" Castilian translation. The introduction nonetheless acknowledges that "clandestine" Spanish-language editions—such as those produced in Zaragoza, Madrid, and France—have been circulated previously. The translation of the text has been revised by Angels Martínez Castells. A translation of "Our Goals and Methods in the Strasbourg Scandal," which was first published in *Internationale Situationniste* 11 (October 1967), is also included.

* * *

53. *Sobre la miseria en el medio estudiantil: opúsculo situacionista*. Barcelone : Anagrama, 1977. 80 p. Couverture marron.

Dans une brève note introductive, l'éditeur présente son texte comme la première traduction « autorisée » en Castillan. Il reconnait néanmoins la parution d'éditions « clandestines » en Espagne (à Saragosse et à Madrid) et en France. La traduction du texte est mise à jour par Angels Martínez Castells. Cette édition inclut également une traduction de « Nos buts et nos méthodes dans le scandale de Strasbourg », publié dans numéro 11 de la revue *Internationale Situationniste* en Octobre 1967.

54. *La Miseria en el Medio Estudiantil, Considerada Bajo sus Aspectos Económico, Político, Psicológico, Sexual e Intelectual.* Trans. Carme López. Barcelona: Icaria, February 1977.

63 pages. Red cover. This edition was published in the same year as the so-called "first authorized" Castilian edition. Includes a brief introduction. Icaria is an independent publisher specializing in essays and academic literature, particularly related to social sciences, by a wide variety of authors including Herbert Marcuse, Roman Jakobson, and Pier Paolo Pasolini.

* * *

54. *La miseria en el medio estudiantil, considerada bajo sus aspectos económico, político, psicológico, sexual e intelectual.* Barcelone : Icaria, février 1977. 63 p. Couverture rouge.

Edition publiée la même année que la soi-disant « première édition autorisée » en castillan. Courte note de l'éditeur. Nouvelle traduction de Carme López. Maison d'édition indépendante axée sur le domaine des sciences sociales et des essais, Icaria publie des textes d'auteurs très divers, de Herbert Marcuse à Roman Jakobson en passant par Pier Paolo Pasolini.

55. *Sobre la Miseria en el Medio Estudiantil.* Bilbao: n.p., July 1992.

24 pages. Red wrappers. Large format reprint, with a different layout from the Anagrama edition (1977) but the same content. A brief introduction emphasizes the need for an activist reading of the text. The rear wrapper lists the print run (500 copies) and the price (free).

* * *

55. *Sobre la miseria en el medio estudiantil.* Bilbao : s.e., juillet 1992. 24 p. Couverture rouge.

Réédition grand format qui reprend, sous une maquette différente, le contenu de l'édition Anagrama de 1977. Une brève présentation, inédite, insiste sur la nécessité d'une lecture militante du texte. La quatrième de couverture indique le tirage (500 exemplaires) et le prix (gratuit).

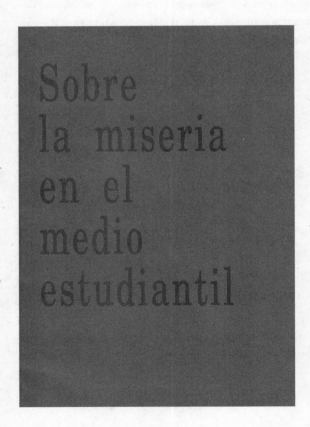

56. *Sobre la Miseria en la Vida Estudiantil*. Xixón: Agitazion/Llar, 1995.

29 pages. Illustrated light brown wrappers with détourned comics from the Japanese manga series Dragon Ball. The front endpaper contains a very brief preface which provides some basic historical context while emphasizing the text's contemporary relevance. The rear wrapper features an excerpt (translated into Spanish) from Raoul Vaneigem's *The Revolution of Everyday Life*: "We don't want a world where the guarantee of not dying of starvation brings the risk of dying of boredom"[26] This slogan would be written on the walls of the Sorbonne in May '68. The image of the front wrapper is provided courtesy of the International Institute of Social History in Amsterdam.

* * *

56. *Sobre la miseria en la vida estudiantil*. Xixón : Agitazion / Llar, 1995. 29 p. Couverture marron clair illustrée d'un comic détourné du manga japonais Dragon Ball.

Brève préface en deuxième de couverture, qui resitue le texte dans son contexte historique tout en insistant sur son actualité. En quatrième de couverture, citation de Raoul Vaneigem (traduite en espagnol), issue de son *Traité de savoir-vivre à l'usage des jeunes générations* : « Nous ne voulons pas d'un monde ou la certitude de ne pas mourir de faim s'échange contre le risque de mourir d'ennui ». Le slogan sera repris sur les murs de la Sorbonne en Mai 68. L'exemplaire ici reproduit provient de l'Institut international d'histoire sociale d'Amsterdam.

SOBRE LA
MISERIA EN LA
VIDA ESTUDIANTIL

Por la profesora emérita:
LA RANA GUSTAVO.

57. *De la Miseria en el Medio Estudiantil, Considerada Bajo sus Aspectos Económico, Político, Psicológico, Sexual e Intelectual.* n.p.: Anagal, 2006.

58 pages. Illustrated green cover. Reprint of the Carme López translation (Icaria, 1977). Illustrations on pages 5, 23, and 39 originate from "In Our Spectacular Society Where All You Can See is Things and Their Price," a 1967 poster announcing the publication of *Internationale Situationniste* 11. A plan to publish a bilingual edition of the text is announced, but we have not yet discovered any evidence this ever materialized.

* * *

57. *De la miseria en el medio estudiantil, considerada bajo sus aspectos económico, político, psicológico, sexual e intelectual.* s.l. : Anagal, 2006. 58 p. Couverture verte illustrée.

Réédition de la traduction de Carme López (Barcelone : Icaria, 1977). Illustrations dans le texte (pages 5, 23 et 39) empruntées à « Dans le décor spectaculaire où le regard ne rencontre que les choses et leur prix », affiche de 1967 qui annonce la parution du onzième numéro de la revue *Internationale Situationniste*. Un projet d'édition bilingue du texte est annoncé par l'éditeur, mais celui-ci ne semble pas avoir abouti.

de la miseria
mustapha khayati
en el medio
Estudiantil
considerada bajo sus
aspectos económico,
político, psicológico,
sexual e intelectual
nómada#7

58. *De la Miseria en el Medio Estudiantil*. Trans. Albert Martínez Pons. Barcelona: El Viejo Topo, 2008.

69 pages. White cover. The preface by Carlos Sevilla Alonso and Miguel Urbán Crespo, "Misery(/ies) of the Present," situates *On the Poverty of Student Life* in its historical context of France in the 1960s, then discusses its continued relevance. The authors emphasize the significance of student movements, providing as a recent example the struggle against the First Employment Contract (CPE) in 2006. Proposed by French Prime Minister Dominique de Villepin, the CPE would have made it easier for employers to lay off workers under the age of twenty-six during a two-year probation period by removing the need to provide reasons for termination. Protests by thousands of students and workers compelled the French government to withdraw the bill. A young activist in 2006, Miguel Urbán Crespo became one of the cofounders of the antiliberal, extreme left-wing movement Podemos in 2015. He was elected as a member of the European Parliament the same year.

* * *

58. *De la miseria en el medio estudiantil*. Barcelone : El Viejo Topo, 2008. 69 p. Couverture blanche.

Nouvelle traduction par Albert Martínez Pons. La préface de Carlos Sevilla Alonso et Miguel Urbán Crespo (« Misère(s) du présent ») resitue *La misère en milieu étudiant* dans son contexte historique avant de s'interroger sur son actualité. Les auteurs reviennent notamment sur la pertinence d'une mouvance étudiante, prenant pour exemple la lutte contre le contrat premier emploi (CPE) en 2006. Annoncé par Dominique de Villepin, alors Premier Ministre, le CPE donne aux employeurs la possibilité de licencier, sans motif, les salariés de moins de 26 ans ayant été au chômage depuis plus de 6 mois, et ce durant une période de consolidation de 2 ans. La forte mobilisation des lycéens et étudiants avait alors forcé Dominique de Villepin à retirer le texte de loi. Jeune activiste en 2006, Miguel Urbán Crespo devient un des co-fondateurs du parti antilibéral Podemos en 2015 ; il siège aujourd'hui au parlement Européen.

DE LA MISERIA EN EL MEDIO ESTUDIANTIL
DE LA MISERIA EN EL MEDIO ESTUDIANTIL
DE LA MISERIA EN EL

DE LA MISERIA EN EL MEDIO ESTUDIANTIL

MEDIO ESTUDIANTIL
DE LA MISERIA EN EL MEDIO ESTUDIANTIL

INTERNACIONAL SITUACIONISTA

Prólogo de
CARLOS SEVILLA ALONSO Y MIGUEL URBÁN CRESPO

EL VIEJO TOPO

59. *Sobre la Miseria en el Medio Estudiantil, Considerada Bajo sus Aspectos Económicos, Políticos, Psicológicos, Sexuales y Particularmente Intelectuales, y Algunas Formas de Tratarla*. Santiago: Difusión Claustrofobia, April 2013.

27 pages. White wrappers illustrated with a photograph of university students, likely from the 1960s. Pirate reprint of the text with the translation by Carme López (Barcelona: Icaria, 1977) by Difusión Claustrofobia, an anti-authoritarian Chilean collective. Includes a brief introduction.

* * *

59. *Sobre la miseria en el medio estudiantil, considerada bajo sus aspectos económicos, políticos, psicológicos, sexuales y particularmente intelectuales, y algunas formas de tratarla*. Santiago : Difusión Claustrofobia, avril 2013. 27 p. Couverture blanche illustrée d'une photographie d'étudiants, probablement des années 60.

Réédition « sauvage » du texte dans sa traduction de Carme López (Barcelone : Icaria, 1977) par Difusión Claustrofobia, un collectif chilien de tendance antiautoritaire. Courte présentation de l'éditeur.

60. *Sobre la Miseria de la Vida Estudiantil, Considerada Bajo sus Aspectos Económico, Político, Psicológico, Sexual e Intelectual.* México: Ratoncito Libertario, June 2013.

31 pages. The cover is illustrated with a photograph of a student smoking his pipe while standing across from a group of policemen. This pirate reprint of the Icaria edition is by the Mexican collective Ratoncito Libertario (or Small Libertarian Mouse). Includes a short introduction.

60. *Sobre la miseria de la vida estudiantil, considerada bajo sus aspectos económico, político, psicológico, sexual e intelectual.* Mexico : Ratoncito Libertario, juin 2013. 31 p. Couverture illustrée d'une photographie d'un étudiant fumant sa pipe devant un groupe de policiers.

Réédition sauvage de l'édition Icaria par le collectif mexicain Ratoncio Libertario (Petite souris libertaire). Courte présentation du texte.

61. *Sobre la Miseria en el Medio Estudiantil.* Argentina: Mariposas del Caos, April 2016.

185 pages. Yellow cover illustrated with a drawing inspired by the famed May '68 poster, "Beauty is in the street," which features a student throwing a cobblestone. This small format reprint of the text does not include a preface or an afterword. The translation is Carme López's (Barcelona: Icaria, 1977), with some corrections. An earlier Argentinian edition (2009) by a mysterious Grupo Anti-Universitario la Miseria is mentioned, but we have not been able to locate a copy.

Mariposas del Caos (or Butterflies of Chaos) is an editorial project that seeks to "contribute to the reflection on the current world order, its destruction, and its suppression."[27] Published authors include Guy Debord, Gilles Dauvé, Anselm Jappe, among others.

* * *

61. *Sobre la miseria en el medio estudiantil.* Argentine : Mariposas del Caos, avril 2016. 185 p. Couverture jaune illustrée inspirée d'une des plus célèbres affiches de Mai 68 (« La beauté est dans la rue »).

Réédition du texte en petit format, sans préface ou postface. Reprend la traduction de Carme López (Barcelone : Icaria, 1977), à laquelle sont faites quelques corrections. Une première édition argentine, produite en 2009 par un mystérieux Grupo Anti-Universitario la Miseria est indiquée, mais on n'a pas pu en retrouver la trace.

Mariposas del Caos (Les papillons du chaos) est un projet éditorial qui a pour but de « contribuer à la réflexion sur l'ordre actuel du monde, sa destruction, et son dépassement ». On retrouve au catalogue des textes de Guy Debord, Gilles Dauvé, Anselm Jappe, etc.

Sobre la
miseria
en el medio
estudiantil

Internacional Situacionista
y estudiantes de Estrasburgo

62. *Sobre la Miseria en el Medio Estudiantil, Considerada Bajo sus Aspectos Económico, Político, Psicológico, Sexual y Especialmente Intelectual y de Algunos Medios Para Remediarla*. Madrid: Ediciones Cuarto Asalto, April 2016.

96 pages. Grey cover. This edition by a Madrid-based collective includes a brief introductory note explaining how the editorial project originated through a series of debates and reflections on the university, and explains its goal to contextualize *On the Poverty of Student Life* fifty after its initial publication. This introduction is followed by an extensive prologue titled, "Fifty Years Later, the Misery Has Worsened," which reevaluates and essentially rewrites the 1966 pamphlet for a contemporary audience. It opens with the statement: "We might very well say, and no-one would disagree with us, that as college tuition rises, freedom of speech declines" (11). Also included are translations by Carlos Pfretzschner of "The Return of the Durutti Column" and *On the Poverty of Student Life*. The book is illustrated throughout with photographs of May '68 rioters as well as photographs of violent demonstrations involving the Japanese Zengakuren.

***

62. *Sobre la miseria en el medio estudiantil, considerada bajo sus aspectos económico, político, psicológico, sexual y especialmente intelectual y de algunos medios para remediarla*. Madrid : Ediciones Cuarto Asalto, avril 2016. 96 p. Couverture grise.

Réédition du texte par un collectif madrilène. Une brève note précise l'origine du projet éditorial (un ensemble de débats et réflexions sur l'Université) et l'ambition de l'ouvrage (contextualiser le texte cinquante après sa première parution). Elle est suivie d'un long prologue (« Cinquante ans plus tard, la misère a empiré ») – en fait une véritable réécriture du texte adapté au contexte actuel, et qui s'ouvre avec une phrase qui s'inspire du pamphlet de 1966 : « Nous pouvons affirmer, sans grand risque de nous tromper, que à mesure que les frais d'inscription universitaires augmentent, la liberté de penser diminue » (p. 11). On retrouve également « Le retour de la colonne Durutti » dans une traduction de Carlos Pfretzschner, et une traduction de la version originale du texte. Le tout est illustré de photographies du Mai 68 français mais également de violentes manifestations des Zengakuren japonais.

63. *De la Miseria en el Medio Estudiantil*. Trans. Diego Luis Sanromán. Logroño: Pepitas de Calabaza, 2018.

134 pages. Fuchsia cover with illustrations inspired by a May '68 poster entitled "A Youth Too Often Worried by the Future." This reprint of *On the Poverty of Student Life* is augmented by "Anatomy of a Scandal," an introduction to and analysis of the original text by Miguel Amorós, a Spanish anarchist associated with The Encyclopedia of Nuisances. Amorós corresponded with Guy Debord in the early 1980s.

For the first time, there is also a Castilian translation of the postscript to the first English edition, "If You Make a Social Revolution, Do It for Fun!" Other writings related to *On the Poverty of Student Life*—including "The Return of the Durutti Column," "The Tortoise in the Tank: Dialectic of the Robot and the Signal," and "Our Methods and Goals in the Strasbourg Scandal"—are reproduced as an appendix. Also included are texts by Daniel Guérin on the SI, correspondence related to the reprinting of *On the Poverty of Student Life* by Champ Libre, as well as other relevant texts. This seems to be the most comprehensive Spanish-language edition to date.

* * *

63. *De la miseria en el medio estudiantil.* Logroño : Pepitas de Calabaza, 2018. 134 p. Couverture fuchsia illustrée inspirée d'une célèbre affiche de Mai 68 (« Une jeunesse que l'avenir inquiète trop souvent »).

Réédition de *La misère en milieu étudiant* dans une nouvelle traduction de Diego Luis Sanromán. Le texte est enrichi de « Anatomie d'un scandale », une présentation du texte par Miguel Amorós. Libertaire espagnol proche de l'Encyclopédie des Nuisances, Amorós a entretenu une correspondance avec Guy Debord au début des années 80.

Pour la première fois, on retrouve également une traduction en castillan de la postface de l'édition anglaise (« Si vous faites une révolution sociale, faites-la pour le plaisir ! »). D'autres documents liés à *La misère* sont reproduits en annexe, dont « Le retour de la colonne Durutti », « La tortue dans la vitrine : la dialectique du robot et du signal », et « Nos méthodes et nos fins dans le scandale de Strasbourg ». On retrouve également un texte de Daniel Guérin sur l'IS, la correspondance relative à la réédition de *La misère* chez Champ Libre, et enfin une postface qui revient sur le pamphlet avec cinquante ans de recul. Il s'agit vraisemblablement de l'édition espagnole la plus aboutie à ce jour.

64. *Aviso a Escolares y Estudiantes de Instituto (1968–2018) / De La Miseria en el Medio Estudiantil, Considerada Bajo sus Aspectos Económico, Político, Psicológico, Sexual y Especialmente Intelectual, y de Algunos Medios Para Remediarla.* Trans. Irma Vep and Juan-José Moreno. Palma: Collectiu Aurora Picornel, 2018.

83 pages. Black cover. This volume pairs Raoul Vaneigem's "A Warning to Students of All Ages" (1995) and "On the Poverty of Student Life." Interspersed are several color images of posters from May '68. Information about the publication of "On the Poverty of Student Life" and bibliographic details about Raoul Vaneigem are included at the end.

* * *

64. *Aviso a escolares y estudiantes de instituto (1968-2018) / De la miseria en el medio estudiantil, considerada bajo sus aspectos económico, político, psicológico, sexual y especialmente intelectual, y de algunos medios para remediarla.* Palma : Collectiu Aurora Picornel, 2018. 83 p. Couverture noire.

Le volume rassemble deux textes : « Avertissement aux écoliers et lycéens » (1995), de Raoul Vaneigem, et « De la misère en milieu étudiant », dans la traduction de Irma Vep et Juan-José Moreno. Reproductions de plusieurs affiches de Mai 68 dans le texte. En fin d'ouvrage, on retrouve des informations concernant la parution de « La misère » ainsi que des repères bibliographiques sur Raoul Vaneigem.

aviso
a escolares
y estudiantes de instituto
1968 – 2018

de la miseria
en el medio
estudiantil

considerada bajo sus aspectos económico, político, psicológico, sexual y especialmente intelectual, y de algunos medios para remediarla

Portuguese

(Portugal)

65. *A Miséria No Meio Estudantil*. Portugal: n.p., c. 1970.

48 pages. Illustrated red wrappers. This edition is augmented by a brief introduction that explains the relevance of *On the Poverty of Student Life* to Portuguese concerns of the early 1970s. Detailed endnotes. The front and rear wrappers feature excerpts from *Survival and its False Dilemma*, a comic dated December 1967 that promotes the publication of *The Revolution of Everyday Life* by Raoul Vaneigem. The image of the front wrapper is courtesy of the International Institute of Social History in Amsterdam.

***

Portugais

(Portugal)

65. *A miséria no meio estudantil.* Portugal : s.e., début des années 70. 48 p. Couverture rouge illustrée.

Edition enrichie d'une brève introduction qui fait le lien entre *La misère en milieu étudiant* et le contexte portugais du début des années 1970. Notes exhaustives en fin d'ouvrage. Les première, troisième et quatrième de couverture reproduisent des extraits de « La survie et sa fausse contestation », bande dessinée détournée datant de décembre 1967 et qui annonce la parution du *Traité de savoir-vivre à l'usage des jeunes générations* de Raoul Vaneigem. L'exemplaire ici reproduit provient de l'Institut international d'histoire sociale d'Amsterdam.

66. *A Miséria No Meio Estudantil, Considerando Sob os Seus Aspectos Económico, Político, Psicológico, Sexual e Particularmente Intelectual, e de Algumas Formas de a Solucionar.* Ed. Jorge de Lima Alves. Trans. Angela Pinto. Cascais: Pasquim, April 1978.

49 pages. White cover. In this edition there is no preface, afterword, nor any illustrations.

* * *

66. *A miséria no meio estudantil, considerando sob os seus aspectos económico, político, psicológico sexual e particularmente intelectual, e de algumas formas de a solucionar.* Cascais : Pasquim, avril 1978. 49 p. Couverture blanche.

Traduction de Angela Pinto, revue par Jorge de Lima Alves. Edition à minima : aucune préface, postface ou illustration.

67. *Da Miséria No Meio Estudantil & de Alguns Meios Para a Prevenir*. Trans. Júlio Henriques. Coimbra: Fenda, 1983.

43 pages. White wrappers illustrated with a series of nearly identical prints of what appears to be Chekhov showing his teeth. In a "Translator's Note," Henriques notes that *On the Poverty of Student Life* previously circulated in Portugal, but claims that his translation is the first intelligible one. Also included is the introduction from the first English edition (1967). For the first time, there is also a Portuguese translation of the postscript from *Ten Days That Shook the University*, "If You Make a Social Revolution, Do It for Fun!"

* * *

67. *Da miséria no meio estudantil & de alguns meios para a prevenir*. Coimbra : Fenda, 1983. 43 p. Couverture blanche illustré d'une série d'images pouvant représenter Tchekhov en train de sourire.

Traduction de Júlio Henriques. Dans une « Note du traducteur », Henriques explique que *La misère en milieu étudiant* a déjà circulé au Portugal, mais qu'il s'agit ici de la première traduction lusitanienne lisible. Reproduit l'introduction qui figure dans la l'édition originale anglaise (1967). Pour la première fois, on retrouve également une traduction portugaise de la postface de l'édition anglaise (« Si vous faites une révolution sociale, faites-la pour le plaisir ! »).

Da miséria
no meio estudantil

& de alguns meios
para a prevenir

Fenda, Edições
na cidade de Coimbra

68. *Da Miséria No Meio Estudantil*. Trans. Júlio Henriques, Maria Afonso. Lisbon: Antigona, 2018.

128 pages. White cover illustrated with a détourned comic. Introduction by Maria Afonso. A rich appendix includes several documents, many of which have been translated for the first time into Portuguese: "The Return of the Durutti Column" by André Bertrand; excerpts from correspondence between Guy Debord and Mustapha Khayati; a letter from Daniel Joubert to Pascal Dumontier dated November 19, 1990; and the essay "Our Goals and Methods in the Strasbourg Scandal."

* * *

68. *Da miséria no meio estudantil*. Lisbonne : Antigona, 2018. 128 p. Couverture blanche illustrée d'une bande dessinée détournée.

Reprend la traduction de Júlio Henriques (revue par Maria Afonso), qui propose également une préface au texte. On retrouve en outre l'introduction à l'édition originale anglaise. En Annexe, de nombreux documents, souvent inédits en portugais : « Le retour de la colonne Durutti » d'André Bertrand, des extraits de la correspondance de Guy Debord avec Mustapha Khayati, une lettre de Daniel Joubert à Pascal Dumontier datée du 19 Novembre 1990, et le texte « Nos buts et nos méthodes dans le scandale de Strasbourg ».

DA MISÉRIA NO MEIO ESTUDANTIL

TRADUÇÃO JÚLIO HENRIQUES

ANTÍGONA

Italian

(Italy)

69. *Della Miseria Nell'Ambiente Studentesco: lo Scandalo Nell'Università di Strasburgo Novembre 1966.* Milan: Feltrinelli, December 1967.[28]

58 pages. Light green wrappers. First Italian edition, which Guy Debord references in a letter to J.V. Martin on December 22, 1967.[29] Collaborators Anna Bravo, Giovanni Butrico, Daniela Marin, and Luisella Passerini translated the text and edited the preface.

Italien

(Italie)

69. *Della miseria nell'ambiente studentesco : Lo scandalo nell'Università di Strasburgo novembre 1966.* Milan : Feltrinelli, décembre 1967. 58 p. Couverture vert clair.

Edition originale italienne, parue chez Feltrinelli, à laquelle Guy Debord fait référence dans une lettre à J.V. Martin du 22 décembre 1967. Anna Bravo, Giovanni Butrico, Daniela Marin et Luisella Passerini collaborent à la traduction et corédigent la préface.

70. *Della Miseria Nell'Ambiente Studentesco*. Cosenza: Gruppo Anarchico M. Bakunin, November 1969.

32 pages. Illustrated white wrappers. Pirate Italian edition distributed by Luigi Lo Celso during the Cosenza student protests in fall 1969. Lo Celso uses the Feltrinelli translation, adding detailed explanatory notes clarifying the historical context and anchoring the text in Situationist thought. In the appendix are two anarcho-Situationist inspired texts: "Revolution is Necessary" and "Call to Workers and Students." The text has two illustrations, one of which shows a CEO wiping his buttocks with toilet paper representing workers' rights.

* * *

70. *Della miseria nell'ambiente studentesco*. Cosence : Gruppo Anarchico M. Bakunin, novembre 1969. 32 p. Couverture blanche illustrée.

Edition pirate italienne distribuée par Luigi Lo Celso lors des grèves étudiantes qui secouent Cosenza à l'automne 1969. Lo Celso reprend la traduction italienne chez Feltrinelli, complétant celle-ci de riches notes explicatives qui clarifient le contexte historique et ancrent le texte dans la pensée situationniste. En postface, deux courts textes d'inspiration anarcho-situationniste : « La révolution est nécessaire » et « Appel aux travailleurs et aux étudiants ». Deux illustrations dans le texte, dont une qui représente un patron essuyant son derrière avec du papier toilette estampillé « droit des travailleurs ».

71. *Sulla Miseria Dell'Ambiente Studentesco.* Trento: Necronomicon, 1975.

23 pages. No wrappers (stapled sheets). The cover page illustration is a full-length portrait of Lenin juxtaposed with the logo of the Italian tire manufacturer Pirelli. This Italian pirate edition uses the Feltrinelli translation (1967) and the detailed notes from the Gruppo Anarchico M. Bakunin edition (1969).

* * *

71. *Sulla miseria dell'ambiente studentesco.* Trente : Necronomicon, 1975. 23 p. Pas de couverture (feuillets agrafés). En première page, portrait en pied de Lénine et du logo du fabricant de pneumatiques italien Pirelli. Edition pirate italienne qui reprend la traduction chez Feltrinelli (1967) et les notes détaillées de l'édition par le Gruppo Anarchico M. Bakunin (1969).

72. *Della Miseria Nell'Ambiente Studentesco*. Turin: Nautilus, 1988.

28 pages. Illustrated yellow wrappers. Reprints the Feltrinelli translation but omits all explanatory notes. This edition includes a brief introduction liberally adapted from the book *Ben Venga Maggio e'l Gonfalon Selvaggio!* [*Come Well, May, and Wildness!*] by Mario Lippolis, published the year before. The title references a fifteenth-century poem *"Ben Venga Maggio"* ["Come May"] by Angelo Poliziano. There are two or three small illustrations in the text.

* * *

72. *Della miseria nell'ambiente studentesco*. Turin : Nautilus, 1988. 28 p. Couverture illustrée jaune.

Réédition qui reprend la traduction italienne chez Feltrinelli mais omet toute note explicative. Brève note d'introduction librement adaptée de *Ben venga maggio e'l gonfalon Selvaggio !* de Mario Lippolis, paru l'année précédente. Le titre de l'ouvrage est inspiré du poème italien du XVème siècle « Ben venga maggio » par Angelo Poliziano. Trois modestes illustrations sont présentes dans le texte.

73. *Della Miseria Nell'Ambiente Studentesco*. Turin: Nautilus, April 1995.

46 pages. Green wrappers illustrated with excerpts from the détourned comic strip "Survival and Its False Dilemma." The translation is identical to the 1988 edition, without the introduction. In lieu of illustrations, eight central pages feature eleven photographs from the May '68 riots.

* * *

73. *Della miseria nell'ambiente studentesco*. Turin : Nautilus, avril 1995. 46 p. Couverture verte illustrée d'extraits de la bande dessinée détournée « La survie et sa fausse contestation ».

Nouvelle édition chez Nautilus. La traduction est identique à celle de l'édition de 1988, mais ne reprend pas la note d'introduction. Au lieu d'illustrations dans le texte, on retrouve, dans les huit pages centrales du livre, une douzaine de photographies de Mai 1968.

German

(Germany, Switzerland)

74. *Das Elend der Studenten*. Berlin: Situationistische Internationale, June 1968.[30]

28 pages. Grey wrappers illustrated with a détournement of "Jesus Risen Between Saints Andrew and Longinus," a 1472 print by Andrea Mantegna.[31] This first German translation—which is more of a loose adaptation of the original pamphlet—was published in West Berlin. Guy Debord references it in a letter to J.V. Martin from December 22, 1967: "We now have reliable contacts in Berlin that are working on a translation of *On the Poverty of Student Life* and other texts."[32] The text is augmented by explanatory notes. The first, dated June 1968, situates the text in its historical context of France in the 1960s. It also mentions the publication of *The Society of the Spectacle*.[33] Another note discusses the concept of the spectacle.

* * *

Allemand

(Allemagne, Suisse)

74. *Das Elend der Studenten*. Berlin : Situationistische Internationale, juin 1968. 28 p. Couverture grise illustrée d'un détournement du « Christ ressuscité entre Saint André et Longin », gravure exécutée en 1472 par Andrea Mantegna.

Edition originale allemande publiée à Berlin-Ouest, à laquelle Guy Debord fait référence dans une lettre à J.V. Martin du 22 Décembre 1967 : « Nous avons maintenant des contacts solides à Berlin, qui traduisent *La misère* et d'autres textes ». Il s'agit en fait d'une adaptation libre du pamphlet strasbourgeois. Le texte est enrichi de deux notes explicatives. La première, datée du 1er juin 1968, situe le texte dans son contexte historique. Elle mentionne également la parution de *La société du spectacle*. La seconde présente le concept de spectacle.

75. *Das Elend der Studenten und der Beginn einer Epoche*. Düsseldorf: Projektgruppe Gegengesellschaft, September 1970.

39 pages. Grey wrappers are illustrated with a photograph of a large gathering of students. This anonymous German translation is more faithful to the original text. It is augmented by a few illustrations, including two photos of student demonstrations. There are also partial translations of two texts by Raoul Vaneigem that were published in *Internationale Situationniste* 12 (September 1969), the journal's final issue: "The Beginning of an Epoch" and "Notice to the Civilized Regarding Generalized Self-Management." The last few pages list postal addresses of the Situationist International in France, Italy, Denmark, and the United States, as well as the latest publications by Debord, Vaneigem, and Viénet.

* * *

75. *Das Elend der Studenten und der Beginn einer Epoche*. Düsseldorf : Projektgruppe Gegengesellschaft, septembre 1970. 39 p. Couverture grise illustrée d'une photographie d'un large groupe d'étudiants.

Seconde édition allemande et nouvelle traduction anonyme, beaucoup plus fidèle au texte original. L'ouvrage est enrichi de quelques illustrations, dont deux photographies de manifestations étudiantes. On retrouve également la traduction de deux textes parus dans le douzième et dernier numéro de la revue *Internationale Situationniste* en septembre 1969 : « Le commencement d'une époque » (extraits) et « Avis aux civilisés relativement à l'autogestion généralisée » par Raoul Vaneigem. Les dernières pages recensent les adresses de l'Internationale Situationniste (en France, en Italie, au Danemark, et aux États-Unis) ainsi que les ouvrages de Debord, Vaneigem et Viénet.

DAS ELEND DER STUDENTEN
UND DER BEGINN EINER EPOCHE

Situationistische Internationale   1,60

76. *Über das Elend im Studentenmilieu, Betrachtet unter seinen Okonomischen, Politischen, Psychologischen, Sexuellen und Besonders Intellektuellen Aspekten und über Einige Mittel, Diesem Abzuhelfen.* Ed. and trans. Pierre Gallissaires. Hamburg: Nautilus, 1977.

71 pages. Illustrated red cover depicting an autonomous floating hand placing a jackhammer above a hole inside of a severed head. The text is followed by several translations and other documents: "Our Goals and Methods in the Strasbourg Scandal"; a piece on the exclusion of the "Garnaultins" (Strasbourg students who had initially been close to the Situationists); a poster of "The Return of the Durutti Column"; and correspondence between Mustapha Khayati and Gérard Lebovici regarding the reprint of the Strasbourg pamphlet by Champ Libre in 1976. At the end of the book are public announcements for German translations of articles from *Internationale Situationniste* as well as for *The Revolution of Everyday Life*.[34]

* * *

76. *Über das Elend im Studentenmilieu, betrachtet unter seinen ökonomischen, politischen, psychologischen, sexuellen und besonders intellektuellen Aspekten und über einige Mittel, diesem Abzuhelfen.* Hambourg : Nautilus, 1977. 71 p. Couverture rouge illustrée représentant une main anonyme, suspendue, qui place un marteau-piqueur au-dessus du trou d'une tête coupée.

Édité par l'anarchiste Pierre Gallissaires, qui fait également office de traducteur, le texte est suivi de traductions de plusieurs autres documents : du tract-affiche « Le retour de la colonne Durutti », du texte « Nos buts et nos méthodes dans le scandale de Strasbourg », du tract d'exclusion des « garnaultins », et de la correspondance entre Mustapha Khayati et Gérard Lebovici autour de la réédition du pamphlet strasbourgeois chez Champ Libre en 1976. En fin d'ouvrage, on trouve des annonces publicitaires pour la traduction allemande d'articles de la revue *Internationale Situationniste* ainsi que du *Traité de savoir-vivre à l'usage des jeunes générations.*

77. *Das Elend der Studenten und der Beginn einer Epoche.* Lucerne: Libertaire, 1990.

44 pages. Orange wrappers illustrated with a photograph of students. Pirate of the 1970 edition by Projektgruppe Gegengesellschaft. The layout is slightly different, but the translations and illustrations are identical.

* * *

77. *Das Elend der Studenten und der Beginn einer Epoche.* Lucerne : Libertaire, 1990. 44 p. Couverture orange illustrée d'une photographie d'étudiants.

Réédition sauvage de l'édition de 1970 par Projektgruppe Gegengesellschaft. La mise en page est légèrement différente, mais les traductions et illustrations sont identiques.

78. *Über das Elend im Studentenmilieu.* Lucerne: Libertaire, 1994.

33 pages. Orange wrappers illustrated with a photograph of a rioter. Pirate of the 1977 translation by Pierre Gallissaires, without any additions.

* * *

78. *Über das Elend im Studentenmilieu.* Lucerne (Suisse) : Libertaire, 1994. 33 p. Couverture orange illustrée d'une photographie d'un manifestant.

Réédition sauvage de la traduction de 1977 par Pierre Gallissaires, sans autre ajout.

Dutch

(Belgium)

79. *Over de Ellende in het Studentenmilieu.* Antwerp: Eigentijds Archief, 1977.

35 pages. White wrappers. First and only known Dutch edition. In the appendix, there are translations of the text "Our Goals and Methods in the Strasbourg Scandal" (first published in *Internationale Situationniste* 11) and a list of several French-language publications by the Situationist International. The rear wrapper features an excerpt from the summary order, dated December 13, 1966, by the Strasburg District Court (with Judge Llabador presiding).

* * *

Neerlandais

(Belgique)

79. *Over de ellende in het studentenmilieu.* Anvers : Eigentidjs Archief, 1977. 35 p. Couverture blanche.

Première (et unique) édition en néerlandais dont on ait retrouvé la trace. En annexe, on retrouve une traduction du texte « Nos buts et nos méthodes dans le scandale de Strasbourg » (paru dans *Internationale Situationniste* 11) et une liste de quelques publications de l'Internationale Situationniste en langue française. La quatrième de couverture reproduit, en néerlandais, un extrait de l'ordonnance de référé rendue le 13 décembre 1966 par le Tribunal de Grande Instance de Strasbourg, présidé par le Juge Llabador.

over
de ellende
in het studentenmilieu

EIGENTIJDS ARCHIEF

Danish

(Denmark)

80. *Elendigheden i Studentens Milieu / Situationistisk Revolution 2. Randers:* Situationistisk Internationale, November 1968.[35]

48 pages. Beige wrappers illustrated with a reproduction of covers of other editions of the text. First edition in Danish. The pamphlet takes up about two-thirds of the second issue of the journal *Situationistisk Revolution (5–31)*. An introduction precedes the text (3–4). There are also translations of several Situationist writings, including "Minimum Definition of Revolutionary Organizations," "In Our Spectacular Society Where All You Can See is Things and Their Price," "Theses on the Cultural Revolution," and some leaflets from the Council for Maintaining the Occupations (CMDO). The whole book is richly illustrated, including images from "The Return of the Durutti Column," photographs of Zengakuren demonstrations in Japan, images of a Situationist leaflet distributed in Denmark, and CMDO posters, among others. Forthcoming works from the Scandinavian section of the Situationist International are also listed at the end.

* * *

Danois

(Danemark)

80. *Elendigheden i studentens milieu / Situationistisk Revolution 2.* Randers : Situationistisk Internationale, novembre 1968. 48 p. Couverture beige illustrée reproduisant les couvertures de quelques autres éditions du texte.

Première édition en danois, qui occupe les deux-tiers du second numéro de la revue Situationistisk Revolution (p. 5-31). Le texte est précédé d'une introduction (p. 3-4). On retrouve également des traductions de quelques documents situationnistes, dont l'article « Définition minimum des organisations révolutionnaires », l'affiche « Dans le décor spectaculaire où le regard ne rencontre que les choses et leur prix », le texte « Thèses sur la révolution culturelle », et quelques tracts du Conseil pour le maintien des occupations (CMDO). Le tout est richement illustré : vignettes tirées de « Le retour de la colonne Durutti », photographie d'une manifestation des Zengakuren au Japon, reproduction d'un tract situationniste distribué au Danemark, affiches du CMDO... Enfin, on retrouve en fin d'ouvrage une liste d'ouvrages en préparation auprès de la section scandinave de l'Internationale Situationniste.

ELENDIGHEDEN
I STUDENTENS
MILIEU

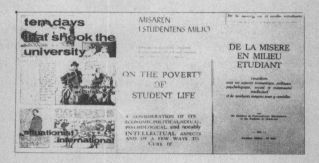

SITUATIONISTISK
REVOLUTION

2

kr. 5.00

81. *Elendigheden i Studentens Milieu, Betragtet ud fra dens Økonomiske, Politiske, Psykologiske, Sexuelle og frem for alt Intellektuelle Synsvinkler og Nogle Veje til dens Helbredelse.* Denmark: Institut for Selvstyre, March 1971.

31 pages. Pirate reprint of the Danish translation published in *Situationistisk Revolution* (1968). The image of the front wrapper is provided courtesy of the Royal Danish Library. We have not been able to find any information about the group that produced this edition.

Denne tekst er skrevet af

MUSTAPHA KHAYATI

medlem af

SITUATIONISTISK INTERNATIONALE

i forbindelse med studenter-
oprøret på Strassbourg Univer-
sitet i november 1966

Her gengivet efter tidsskriftet
SITUATIONISTISK REVOLUTION
nr. 2, 1968

produceret marts 1971 af
INSTITUT FOR SELVSTYRE

81. *Elendigheden i studentens milieu, betragtet ud fra dens økonomiske, politiske, psykologiske, sexuelle og frem for alt intellektuelle synsvinkler og nogle veje til dens helbredelse.* Danemark : Institut for Selvstyre, mars 1971. 31 p.

Réédition sauvage de la traduction danoise parue dans *Situationistisk Revolution* trois ans plus tôt. L'exemplaire ici reproduit est conservé à la Bibliothèque Royale du Danemark. On ne sait rien du mystérieux groupe qui produit cette édition.

SITUATIONISTISK REVOLUTION

ELENDIGHEDEN I STUDENTENS MILIEU

BETRAGTET
UD FRA DENS ØKONOMISKE, POLITISKE,
PSYKOLOGISKE, SEXUELLE OG FREM FOR
ALT INTELLEKTUELLE SYNSVINKLER
OG NOGLE VEJE TIL DENS
HELBREDELSE

5

Swedish

(Sweden)

82. *Misären i Studentens Miljö, Betraktad ur Sina Ekonomiska, Psykologiska, Sexuella och Framför Allt Intellektuella Synvinklar Samt Om Några Medel Att Avhjälpa Den.* Trans. Gunnar Sandin and Anders Löfqvist. Stockholm: Syndikalistiska Grupprörelsen, April 1967.[36]

23 pages. White wrappers. First Swedish edition. There is a short preface by the translators, who were members of Syndikalistiska Grupprörelsen—the youth-wing of the Sveriges Arbetares (Central Organization of the Workers of Sweden). The group was active between 1958 and 1970.

* * *

Suedois

(Suède)

82. *Misären i studentens miljö, Betraktad ur sina ekonomiska, psykologiska, sexuella och framför allt intellektuella synvinklar samt om några medel att avhjälpa den.* Stockholm : Syndikalistiska Grupprörelsen, avril 1967. 23 p. Couverture blanche.

Edition originale suédoise. Traduction de Gunnar Sandin et Anders Löfqvist. Brève préface des traducteurs, membres du Syndikalistiska Grupprörelsen, mouvement de jeunesse de Sveriges Arbetares (Organisation Centrale des Travailleurs de Suède). Le groupe opère entre 1958 et 1970.

MISÄREN
I STUDENTENS MILJÖ

Betraktad ur sina ekonomiska, psykologiska,
sexuella och framför allt intellektuella synvinklar
samt om några medel att avhjälpa den

Lilla **TUVA** serien   Nummer 1
2 kr + oms.

Russian

(Russia)

83. О нищете студенческой жизни. Trans. Stepan Mikhaïlenko. Moscow: Gileia, 2012.

90 pages. Grey cover illustrated with a détourned comic strip. Translations, notes, and postface by Stepan Mikhaïlenko. The appendix includes several relevant documents (translated into Russian): "The Return of the Durutti Column"; an excerpt from the summary order issued on December 13, 1966 by the Strasbourg District Court; and correspondence between Mustapha Khayati and Gérard Lebovici regarding the reissue of the Strasbourg pamphlet by Champ Libre in 1976. An afterword discusses the historical context in which the pamphlet came to be. Print run: 1,000 copies.

***

Russe

(Russie)

83. О нищете студенческой жизни. Moscou: Gileia, 2012. 90 p. Couverture grise illustrée d'une bande dessinée détournée.

Traduction, notes explicatives et postface de Stepan Mikhaïlenko. Une annexe regroupe plusieurs documents importants, traduits pour l'occasion en russe : le tract-affiche « Le retour de la colonne Durutti » ; un extrait de l'ordonnance de référé rendue le 13 décembre 1966 par le Tribunal de Grande Instance de Strasbourg ; et la correspondance entre Mustapha Khayati et Gérard Lebovici autour de la réédition du pamphlet chez Champ Libre en 1976. Une postface résume le contexte historique dans lequel le pamphlet voit le jour. Tirage à 1.000 exemplaires.

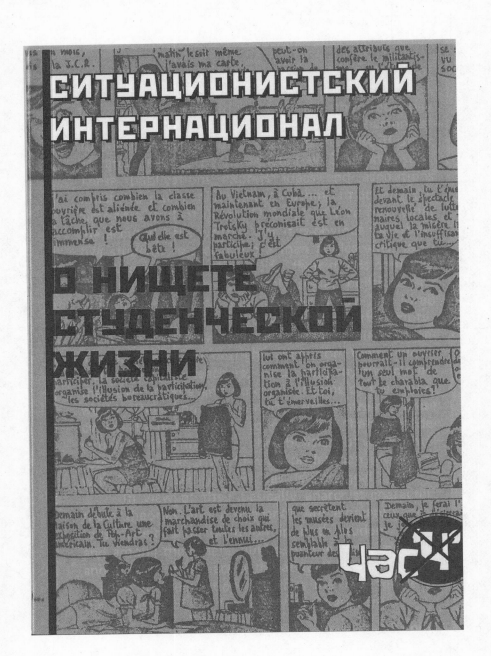

Greek

(Greece)

84. Πεζοδρόμιο 1: Η μιζέρια των φοιτητικών κύκλων. Athens: Pezodromio, April 1973.

34 pages. Beige cover. This is, in all likelihood, the original Greek translation. Published as a special issue of the periodical *Pezodromio: Cahiers d'Études Antiautoritaires*. Includes "Our Goals and Methods in the Strasbourg Scandal" as a preface.

Grec

(Grèce)

84. Πεζοδρόμιο 1 : Η μιζέρια των φοιτητικών κύκλων. Athens: Pezodromio, Avril 1973. 34 p. Couverture beige.

Il s'agit vraisemblablement de l'édition originale en Grec, publiée comme numéro spécial de la revue *Pezodromio : cahiers d'études antiautoritaires*. En guise de préface, on retrouve le texte « Nos buts et nos méthodes dans le scandale de Strasbourg ».

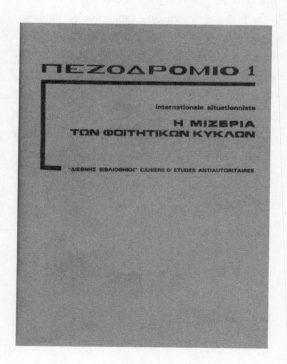

85. Για την αθλιότητα των φοιτητικών κύκλων. Trans. Nikos V. Alexious and Dionysēs Chalkias. Athens: Eleftheros Typos, 1992.

72 pages. Yellow cover. The text is followed by the postscript to the original English edition ("If You Want to Make a Social Revolution, Do It for Fun") as well as an appendix that includes the following documents: "Our Goals and Methods in the Strasbourg Scandal"; "The Return of the Durutti Column"; covers from English, Swedish, American, Spanish, and French editions; and a fake obituary of Guy Debord, dated January 3, 1967, which was distributed by Strasbourg students whom Debord had separated from at the end of 1966 (the infamous "Garnaultins"). The entire text is translated into Greek except for "The Return of the Durutti Column," which interestingly is translated into Italian.

* * *

85. Για την αθλιότητα των φοιτητικών κύκλων. Athènes: Eleftheros Typos, 1992. 72 p. Couverture jaune.

Traduction de Nikos V. Alexious et Dionysēs Chalkias. Le texte est suivi de la postface anglaise (« Si vous faites une révolution sociale, faites-la pour le plaisir ») ainsi que d'une annexe regroupant les documents suivants: « Nos buts et nos méthodes dans le scandale de Strasbourg »; « Le retour de la colonne Durutti » ; les couvertures des éditions anglaise, suédoise, américaine, espagnole et française du texte ; et un faux faire-part de décès de Guy Debord, daté du 3 Janvier 1967, distribué par les étudiants strasbourgeois dont s'était distancié Debord fin 1966 (les célèbres « garnaultins »). L'ensemble est traduit en grec, à l'exception de « Le retour de la colonne Durutti », étrangement proposé dans sa version italienne.

86. Για την αθλιότητα των φοιτητικών κύκλων. Trans. Nikos V. Alexious and Dionysēs Chalkias. Athens: Eleftheros Typos, December 2004.

72 pages. Black cover with graffiti of well-known May '68 slogan: "Culture is the inversion of life." This is a reprint of the edition described in the previous entry, with a different cover but otherwise identical contents.

* * *

86. Για την αθλιότητα των φοιτητικών κύκλων. Athènes: Eleftheros Typos, Décembre 2004. 72 p. Couverture noire illustrée qui reproduit le graffiti « La culture est l'inversion de la vie », un des slogans les plus populaires de Mai 68.

Réimpression à l'identique du précédent, sous une couverture différente.

internationale situationniste

ΓΙΑ ΤΗΝ ΑΘΛΙΟΤΗΤΑ
ΤΩΝ ΦΟΙΤΗΤΙΚΩΝ ΚΥΚΛΩΝ

ΕΚΔΟΣΗ Β΄

Serbo-Croatian

(Serbia and former Yugoslavia)

87. "Beda Studentskog Života." *Film i Revolucija Danas*. Trans Svetlana Gligorijevic and Vesna Devic. Belgrade: Hrabri novi svet (FEST), 1971.

Light brown cover. This first Serbian edition was published in a collection of avant-garde texts created for promotional distribution at the festival "Cinema is Revolution" in Belgrade. Translation by Svetlana Gligorijevic and Vesna Devic, based on the first English edition from 1967. Includes the postscript "If You Make a Social Revolution, Do It for Fun!"

* * *

Serbo-Croate

(Serbie et ex-Yougoslavie)

87. « Beda studentskog života ». *Film i revolucija danas*. Belgrade: Hrabri novi svet" (FEST), 1971. Couverture marron clair.

Traduction de Svetlana Gligorijevic et Vesna Devic. Première édition en serbo-croate, publiée dans un recueil de textes d'avant-garde distribué à l'occasion du festival « le cinéma est la révolution » à Belgrade, Yougoslavie. L'éditeur traduit le texte dans son intégralité mais omet le titre. La traduction est réalisée à partir de l'édition originale anglaise de 1967, comme le témoigne l'ajout de la postface « Si vous faites une révolution sociale, faites-la pour le plaisir ! ».

FILM I
REVOLUCI
JA
DANAS©

1. STA JE PROGRES
   U UMETNOSTI?
2. KAD PRICAM
   U SNU
3. ISTOCNI VETAR
4. ZAN-LIK GODAR
5. FILM I REVOLUCIJA
6. LENI I VUK
7. UVOD ZA »NULU
   IZ VLADANJA«
8. NARODE,
   SPREMI SE . . .
9. REVOLUCIONARNO
   PISMO BR. 3
10. PRIRUCNIK
    ZA GRADSKOG
    TERORISTU
11. NASILJE JE
    UBIJANJE
    MASINAMA
    IZ DALJINE
12. STA ZELIMO,
    U STA VERUJEMO
13. PRAVILA PARTIJ
    CRNIH PANTERA
14. PORUKA AMERICI
15. IZLAZ ZA SLUCAJ
    OPASNOSTI
16. FEMINISTKINJE.
    POLITICKA
    ORGANIZACIJA
    ZA PONISTAVANJE
    POLNIH ULOGA
17. SEKSUALNA
    POLITIKA:
    MANIFEST
    ZA REVOLUCIJU
18. MANIFEST
    CRVENIH CARAPA
19. MANIFEST KUCKI
20. TELEVIZIJA
    KAO SKUP
    GRABANA
21. TELEVIZIJA
    I BOLESNIKOVA
    SLIKA O SEBI
22. OPSTA
    DELATNOST,
    NACELA I PRAVILA
    ZAJEDNICE
    ZA PROUCAVANJE
    NARKOTIZOVANJA
    OMLADINE
23. STA JE LSD?
24. POLITIKA
    EKSPANZIJE
    SVESTI
25. PUTOVANJE
    KROZ VREME
    I ZAMENA UMA
26. ELEKTRONSKI
    ZEN
27. GERILSKA
    TELEVIZIJA
28. ENDI VORHOL
29. PRAZAN PROSTOR
    KAO
    KOMUNIKACIJA
30. UMETNOST —
    NEUMETNOST
31. ZASTO PLEME?
32. ZELIMO NACIJU
    PESNIKA
33. NASA ZEMLJA JE
    EKSPERIMEN-
    TALNA
    LABORATORIJA
34. STA JE REVOLUCI-
    ONARNI FILM?
35. PROIZVODACI
    REALNOSTI
36. ISCEREN
    GANGSTERI
    PONOVO JASU
37. SITUACIO-
    NISTICKA
    INTERNACIONALA
38. LEVI FRONT
39. KULTURNA
    REVOLUCIJA
40. AKCIJA »TOTAL«
41. PRAVO
    NA LENJOST
42. SOCIJALISTICKO
    DRUSTVO
43. NOVAC, NEKADA
    UPOTREBLJIVO
    SREDSTVO
44.
45. FILM KAO POEMA
    PROMENE
46. FILM
    I VESTICLUK
47. POSTALI SU ONI
    STO SU V GLI
48. UMETNOST
    PRED NAMA
49. MOZAK
50. COVEKOV SISTEM
    TOTALNE
    KOMUNIKACIJE

IZBOR DUSAN MAKAVEJEV LAZAR STOJANOVIC
DIZAJN FLORIJAN HAJDU
IZDAVAC MEDUNARODNI FILMSKI FESTIVAL »HRABRI NO
VI SVET« BEOGRAD KNEZ MIHAJLOVA 19
• TAMPA: GRAFICKO PREDUZECE »BUDUCNOST« ZRENJANIN
LISTINA BR. 14 »SVJETLOST« SARAJEVO

MATERIJAL ZA SIMPOZIJUM »FILM« U DRUŠTVENOM ŽIVOTU
PROTAČASIMA JANUAR 1971.

NE, ALI GLEDAO SAM FILM

preveo Nikola Čaluperk

37. SITUACIO NISTIČKA INTERNA CIONALA

UČINITI SRAMOTU JOŠ SRAMNIJOM, JAVNOM

88. *Beda Studentskog Života*. Ed. and trans. Aleksa Golijanin. Belgrade: Anahija/ Blok 45, 2004.

67 pages. White wrappers illustrated with a black-and-white photograph of a naked woman.

* * *

88. *Beda studentskog života*. Belgrade : Anarhija / Blok 45, 2004. 67 p. Couverture blanche illustrée d'une photographie érotique en noir et blanc.

Traduction, préface et postface d'Aleksa Golijanin.

Situacionistička internacionala
BEDA STUDENTSKOG ŽIVOTA
1966.

anarhija/ blok 45

89. *Beda Studentskog Života*. Belgrade: CLS, 2008.

99 pages. Cover illustrated with a photograph of a large gathering of students. Pirate edition of the translation by Aleksa Golijanin with a new preface from Centar za Liberterske Studije (or Center for Libertarian Studies) dated October 2008. This edition also includes a translation of the text "Our Goals and Methods in the Strasbourg Scandal" in *Internationale Situationniste* 11 (October 1967) by an anonymous translator. In the appendix, there are two texts by Karl Marx on alienated labor.

* * *

89. *Beda studentskog života*. Belgrade : CLS, 2008. 99 p. Couverture illustrée d'une photographie d'un large groupe d'étudiants.

Réedition sauvage de la traduction de Aleksa Golijanin, avec une nouvelle préface du Cenar za liberterske studije (Centre d'études libertaires) datée d'octobre 2008. Reproduit également une traduction anonyme du texte « Nos buts et nos méthodes dans le scandale de Strasbourg » (paru dans *Internationale Situationniste* 11, octobre 1967). En annexe, deux textes de Karl Marx sur le travail aliéné.

Beda
studentskog
života

90. *Beda Studentskog Života, Razmotrena u Njenim Ekonomskim, Političkim, Socijalnim, Psihološkim, Seksualnim i Posebno Intelektualnim Aspektima, uz Skroman Predlog za Njeno Ukidanje.* Belgrade: Anarhija/Blok 45, 2012.

34 pages. Grey wrappers with a May '68 poster illustrating "A youth too often worried about the future." Later edition by Anarhija/Blok 45, using the translation by Aleksa Golijanin. The edition has a short preface.

***

90. *Beda studentskog života, razmotrena u njenim ekonomskim, političkim, socijalnim, psihološkim, seksualnim i posebno intelektualnim aspektima,· uz skroman predlog za njeno ukidanje.* Belgrade : Anarhija / Blok 45, 2012. 34 p. Couverture grise illustrée d'une affiche de Mai 68 : « Une jeunesse que l'avenir inquiète trop souvent ».

Reprend la traduction en serbo-croate de Aleksa Golijanin (2008). Court prologue.

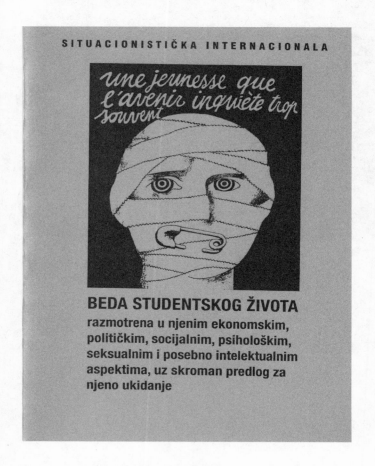

Slovenian

(Slovenia)

91. "O Bedi Študentskega Življenja (z Ekonomskega, Političnega, Psihološkega, Seksualnega in Predvsem Intelektualnega Vidika, s Skromnim Predlogom za Njegovo Izboljšanje)." Trans. Klavdija Poropat. *Časopis za Kritiko Znanost* 25, no. 182 (1997): 75–97.

Illustrated cover. First edition in Slovenian, published by a social science periodical in Ljubljana. The translation by Poropat was based on Ken Knabb's English translation in his *Situationist International Anthology.* [37]

***

Slovène

(Slovénie)

91. « O bedi študentskega življenja (z ekonomskega, političnega, psihološkega, seksualnega in predvsem intelektualnega vidika, s skromnim predlogom za njegovo izboljšanje) ». *Časopis za kritiko znanosti*, vol. 25, issue 182. Ljubljana: Študentska založba, 1997. p. 75-97. Couverture illustrée.

Traduction de Klavdija Poropat à partir de la traduction anglaise de Ken Knabb dans *Situationist International Anthology*. Edition originale en slovène, publiée dans une revue de sciences sociales.

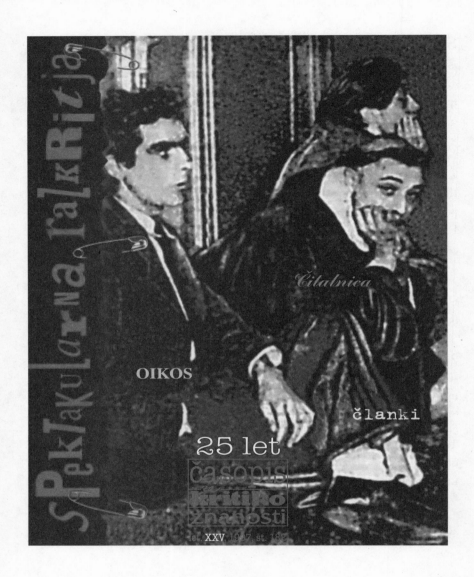

O bedi študentskega življenja

(z ekonomskega, političnega, psihološkega, seksualnega in predvsem intelektualnega vidika, s skromnim predlogom za njegovo izboljšanje)[1]

OSRAMOTITI SRAM Z NJEGOVIM JAVNIM RAZGALJENJEM

Nič ne tvegamo, če zapišemo, da je poleg policaja in duhovnika v Franciji najbolj univerzalno prezirano bitje prav študent. Toda razlogi za njegovo zaničevanje so pogosto napačni in le odsevajo dominantno ideologijo. Razlogi, zaradi katerih ga revolucionarna misel upravičeno zaničuje, pa ostajajo potlačeni in neizrečeni. Kakor koli že, goreči pristaši lažne opozicije se zavedajo teh napak – napak, ki so tudi njihove. Svoje dejansko zaničevanje sprevračajo v pokroviteljsko občudovanje. Tako se nemočna levičarska inteligenca (od *Les Temps Modernes* do *L'Express*) vzneseno navdušuje nad t. i. "študentskim uporom", dejansko propadajoče birokratske organizacije (od "Komunistične" partije do Nacionalne zveze študentov Francije) pa ljubosumno tekmujejo za "moralno in materialno" podporo študentov. Pokazali bomo, čemu tako zanimanje za študente in njegovo ukoreninjenost v dominantni realnosti čezmerno razvitega kapitalizma. Pamflet bomo uporabili za postopno razkrivanje razlogov tega zanimanja: odtujitvi nujno sledi njena ukinitev.

[1] *Pamflet je nastal novembra 1966 s sodelovanjem med člani SI – predvsem Mustapha Khayatija – in AFGES (Zveza študentov v Strassbourgu). Vzeli smo ga iz zbornika **Situationist Anthology**, ki ga je uredil Ken Knabb (Bureau of Public Secrets, Berkley, ZDA 1989). Slovenski prevod je nastal na podlagi Knabbovega prevoda v angleščino. Za razloge, čemu je temu tako, glej ustrezno opombo v tekstu Stewarta Homea v tej publikaciji. Za drugačno obrazložitev pa paragraf 207 v Debordovem tekstu (prav tako v tej publikaciji). Knabbove opombe smo iz prevoda izpustili. (Op. ur.)*

Polish

(Poland)

92. *Nędza Studenckiego Zycia, Jej Ekonomiczne, Polityczne, Psychologiczne i Przede Wszystkim Intelektualne Aspekty.* Poland: Wydawnictwo Utopia, n.d.

Illustrated yellow wrappers with drawing of a sheep wearing a suit. Polish edition with no publication information available. The image of the front wrapper is provided courtesy of the Beinecke Library at Yale University.

Polonais

(Pologne)

92. *Nędza studenckiego życia, jej ekonomiczne, polityczne, psychologiczne i przede wszystkim intelektualne aspekty.* Pologne : Wydawnictwo Utopia, s.d. Couverture jaune illustrée d'un mouton portant un costume et une cravate.

Traduction en polonaise dont on ne connait pas la date de publication. Illustration reproduite avec la permission de la Bibliothèque Beinecke de l'Université de Yale.

Nędza studenckiego życia

jej ekonomiczne, polityczne, seksualne,
psychologiczne i przede wszystkim
intelektualne aspekty

Wydawnictwo Utopia

Korean

(South Korea)

93. *De la Misère en Milieu Étudiant* / 비참한 대학 생활. Ed. and trans. Yugi Min. Seoul: Chaek Sesang, 2016.

168 pages. Illustrated mauve cover. The Korean translation, notes, foreword, and afterword are by Yugi Min. This edition commemorates the fiftieth anniversary of *On the Poverty of Student Life*. It includes a Korean wraparound band that reads, 청춘이여 저항하라! ("Resist, youth!")

* * *

Coréen

(Corée du Sud)

93. *De la misère en milieu étudiant* / 비참한 대학 생활. Seoul : Chaek Sesang, 2016. 168 p. Couverture mauve illustrée.

Traduction en coréen, notes, préface et postface de Yugi Min. Cette édition commémore le cinquantième anniversaire de la parution de *La misère en milieu étudiant*. Bandeau en coréen : 청춘이여 저항하라 ! (« Jeunes, résistez ! »)

Chinese

(United Kingdom, France, Hong Kong)

94. 論ㄚ畜ㅜ之貧乏. Ed. René Viénet. Hong Kong: Champ Libre, December 1972.

93 pages. Black cover. This trilingual edition in French, Chinese, and English was published by Champ Libre as part of the "Bibliothèque Asiatique" (Asian Library) series under the direction of René Viénet. This first Chinese language translation of the pamphlet was printed in a run of 5,000 copies in Hong Kong. On the title page, three of the Chinese characters (大學生) are deliberately turned upside down—a sarcastic typographical allusion to "Révo. Cul.," a neologism from *Révo. Cul. Dans le Chine Pop.*[38] Upside-down characters, here, are intended to reference the Cultural Revolution during which tortured victims would have their names turned upside down, crossed out, and pinned to their chests. This reference is meant to be taken ironically and in opposition to the Cultural Revolution, which Viénet calls counterrevolutionary and anticultural. The preface by Lu Zhishen (a pseudonym taken from the fourteenth-century Chinese novel Waterside [水滸傳]) considers *On the Poverty of Student Life* in relation to Hong Kong in the 1970s. It calls local students to action. Following the Chinese translation, the book "reproduces Mustapha Khayati's text as it was issued in Strasbourg in 1966, with the exception of some forty lines concerning a Japanese Leninist organization whose bureaucratic entrails had, at the time, been mistaken by the author and his friends for proletarian lanterns" (2). The omitted text, which praises the Japanese Zengakuren, is also taken out of some English translations. Khayati is confirmed as the primary author of the text, as was the case in Viénet's *Enragés et Situationnistes dans le Mouvement des Occupations.*[39] This did not sit well with Debord, who according to Viénet, seems to have requested the removal of the pamphlet from the Champ Libre catalogue.[40]

Chinois

(Royaume-Uni, France, Hong Kong)

94. 論 丫畜王 之貧乏. Hong Kong : Champ Libre, décembre 1972. 93 p. Couverture noire.

Edition trilingue français-chinois-anglais, publiée dans la collection « Bibliothèque Asiatique » aux éditions Champ Libre par les soins de René Viénet. Il s'agit de la première édition en langue chinoise de cette brochure. L'impression fut réalisée à Hong Kong et tirée à 5.000 exemplaires. Le titre, sur la couverture et sur la page de titre, comporte un « renversement » (cul par dessus tête) délibéré de trois caractères chinois (大學生 pour le mot étudiant), une allusion typographique sarcastique évoquant pour Viénet la *Révo. cul.* (Ce néologisme sera lancé par son édition de *Révo. cul. dans la chine pop.*, en 1974) i.e. la (contre) révolution (anti) culturelle, alors encore en cours, où les noms des victimes torturées étaient ainsi renversés, et rayés, sur les pancartes épinglées sur le torse des victimes. La préface de Lu Zhishen – un pseudonyme tiré du roman du XIVème siècle *Au bord de l'eau* (水滸傳) – replace *La misère en milieu étudiant* dans le contexte hongkongais des années 70 et lance un appel aux étudiants de Hong Kong. Cette édition prévient le lecteur qu'elle « reproduit à la suite de la traduction chinoise le texte [français] de Mustapha Khayati tel qu'il fut édité à Strasbourg en 1966, à l'exception d'une quarantaine de lignes consacrées à une organisation léniniste japonaise dont les vessies bureaucratiques avaient, à l'époque, été prises par l'auteur et ses amis pour des lanternes prolétariennes » (p. 2). Le paragraphe en question – un éloge des Zengakuren japonais – est également supprimé dans quelques traductions anglaises. Mustapha Khayati est présenté comme instigateur et principal auteur du texte, comme il l'avait été dès 1968 dans *Enragés et situationnistes dans le mouvement des occupations.* Ce qui n'est pas sans causer l'ire de Debord. Selon Viénet, il semble que ce soit Debord qui aurait, par la suite, exigé que cette édition chinoise disparaisse du catalogue de Champ Libre.

創勢國際成員
及史特拉斯堡大學生作

論學生之貧乏

——從經濟、政治、
心理、兩性關係
特別是思想方面觀之
及
一些補救辦法

EDITIONS CHAMP LIBRE

95. 論大學生之貧乏. London: Spectacular Times, 1986.

29 pages. White wrappers. Modified version of the original Chinese translation from 1972. The (pseudonymous) preface from Lu Zhishen is included.

* * *

95. 論大學生之貧乏. Londres: Spectacular Times, 1986. 29 p. Couverture blanche.

Reprend, avec des modifications, la première traduction chinoise de 1972. On retrouve la préface signée du pseudonyme Lu Zhishen.

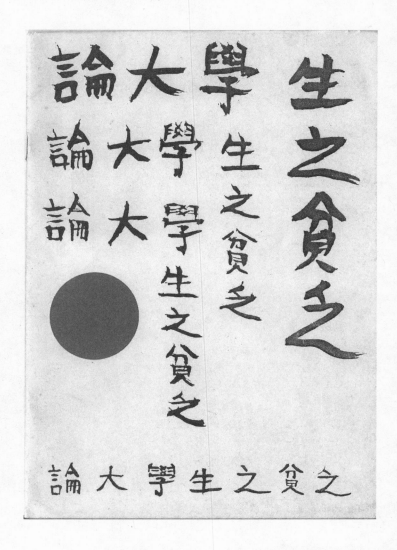

96. 論大學生之貧乏. Paris: Bibliothèque Fantastique, April 2010.

32 pages. White wrappers. Pirate reprint of the Chinese translation from the trilingual 1972 edition. Includes the preface by Lu Zhishen.

* * *

96. 論大學生之貧乏. Paris: Bibliothèque Fantastique, Avril 2010. 32 p. Couverture blanche.

Réimpression pirate de la traduction chinoise de l'édition trilingue de 1972, complète de sa préface de Lu Zhishen.

論大學生之貧乏

一從經濟、政治、心理、兩性關係

特別是思想方面觀之

及

一些補救辦法

創勢國際成員及史特拉斯堡大學生作

不留版權　　歡迎翻印

法文初版：一九六六年十一月　史特拉斯堡學生會

中文初版：一九七二年十二月　魯　智　深　譯

Japanese

(Japan)

97. "学生の情況の悲惨さについて." 構造 [*Structure*] 2, no. 29 (1970): 182–201.

Illustrated wrappers. First Japanese translation of the text in an anarchist journal. Also included are articles by Michiyo Yamamoto, "The University of Tokyo Struggle and Me" and "Nihon University Struggle Activities and Thoughts."

***

Japonais

(Japon)

97. « 学生の情況の悲惨さについて ». 構造 (*Structure*) 2, no. 29. Tokyo, 1970. p. 182-201.

Traduction originale en japonais dans une revue anarchiste nipponne. On retrouve également deux articles de Michiyo Yamamoto sur les luttes étudiantes au Japon : « Mon rôle dans la révolte de l'Université de Tokyo » et « Activités et pensées subversives à l'Université Nihon ».

98. 学生の情況の悲惨さについて. Tokyo: Rosai International, 1978.

11 pages. Yellow cover. Reprint of the original Japanese translation as a pamphlet by Tommy Haruki. Haruki corresponded regularly with American translator Ken Knabb. When Knabb visited him and other Japanese anarchists in Kyoto and Osaka , they discussed the translation together.[41]

* * *

98. 学生の情況の悲惨さについて. Tokyo : Rosai International, 1978. 11 p. Couverture jaune.

Tommy Haruki reproduit la traduction originale en japonais sous forme de pamphlet. Haruki correspondait régulièrement avec le traducteur américain Ken Knabb. Lors d'un voyage au Japon, Knabb rendit visite à celui-ci et à d'autres anarchistes japonais à Kyoto et à Osaka. Haruki et Knabb travaillèrent alors ensemble à la traduction du texte en japonais.

Farsi

(United Kingdom)

درباره فقر و فلاکت زندگی دانشجویی: از لحاظ اقتصادی، سیاسی، روانشناختی جنسی و خصوصاً 99. فکری و پیشنهادی فروتنانه برای علاج آن .London: Melancholic Troglodytes, 2001.

30 pages. Illustrated pink wrappers. Original Farsi translation, published in the United Kingdom by Melancholic Troglodytes. The translation is from the English language editions by Black & Red (1983) and Ken Knabb (1989). Numerous détourned comics in Farsi and English.

***

Farsi

(Royaume-Uni)

درباره فقر و فلاکت زندگی دانشجویی: از لحاظ اقتصادی، سیاسی، روانشناختی جنسی و خصوصاً 99. فکری و پیشنهادی فروتنانه برای علاج آن .Londres: Melancholic Troglodytes, 2001. 30 p. Couverture rose illustrée.

Traduction originale en Farsi, publiée au Royaume Uni par le groupe Melancholic Troglodytes. Traduction faite à partir des éditions anglo-saxonnes par Black & Red (1983) et Ken Knabb (2001). Nombreux comics détournés en Farsi et en anglais.

No, no, no mate, you're holding it back to front! For this, is the Farsi translation of the infamous Situationist text *On the Poverty of Student Life* (Mustapha Khayati, 1966). Although slightly dated and perhaps even superceded by events in the 'west', the text deals intelligently with a number of issues close to the hearts and minds of young Iranian proletarians, which is why *Melancholic Troglodytes* considered it worthy of a wider distribution. The present translation is based on two templates: *Black & Red* (Detroit: 1983) and the *Situationist Internationalist Anthology* (Ken Knabb: 1989). Our thanks to both.

Past issues still available:
No. 1: Fatwaing the Ayatollahs: The Kamikaze Warrior of Allah; Psycho-Geography; Satanic Film Theses; Mithra, the Persian Matador; Robin Hood and Film; The Zanj Slaves' Rebellion.
No. 2: Afghanistan; Circumcision: Three Strikes and you're out as Strategy; Critique of Zarathushtra; Dolls as Cultural Artifacts; Pseudo-Potlatch; Critique of Nation of Islam; Chess and History.
No. 3: Critique of Star Trek; Bourgeois Nature of Brecht and Godard; Auteur Theory Updated; Base-Structure –Superstructure and Film Analysis.
No. 4: Critiques of Timpanaro, Kovel, Bhavnani & Davies, C. G. Spivak; Kritische Psychologie, Riegel, Feuerbach and Critical Psychology.

Current issue:
No. 5: On the Poverty of Student Life (Mustapha Khayati, 1966).

Forthcoming issues:
No. 6: Consciousness and Empowerment Amongst Proletarian Collectivities (Voloshinov, Vygotsky, Bakhtin, and Leontiev).
No. 7: Marxist Critiques of Austrian Fascism; Cybersex; Water Disputes in the Middle East; Psychoanalytic Film Analysis; Yezidi 'Devil-Worshippers': Spiritual Atheism.

Back issues available for £2.00 + P&P (Cash, or blank cheque please) from: **Melancholic Troglodytes, Box no. 44, 136-138 Kingsland High Street, London E8 2NS, United Kingdom.**

Price: £2.00

100. ‏فروتنانه برای علاج آن‏. Trans. Omid Shams. Iran: Ketabnak/Problematicaa, n.d.

44 pages. Illustrated cover. This text, produced by the collective Problematicaa, addresses the concept of translation in their manifesto: "The translators . . . are fascinated with the Other's discourse. For them, thought is another word for translation, or to put it better, thought is impossible without translation."[42]

* * *

100. ‏درباره فقر و فلاکت زندگی دانشجویی: از لحاظ اقتصادی، سیاسی، روانشناختی جنسی و‏ ‏خصوصاً فکری و پیشنهادی فروتنانه برای علاج آن‏. Trans. Omid Shams. Iran: Ketabnak / Problematicaa, s.d.. 44 p. Couverture illustrée.

Cette traduction est l'œuvre du collectif Problematicaa, qui s'intéressent au concept de la traduction dans leur manifeste : « Les traducteurs [...] sont fascinés par le discours de l'Autre. De leur point de vue, pensée et traduction sont synonymes. Pour dire les choses plus clairement, la pensée est impossible sans traduction ».

درباره‌ی فقر و فلاکت زندگی دانشجویی

مصطفی خیاطی

ترجمه‌ی امید شمس

کتاب سبز

A few texts inspired by "On the Poverty of Student Life"

1. "The Poverty of Arab Studies" (Misère des Études Arabes / عربية [...]حول رال).
Box 8, *Writings about Arab Lands*. Beinecke Rare Book and Manuscript Library,
Yale University: Khayati Papers.

In the Khayati Papers at the Beinecke Library at Yale University, there is a written
text in French and Arabic that Khayati prepared for An-Nidhal, a Tunisian
revolutionary periodical. In this short article, he indicts the Arab Nationalism
and Marxism of Lutfallah Soliman and others.

* * *

Quelques textes inspirés de « La Misère en Milieu Étudiant »

1. *De la misère des études arabes* / عربية [...]حول رال. Boite 8, Ecrits sur les Pays Arabes.
Bibliothèque Beinecke des Livres Rares et des Manuscrits, Université de Yale :
Fonds Khayati.

Dans les archives de Mustapha Khayati conservées à la bibliothèque Beinecke de
l'Université de Yale, on retrouve un texte écrit en français et en arabe que Khayati
a préparé pour *An-Nidhal*, une revue révolutionnaire tunisienne. Dans ce court
article, il critique entre autres le nationalisme arabe et le marxisme de Lutfallah
Soliman.

حول دراسة عربية

ـ تقرير كان حول نفس الموضوع = عدد خاص عن سلامة لطفالله

. بعد الاطلاع على العدد الأول من "دراسات عربية" . نقول اجابتنا إلى ماكان قد تعلّنا حول العدد العشرين نفس النشرية

٢) ان النشرية محتواها ومفاهيها و برموزها البشرية (دون الحديث عن البرامج التي تركّها في المناولة الجنوب التي تغر لها والتي سوف ضد اليها) رجعية بجوهرها . وهذه يعطي مظهرها وانتهازية مؤقتة في أسلوبها و نوايا اصحابها .

٣) ان الموضوع عن عبر الانتشار و نظامير هذا الشكل الموّح . بدعوى أنّه أربعة الغربية تركّز كل جهودنا ط عليه . يوحي بشكل ساخر مع التخلف النظري الذي جاء ل ليغطي صاحب الدختاسية . ويعكس الموقع الطبقي و الطبقس المتدني في حركة الثورة العربية . هذا إذا سلمنا بنزاهة و اخلاص ساحب المجلة ولم نبحث عن القوى التي تركه وراءها المظهر الأولى في مارجة الثورة العربية المدربة ، وليس هنا يتسرّم ٤) ان نكون عارفة هذه المجلة لحظ هءا جزء كصولة لدفع الغبار عن البورجوازية الصغرى التي اخترته ياتجا ... برامجها و استقدميّها و انطلقت كايتنا من تعمّق ان و طلبت من مطالب الثورة الثورة العربية المعاصرة ، وتشكل بالتالي واجهة وطائفية لهذه الاهتمام المنفتح ؟ عام الرأي العام الأوروبي . نفهم عن ناشرها المظهر الثورى في أوساط المثقفين العرب الذين لم تمنع من اختياراتهم لعلّم يعد ٥) إذا ما تبرى تظهرغ يديولوجي لواقع . مضاد الثورة من وأصبح كل النّار العربي مجاربته لدوام حضارة ، ط المتمركة - ولكانت ليبرالية "تقدمية" . ٦) ان مشروعه شعل "انفال" . وسط مجموعة من طبقات علوية بادس و التخلف الفكرى و الانتهازية الأجيرة هو محاولة مفتوحة . لنشر ثورة البرجوازية الصغرى بثوب يسهل عليه تزوية . للغة . و يعطيحاها نه "جذرية" . فقد تكون نحن أكثر تسرّعية ها

لكن هذا زرى ما يلي :

٧) قطع جميع العلقات مع المدعوّ سي لطفالله بكم تماجي موأصفنا (القناصري) ويكن مراقبة الكريم والعلمية المضادة للثورة . وليست هنا لم تكون نتصل من عير على أي مستوى ، بل بالعكس لا بد نقاومه كل نقاوم الأحزاب الاصلاحية و الحركية القائمة .

٨) لنشر شال تقدي بقدي لا يبقى لي شكلي لتنا نعاديه سياسيا وتقاوى مشروعه الانتهازية المشبوهة .

2. *De la Misère en Milieu Lycéen (et Autres Scolarisés)*. Paris: Maspero, 1969.

16 pages. Yellow-green wrappers. Supplement to the fourth issue of *Passer Outre*. The text, which translates as *On the Poverty of High School Life (and High School Students)*, is a scathing critique of the high school milieu. The layout, style, and content are clearly inspired by the 1966 Situationist pamphlet. "In addition to its unchangeability as an institution, high school appears to be characterized by its similarity to the superstructural whole of society and its immediate corollary: the aberration of its physical and mental alienation" (3). Dominique Lacout, now retired from his professorship at the École Normale Supérieure, is one of the authors of this collectively written text.

* * *

2. *De la misère en milieu lycéen (et autres scolarisés)*. Paris : Maspero, 1969. 16 p. Couverture jaune-vert.

Supplément au no. 4 de *Passer outre*. Le texte est une attaque frontale contre le milieu lycéen. La maquette, le style, et le contenu s'inspirent ouvertement du pamphlet situationniste de 1966. « Ce qui caractérise à priori le lycée c'est, outre le caractère d'immuabilité de son institution, sa similitude avec l'ensemble superstructurel de la société et son corollaire immédiat : l'aberration de sa double aliénation physique et mentale » (p. 3). Dominique Lacout, ancien professeur de philosophie à l'École Normale Supérieure, est un des auteurs de ce texte collectif.

Comités d'Action Lycéens

(actuelle tendance révolutionnaire)

DE LA MISÈRE EN MILIEU LYCÉEN

(et autres scolarisés)

1969

Supplément n° 4 de "Passer Outre"

1ᶠ

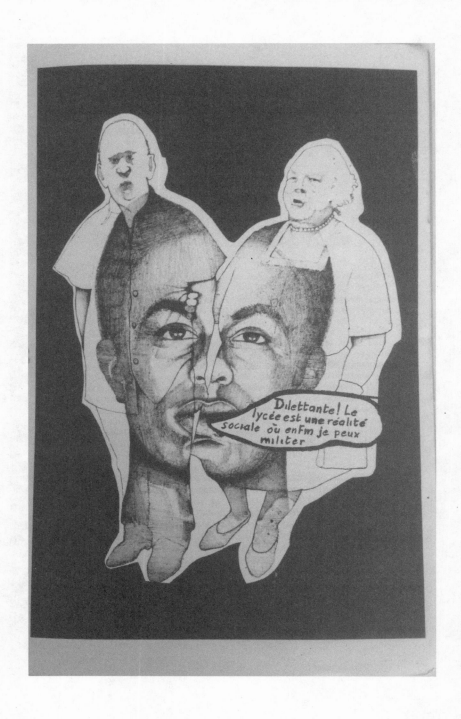

3. "Les Affranchies du Vieux Monde." *De la misère en milieu féministe ou la pouffiasserie à visage humain*. Paris: Editions les Emissions des Femmes, November 1977.

31 pages. Black wrappers with pink text. The title translates as *On the Poverty of Feminism or the Bitch with a Human Face*. Overtly inspired by *On the Poverty of Student Life*, this pamphlet contains a violent attack against second-wave feminism in the aftermath of May 1968. The text opens with: "We might very well say, and no one would disagree with us, that, unlike the policeman, the priest, and the student, the 'emancipated woman' is the most universally revered creature" (3). This clearly echoes the opening lines of the 1966 Situationist pamphlet: "We might very well say, and no-one would disagree with us, that the student is the most universally despised creature in France, apart from the priest and the policeman." The authors argue that so-called "liberation movements" alienate men and women alike by confining them to new roles within the capitalist system.

* * *

3. *De la misère en milieu féministe ou la pouffiasserie à visage humain*. Paris : Editions les émissions des femmes, novembre 1977. 31 p. Couverture noire avec texte en rose.

Très ouvertement inspiré de *La misère en milieu étudiant*, ce brûlot s'en prend violemment au féminisme de la « deuxième vague » de l'après-Mai 68. L'ouvrage s'ouvre par ces lignes : « Nous pouvons affirmer sans grand risque de nous tromper que la femme 'émancipée' est, à l'encontre du policier, du prêtre et de l'étudiant, l'être le plus universellement adulé » (p. 3). La référence au pamphlet situationniste est évidente ; ce dernier débute ainsi : « Nous pouvons affirmer, sans grand risque de nous tromper, que l'étudiant en France est, après le policier et le prêtre, l'être le plus universellement méprisé ». Pour les auteurs, les mouvements dits de « libération des femmes » imposent à chacun un nouveau rôle dans l'univers capitaliste moderne.

de

LA MISERE EN MILIEU FEMINISTE

ou

la pouffiasserie à visage humain

par

les affranchies du vieux monde

LES EMISSIONS DES FEMMES

Endnotes

1   Jean-Jacques Raspaud and Jean-Pierre Voyer, L'internationale situationniste : Protagonistes, chronologie, bibliographie (Paris: Champ Libre, 1972), 119.

2   André Bertrand and André Schneider, Le scandale de Strasbourg mis à nu par ses célibataires, même (Montreuil: L'Insomniaque, 2018), 25.

3   Louis-Jean Marty, email message to Mehdi El Hajoui, May 9, 2016.

4   Mustapha Khayati, "Letter to Champ Libre, October 12, 1978," in Champ Libre, Correspondance, Vol. 1 (Paris: Champ Libre, 1978).

5   See QCQ Zanzara, https://infokiosques.net/imprimersans2.php3?id_article=55.

6   Éric Brun, Les situationnistes. Une avant-garde totale (Paris: Centre National de la Recherche Scientifique, 2014).

7   Raspaud and Voyer, L'internationale situationniste, 135.

8   Raspaud and Voyer, L'internationale situationniste, 122.

9   John Reed, Ten Days That Shook the World (New York: Boni & Liveright, 1919).

10 Raspaud and Voyer, L'internationale situationniste, 122.

11 Raspaud and Voyer, L'internationale situationniste, 120.

12 Samuel Rawson Gardiner, A Student's History of England from the Earliest Times to 1885: B.C. 55–A.D. 1509 (London: Longmans, Green, & Company, 1896), 93.

13 Raspaud and Voyer, L'internationale situationniste, 120.

14 Gardiner, A Student's History of England, 93.

15 Raspaud and Voyer, L'internationale situationniste, 120.

16 Raspaud and Voyer, L'internationale situationniste, 126.

17 Lord Byron, Sardanapalus: A Tragedy (London: John Murray, 1821), https://archive. org/details/sardanapalustrag01byro/page/n3/mode/2up.

18 Thomas J. Clark, The Absolute Bourgeois (Berkeley: University of California Press, 1999).

19 Raspaud and Voyer, L'internationale situationniste, 133.

20 Guy Debord, The Society of the Spectacle (Detroit: Black & Red, 1970).

21 Lorraine Perlman, Having Little, Being Much: A Chronicle of Fredy Perlman's Fifty Years (Detroit: Black & Red, 1989).

22 Christopher Gray, Leaving the 20th Century: The Incomplete Work of the Situationist International (London: Free Fall Publications, 1974).

23 Jonathan Swift, A Modest Proposal for Preventing the Children of Poor People from Being a Burthen to Their Parents or Country, and for Making Them Beneficial to the Publick (London: J. Roberts, 1729).

24 Ken Knabb, Situationist International Anthology: Revised and Expanded Edition (Berkeley: Bureau of Public Secrets, 2007).

25 Raspaud and Voyer, L'internationale situationniste, 131–132.

26 Raoul Vaneigem, Traité de savoir-vivre à l'usage des jeunes générations (Paris: Gallimard, 1967).

27 Mariposas del Caos, "2017 Editions," http://edicionesmariposasdelcaos.blogspot. com/.

28 Raspaud and Voyer, L'internationale situationniste, 134.

29 Guy Debord, Correspondance, volume 3 : janvier 1965 - décembre 1968 (Paris: Fayard, 2003), 250.

30 Raspaud and Voyer, L'internationale situationniste, 131.

31 Workshop of Andrea Mantegna, Risen Christ Between Saints Andrew and Longinus, c. 1472. See https://www.artic.edu/artworks/4293/risen-christ-between-saints-andrew-and-longinus.

32 Debord, Correspondance, vol. 3, 250.

33 Guy Debord, La Société du spectacle (Paris: Buchet-Chastel, 1967).

34 Vaneigem, Traité de savoir-vivre à l'usage des jeunes générations.

35 Raspaud and Voyer, L'internationale situationniste, 121.

36 Raspaud and Voyer, L'internationale situationniste, 135.

37 Ken Knabb, Situationist International Anthology: Revised and Expanded Edition (Berkeley: Bureau of Public Secrets, 2007).

38 Hector Mandares, Révo. cul. dans la Chine pop : anthologie de la presse des Gardes rouges (Paris: Champ Libre, 1974.)

39 René Vienet, Enragés et situationnistes dans le mouvement des occupations (Paris: Gallimard, 1968), 250.

40 René Viénet, email message Anna O'Meara, September 4, 2021.

41 Ken Knabb, "Confessions of a Mild-Mannered Enemy of the State," in Public Secrets: Collected Skirmishes of Ken Knabb (Berkeley: Bureau of Public Secrets, 1997), http://www.bopsecrets.org/PS/autobio.htm.

42 "Manifest," Problematicaa, http://problematicaa.com/m/a-manifesto-for-problematica/.

Glossary

AFGES (Association Fédérative Générale des Étudiants de Strasbourg): Founded in 1923, the Strasbourg-based student union acts as the local arm of the nationwide UNEF (Union Nationale des Étudiants de France).

Anti-copyright: The original text of *On the Poverty of Student Life* states that "no copyright is held on this text. It can be reproduced by anyone in any form whatsoever." Thus, available reproductions of the text are without express permission from the authors.

Détourned (détournement): Short for "détournement of preexisting aesthetic elements." The integration of present or past artistic productions into a superior construction of a milieu. In this sense, there can be no Situationist painting or music but only a Situationist use of those means. In a more elementary sense, détournement within the old cultural spheres is a method of propaganda, a method which reveals the wearing out and loss of importance of those spheres.

Garnaultins: Strasbourg students who had initially been close to the Situationists and were later marginalized by the SI. The word "Garnaultins" was derived from the name of Jean Garnault, one of the Strasbourg students involved in the "Strasbourg Scandal" of 1966.

Internationale Situationniste: The main vector for Situationist ideas, the periodical ran twelve issues between 1958 and 1969. The text "Our Goals and Methods in the Strasbourg Scandal," which clarifies the context and motivations behind the publication of *On the Poverty of Student Life*, was published in issue #11 in October 1967.

May '68: A series of events that took place across France in May of 1968, beginning with student activism, and leading not only to a general strike but to international revolutionary agitation. Sometimes evaluated as a failure, May '68 is often also seen as an origin-point for many protest movements that followed.

Pirate edition: A nearly identical reproduction of an existing text.

Revolution of Everyday Life, The: The seminal work of Situationist Raoul Vaneigem, this influential text calls for the youth of France to consider the banality of their everyday lives and theorizes ways in which they may be able to start truly living.

Situationist: Relating to the theory or practical activity of constructing situations. One who engages in the construction of situations. A member of the Situationist International.

Situationist International (SI): Founded in Cosio d'Arroscia in 1957, this organization of theoreticians and artists sought to transcend the radical avant-garde approaches of the Surrealists, Dadaists, and Lettrists. The SI piloted key concepts like *spectacle*, *détournement*, and the *revolution of everyday life*. It was dissolved in 1972.

Society of the Spectacle, The: Guy Debord's magnum opus, published in 1967, has remained a highly influential text. In it, he considers the alienating ramifications of an image-dominated society and theorizes that "in modern societies where modern conditions of production prevail . . . everything that was directly lived has moved away into a representation." The author was one of the founders of the Situationist International.

Strasbourg Scandal: In 1966, a handful of students intent on causing disruption were miraculously elected to lead the University of Strasbourg's student council. The Situationists saw an opening; Mustapha Khayati put pen to paper and wrote the bulk of what would soon be advertised as "the most scandalous pamphlet of the century." Ten thousand copies were printed, using up the entire budget of the student union for the academic year, then distributed at the university's convocation ceremony in November 1966. A scandal soon ensued, with the young Turks appearing on the front page of local newspapers and being featured in nationwide daily *Le Monde* and in periodicals like France's *L'Express*, Italy's *L'Europeo*, and more. The operation also made it possible for the Situationist International—then an underground political and artistic movement—to emerge from the confines of the avant-garde.

UNEF (Union Nationale des Étudiants de France): Founded in 1907, UNEF has emerged as the largest national student union in France.

Quelques Definitions

AFGES (Association Fédérative Générale des Étudiants de Strasbourg) : Fondée en 1923, basée à Strasbourg, l'organisation étudiante est rattachée à l'Union Nationale des Etudiants de France (UNEF) qui opère à l'échelle nationale.

Anti-copyright : La version originale de *La Misère en milieu étudiant* indique que le texte « peut être librement reproduit même sans indication d'origine ». Différentes éditions du texte peuvent donc être réalisées sans l'accord des auteurs.

Détourned (détournement) : S'emploie par abréviation de la formule : détournement d'éléments esthétiques préfabriqués. Intégration de productions actuelles ou passées des arts dans une construction supérieure du milieu. Dans ce sens il ne peut y avoir de peinture ou de musique situationniste, mais un usage situationniste de ces moyens. Dans un sens plus primitif, le détournement à l'intérieur des sphères culturelles anciennes est une méthode de propagande, qui témoigne de l'usure et de la perte d'importance de ces sphères.

Garnaultins : Etudiants strasbourgeois proches des situationnistes qui sont ensuite mis à l'écart par l'IS. Le mot « Garnaultins » se réfere à Jean Garnault, l'un des étudiants strasbourgeois impliqués dans le « scandale de Strasbourg » de 1966.

Internationale Situationniste (IS) : Fondée à Cosio d'Arroscia en 1957, cette organisation de théoriciens et d'artistes cherche à dépasser les avant-gardes surréalistes, dadaïstes, et lettristes. Elle inaugure plusieurs concepts clés comme le spectacle, le détournement, et la révolution de la vie quotidienne. L'IS s'autodissout en 1972.

Internationale Situationniste : Principal vecteur des idées de l'Internationale Situationniste, la revue connait douze numéros entre 1958 et 1959. L'article « Nos buts et nos méthodes dans le scandale de Strasbourg », qui décrit le contexte et les motivations ayant donné lieu au texte de *la Misère en milieu étudiant*, est publié dans le numéro onze en octobre 1967.

Mai 68 : Ensemble d'événements qui ont eu lieu en France en Mai 1968, prenant comme point de départ des manifestations étudiantes et conclus par une grève générale en France et à des explosions révolutionnaires à l'international. Bien que Mai 68 soit parfois considéré comme un échec, il impulse de nombreux mouvements de contestation des années 70.

Pirate (édition) : Reproduction à l'identique ou presque d'une édition d'un texte.

Situationniste : Ce qui se rapporte à la théorie ou à l'activité pratique d'une construction des situations. Celui qui s'emploie à construire des situations. Membre de l'Internationale situationniste.

Société du spectacle (La) : Publié en 1967, œuvre phare de Guy Debord, *La Société du spectacle* demeure d'actualité. L'auteur, qui fut l'un des fondateurs de l'IS, dénonce les méfaits d'une société dominée par l'image. Pour Debord, « dans les sociétés dans lesquelles règnent les conditions modernes de production [...] tout ce qui était directement vécu s'est éloigné dans une représentation ».

Scandale de Strasbourg : En 1966, une poignée d'étudiants déterminés à semer la pagaille sont miraculeusement élus à la tête de l'AFGES, l'association étudiante de l'Université de Strasbourg. Les situationnistes y voient une opportunité ; Mustapha Khayati prend la plume et rédige la majeure partie de ce qui sera bientôt annoncé comme « le pamphlet le plus scandaleux du siècle ». Dix mille exemplaires sont imprimés – dilapidant pour l'occasion le budget de l'AFGES pour l'année universitaire 1966-1967 – puis distribués lors de la cérémonie la rentrée solennelle le 22 novembre 1966. On crie au scandale ; les organisateurs apparaissant à la une des journaux locaux, dans les journaux nationaux comme *Le Monde*, et dans des revues comme *L'Express* en France et *L'Europeo* en Italie. Le scandale de Strasbourg permet également à l'Internationale situationniste – mouvement politique et artistique alors encore largement confidentiel – de sortir des confins de l'avant-garde.

Traité de savoir-vivre à l'usage des jeunes générations : Œuvre phare du Situationniste Raoul Vaneigem, le *Traité* appelle la jeunesse française à s'interroger sur la banalité de sa vie et théorise les changements nécessaires (« la révolution de la vie quotidienne ») pour accéder à la vraie vie.

UNEF (Union Nationale des Étudiants de France) : Fondée en 1907, l'UNEF s'est imposée comme le syndicat étudiant dominant à l'échelle nationale.

Acknowledgements

Over the course of the production of this Common Notions edition of *On the Poverty of Student Life*, the editors have had the privilege of hearing from the people best equipped to tell the stories related to the initial and continued proliferation of this pamphlet. We extend our gratitude to the generosity of contributors who have made this edition possible, as well as to the many people who have assisted the production of this text along the way.

Mustapha Khayati helped illuminate the conditions of production and circulation of *On the Poverty of Student Life*. His generosity with his time and support for this project are deeply appreciated. First and foremost, this book is for him.

René Viénet's correspondence regarding the Introduction and the Chinese editions were of great value, contributing significantly to the quality of information in this book. Viénet's prolific work on translations and his investigations of the history of the French Revolution continue to this day.

Donald Nicholson-Smith and **T.J. Clark** both provided critical insight to the first English-language adaptation of *On the Poverty of Student Life* (as *Ten Days That Shook the University*), which they produced more than fifty years ago.

Lorraine Perlman helped the editors understand how a small group of American anarchists in radical publishing played a critical role in the dissemination of Situationist ideas in the United States. Over the years, Black & Red released more editions of *On the Poverty of Student Life* than any other publisher in the world.

Isaac Cronin's many conversations with the editors provided significant information that helped unravel the stories in the Introduction.

Ken Knabb's open and direct communication contributed significantly to the stories in this text, as well as to cultivating an understanding of relevant global connections.

We would like to give special thanks to this book's contributors. Thank you, to **Allan Antliff** from the University of Victoria for conducting an interview with Lorraine Perlman. Thank you to **Zoé Crochon** and **Nadège LeJeune** for their help on the English translation of the Khayati interview, and Nadège, again for assistance with the entries in the French-language bibliography. Thank you to **Luca Vallino** for assistance with Italian translation and his thoughts regarding the Italian editions.

This book could not have been published without the persistent efforts of several archivists, and the contributions of various university collections. We would especially like to thank **Kevin Repp** from the Beinecke Rare Book and Manuscript Library at Yale University. His in-depth understanding of the source material and the archive's collections guided the editors through this project. The Beinecke facsimiles reproduced in this edition are just a small part of the materials that Kevin and his colleagues at Yale have provided to us through scans. Thank you also to **Jessica Tubis** and **Rebecca McGuire** from the Beinecke, who actively contributed to these efforts. We would also like to recognize **Laurence LeBras** from the Fonds Guy Debord in the Bibliothèque Nationale de France, the **Harvard Special Collections**, and **The Bancroft Library** at UC Berkeley. Thank you also to **Thomas Hvid Kromann** from the Royal Danish Library for providing access to an early Danish edition of the pamphlet. For crucial assistance in the review process for the Introduction, many thanks to **Olivier Morel**, **John Teramoto**, and **Anthony Cox**.

Some individuals have been particularly helpful in filling gaps in the bibliography of *On the Poverty of Student Life*. **Aleksa Golijanin** and **Rabitor Trivunac** greatly assisted in finding and understanding Eastern European editions. **Kaveh Nouri** from Melancholic Troglodytes was very helpful in locating one of the Farsi editions. **Coralie De Castro** generously provided a later French edition with illustrations.

The interview, "*On the Poverty of Student Life*, Past and Present," with Mustapha Khayati and Mehdi El Hajoui, was conducted in September 2021 and translated by Zoé Crochon and Nadège LeJeune, with help from the editors and footnotes by Mehdi El Hajoui. "*On the Poverty of Student Life*: The Black & Red Edition," by Allan Antliff, was authored in September 2021. Donald Nicholson-Smith's "*Ten Days That Shook the University*: A Note on an Adaptation" was authored in August 2021. The draft manuscript of the first chapter of *De la misère en milieu étudiant, considérée sous ses aspects économique, politique, psychologique, sexuel et notamment intellectuel et de quelques moyens pour y remédier* is reprinted here, courtesy of the Beinecke.

Our thanks to everyone at **Common Notions Press**, especially Malav Kanuga, Josh MacPhee, and Erika Biddle-Stavrakos, for their enthusiastic support and meticulous focus throughout, and the design team, Morgan Buck and Graciela Vasquez, for putting these stunning pages together.

Finally, thanks to the many people who contributed in one way or another to this project who we may have forgotten to credit. To them, the editors extend both their appreciation and apologies.

About the Editors

Mehdi El Hajoui has been researching and collecting Situationist International texts and ephemera for the last fifteen years. Items from his archive have been exhibited at Indiana University's Lilly Library, the Chicago Architecture Biennial, the Musée d'Art Moderne et Contemporain in Geneva, Berlin's Haus der Kulturen der Welt, and the Power Plant in Toronto. He frequently writes and lectures, and is a board member of Booklyn and Pro Arts Commons, organizations providing support for marginalized artists working at the intersection of art and social change.

Anna O'Meara's research investigates Middle Eastern art and activism between the late 1960's and early 1970's, particularly the work of Mustapha Khayati, as well as the global involvement and ramifications of Situationist film and art. Her translations have been published by Three Rooms Press, Annex Press, BauerVerlag, and Verso.

About the Contributors

Allan Antliff is a professor of Art History and Visual Studies at the University of Victoria and has published extensively on anarchism and the arts. He has been active in the anarchist movement since the 1980s.

Mustapha Khayati was a member of the Situationist International between 1965 and 1969. Although *On the Poverty of Student Life* was a collective endeavor, Khayati wrote nearly all of the pamphlet's content and is considered its main author.

Donald Nicholson-Smith was a member of the Situationist International between 1965 and 1967. He translated and expanded *On the Poverty of Student Life*, or the "Strasbourg pamphlet," in collaboration with fellow Situationist **T.J. Clark** as *Ten Days That Shook the University* (SI, 1967). He has also translated *The Society of the Spectacle* and *The Revolution of Everyday Life*, the cardinal works of Guy Debord and Raoul Vaneigem respectively.

The Situationist International was an international organization of social revolutionaries made up of avant-garde artists, intellectuals, and political theorists. It was prominent in Europe from its formation in 1957 to its dissolution in 1972.

About Common Notions

Common Notions is a publishing house and programming platform that fosters new formulations of living autonomy. We aim to circulate timely reflections, clear critiques, and inspiring strategies that amplify movements for social justice.

Our publications trace a constellation of critical and visionary meditations on the organization of freedom. By any media necessary, we seek to nourish the imagination and generalize common notions about the creation of other worlds beyond state and capital. Inspired by various traditions of autonomism and liberation—in the US and internationally, historical and emerging from contemporary movements—our publications provide resources for a collective reading of struggles past, present, and to come.

Common Notions regularly collaborates with political collectives, militant authors, radical presses, and maverick designers around the world. Our political and aesthetic pursuits are dreamed and realized with Antumbra Designs.

www.commonnotions.org
info@commonnotions.org

Become a Monthly Sustainer

These are decisive times, ripe with challenges and possibility, heartache and beautiful inspiration. More than ever, we are in need of timely reflections, clear critiques, and inspiring strategies that can help movements for social justice grow and transform society. Help us amplify those necessary words, deeds, and dreams that our liberation movements and our worlds so need.

Movements are sustained by people like you, whose fugitive words, deeds, and dreams bend against the world of domination and exploitation.

For collective imagination, dedicated practices of love and study, and organized acts of freedom.

By any media necessary. With your love and support.
Monthly sustainers start at $12 and $25.
Join us at commonnotions.org/sustain.